Y0-BEC-770

SEVEN TREASURE CITIES

OF LATIN AMERICA

SEVEN TREASURE CITIES

OF LATIN AMERICA

By Bertha Kitchell Whyte

OCTOBER HOUSE INC. NEW YORK

CONTENTS

ACKNOWLEDGMENTS

I wish to acknowledge the invaluable help, in Old San Juan, P.R., of Miss Agnes Sherman of Fomento, Francisco Castagnet, and Dr. Ricardo Alegría of the Institute of Culture; in Mérida, of the Fernando Barbachano family; in Cartagena that of Señora Rosa Marie de Ochoa and of ex-Mayor Dr. Harold Calvo; in Tunja that of ex-Judge Jaime Ruiz Ojeda; in Quito, that of Padre Samuel Calvo of the San Franciscan Museum; of Dr. Albert Giesecke of the American Embassy in Lima who supplied me, for four years, with books and clippings about Lima and Cuzco; and Señora Fernando Villaran of that city. I was also fortunate to have the advice and critical judgment of the best Spanish and Latin American art historian in the United States, the late Dr. Martin Soria of Michigan State University who tragically lost his life in a plane crash in Brussels, on February 14, 1961, en route to Madrid by Government invitation to lecture on Velasquez. These unselfish friends supplied me with books and maps and pictures.

I am much indebted to my youthful photographer, Jon Engel, who patiently carried thirty pounds of photographic equipment through tropical cities and those high up in the Andes where we both ignored several attacks of *sirrochi* (mountain sickness). All photographs of South America were taken by him unless otherwise attributed. (Those taken in San Juan and Mérida are my own, unless otherwise specified.)

For assistance in correcting the manuscript I am beholden to Dr. Stephen Borhegyi, director of the Milwaukee Public Museum, Adelaide Harris of Gainesville, Florida; to John Bret Harte; my lawyer husband, Malcolm K. Whyte, and our son John B. Whyte.

To all of these, I dedicate this book.

BERTHA KITCHELL WHYTE

PREFACE

It is a privilege to make a few remarks to the present work on Spanish Colonial Art.

Time, effort, study, have entered into the presentation of a work which is, and will continue to be, outstanding in its field. Bertha Whyte has spent years of painstaking research and study of the artistic traditions developed in several of Spain's colonies in the New World. Every effort has been made to present an ensemble which must appeal to those who are attracted to this cultural field.

Naturally, all possible sites could not be included readily in a single volume, nor could all the phases of art relating to the sites selected be incorporated in the present book.

As a student and patron of art, Bertha Whyte has visited museums of art, private collections, historic homes and other sources.

Her descriptions are intended to be non-technical in order to appeal to lovers of art who have no special training in this field. She wants these readers to acquire a feeling and a respect for Spanish Colonial Art, and to learn that it was not only the Spaniards who contributed to the general picture, but that other European nationals and native artists must be included in any study and description of the art of this era.

Mestizo influence began to show an interesting development towards the end of the seventeenth century and, particularly, during the following century.

Lovers of art will do well to explore personally the centers of Spanish Colonial Art portrayed in this work in order to obtain the full impact and significance of the artistic efforts developed through several centuries by nationals of different countries in the field of Spanish Colonial Art.

Lima, Peru   Dr. Albert A. Giesecke

Rulers in Spain During the Spanish-Colonial Period

Ferdinand of Aragon
      and   } (1479–1516)
Isabella of Castile

Joanna the Mad

Philip I (1504–1506)

Charles the 1st or Emperor V (1516–56) House of Austria

Philip II (1556–98)

Philip III (1598–1621)

Philip IV (1621–1665)

Charles II (1665–1700)

Philip V (1700–1746) (grandson of Louis XIV) House of Bourbon

Ferdinand VI (1746–59)

Charles III (1759–88) decreed expulsion of Jesuits as not owing
    allegiance to the State

Charles IV abdicates in favor of Napoleon

Joseph Napoleon (1808–1814)

Ferdinand VII (1814–1833) (monarchy restored)

Queen Isabella II Regency (1833–43)

INTRODUCTION

In this book about seven Spanish Colonial cities in Latin America, the emphasis is chiefly on the art of the Colonial period and its present remains. The Spanish Colonial period spanned about three hundred years from the Conquest to the Independence, extending roughly from the early sixteenth century to the early nineteenth. Accordingly, the story of the seven cities starts four hundred years ago. From the cities selected you can follow the course of the Spanish Conquest. From Hispaniola it wound to Puerto Rico, to Mexico and Mérida and from there to Cartagena. From Cartagena it went by sea to Portobelo and across the Isthmus of Panama to the Pacific and then southward. Inland, it went to Quito and Tunja and, farther down, it crossed over the Andes to Cuzco. Pizarro, exploring westward out of Cuzco, founded Lima near the coast. Part of the treasure of these cities is their history and the memories of what they once possessed.

It is true that many books have been written which open vistas into this period, but only a few have been translated—and not many Spanish books are properly catalogued in the Latin American libraries. Fortunately, I did find some valuable material in private collections which afforded fascinating glimpses into the Colonial period. The future student will find abundant material if he looks hard enough.

Before discussing the art of the period, some comments on the Spanish Colonial administration and its results are necessary. During his third voyage, Columbus inaugurated slavery on Hispaniola (the large island now divided between the Dominican Republic and Haiti) and instituted the *repartimiento* system. Under this system a Spanish settler was allotted a division of cultivated land and was assigned, as his personal slaves, the Indians who lived on it, with the consent of the native *caciques*, or chiefs. The latter accepted this unhappy arrangement because it excused them from the intolerable gold tribute.★

★ Gold production in general rapidly declined; it was important, for instance, only until about 1551 in Puerto Rico.

Repartimiento was interrelated with another system, called *encomienda. Encomienda* was a land grant with the right to exact tribute from certain groups of Indians while, as said above, *repartimiento* was a grant of Indians for labor. Both theoretically obligated the Spaniards to care for the welfare, spiritual and physical, of the Indians. The *encomendero* was supposed to indoctrinate the Indians into the Catholic Religion and to build a church. The auxiliary *mita* system, which required the Indians to work for the *encomenderos* a certain length of time in either house service, farm labor, public or church work, mines or factories was a form of slavery and a source of discontent, to put it mildly.*

Columbus' object was to earn gold for the Spanish monarchs to justify the cost of his explorations. While he and his family were personally kind to the Indians, many conquistadors were rogues or, as a gentleman of Guayaquil told me, "a lot of greedy riff-raff." Their rapacious cruelty led to the virtual extinction of the Indians on most of the islands of the Caribbean. The Great Navigator was not a good administrator, and his system of *repartimientos* under the *encomenderos* who received, in return for their efforts as discoverers, allotments of land and Indians, was most cruel.

From the first, Pizarro was empowered by Spain to bestow *encomiendas* and *repartimientos* in Peru upon his fellow conquistadors. In 1536, these grants were extended to two generations.

In Peru, under the regime of the Spaniards, the treatment accorded the Indians was harsh and tyrannical. Except for some concern for their immortal souls, the Spaniards looked upon them simply as a source of supply for the manual labor needed to operate mines, factories, and huge estates and to construct new buildings. The Indians were forced to accept this in place of the remarkable Inca system of planned economy, a kind of benevolent socialism. Although the *repartimiento* system in theory benefited the Indians as well as the whites, in practice it subjected the natives to intolerable exactions and ill treatment.

An early protest was raised by Vincente de Valverde, first bishop of Cuzco; a little later Bartolomé de las Casas,† while Bishop of Chiapas, Mexico, appeared

---

* *Cecilia Valdés* (Vantage Press, Inc., New York), a novel written by Cirilo Villarde, a Cuban lawyer, in 1830 and published in entirety in 1872, tells too poignantly of the misery of Cuban slaves. It gives the relationships between Spaniards, Creoles, mulattoes and slaves in Cuba, prior to the freeing of the latter.

† Don Padre Bartolomé de las Casas (1474–1566), a great Dominican and champion of the Indians, wrote between 1527 and 1561 the *History of the Indies*, an invaluable source book; also, a *Very Brief Account of the Destruction of the Indians*.

personally before Charles V and induced him to promulgate the code known as the "New Laws," which modified the existing system. It decreed that all participators in civil wars and all government officials be deprived at once of their grants, and that all grants pass to the Crown on the death of the original owner. Indians were to pay only a fixed sum as tribute (*mita*) and all forced labor was prohibited. Naturally enough, the "New Laws" were completely unpopular with the conquerors and hence became unworkable. They were revoked after only three years.

Sadly, though, Padre Bartolomé's solution was to acquiesce to the importation of slaves from Africa. Indian slaves decreased, but Negro slavery developed and Negro slaves were imported at high prices. Portuguese, Englishmen, Germans and Russians brought most of the slaves to Puerto Rico and Hispaniola, and thence to Cartagena.

In many memoirs and in, for instance, the boys' book *Under Drake's Flag* written by the English naval officer and war correspondent, George Alfred Henty,★ the abhorrence of the English for the cruelty of the Spaniards towards their slaves is recorded. However, in a book written by a Baptist missionary sent to the English island of Jamaica,† it is pointed out that the English were practically as cruel, and differed from the Spaniards mainly in offering no religious instruction in the seventeenth century. The first missionaries to Jamaica in the eighteenth century were stoned by white people, irreligion prevailing.

A few words should be devoted to several Spanish institutions which affected the entire civilization in the Colonial period. The *Audiencia* was the court of appeal but was also used as a check on the governor's power. Its decisions could be appealed to the Council of the Indies (organized in 1542) and to the Crown. The *Audiencias* were governmental commissions with special areas, as well as tribunals of justice. The territories were also designated as *Audiencias*. By assigning powers to the *Audiencias*, the Crown frequently exerted governmental control over officers whose territories fell within their judicial jurisdiction.

The Inquisition was civil and political, as well as religious, in function and was financed by the Crown. The Catholic Church was an instrument of the Crown and, in 1519, the Bishop of Puerto Rico became the Chief Inquisitor. The church was supported, however, by tithes which in the poorer countries were hard to collect. The king demanded one fifth of all the wealth extracted from the New World.

★ Charles Scribner Sons, 1897, New York.
† *Jamaica: Its Past and Present State*, by James J. Phillipe, Paternoster Row, London 1843.

Gold and emerald cross recovered from the wreck of a Spanish ship wrecked circa 1594 on the Bermuda reefs. The emeralds are cabuchon cut from Colombia; the gold is 24 carat. The cross was made by Indians under Spanish supervision for a high Church dignitary.

Gold and pearl buttons. Gold mount was cast in molds made by the lost wax method. The pearls are conch pearls.

After the *flotas*, or convoys, carrying the king's "fifths" from Peru, New Spain (Mexico) and Cartagena were organized, they sailed from Portobelo, Panama, and Vera Cruz, Mexico, for Spain by way of the windward passage. The key to this passage, as well as to the leeward passage, was Puerto Rico; so, San Juan developed in importance and was the object of many raids by the corsairs of Holland, England and France. The windward route carried up as far north as Bermuda. (On the fourth journey of Columbus, one ship was nicknamed "Bermuda" after the owner and shipmaster Francisco Bermudez. The island was probably named after the ship.) Diving among the reefs of Bermuda in January, 1956, Edward Tucker and Robert

An engagement between the English ship Buckington and Dutch ships bearing provisions for Martinique and convoyed by French ships, 1758. This engraving also shows types of ships of the period.

center of the island's Operation Bootstrap—a movement to raise the standard of living by supplementing the old agricultural economy through business and industrial development.

The first view of this island city from the entrance of its beautiful harbor is the dramatic headland crowned with the historic battlements of El Morro Castle. A stone wall surrounds the impressive promontory. On its water side, in addition to classic El Morro, stand the fortress of San Cristóbal and the palaces of La Fortaleza and Casa Blanca. Inside the wall, with its stone watchtowers, are narrow streets overhung with balconies.

Even the balconies have historic character. Those with wooden balusters are the oldest; others displaying cast-iron brackets and railings came from New Orleans during that city's Spanish regime; while another closed wooden type of balcony recalls the style of the Moors. The ingot iron for the wrought-iron grilles, doors and balconies was brought from Spain.

5

El Cabildo, the city hall, is on Baldorioty de Castro Square, or the Plaza de Armas, which was once the marketplace. It is a gracious old building with a fine Spanish wrought-iron wellhead in its patio. Near El Morro on San Sebastian Street, the Church of San José dominates the *plazuela* of that name. In its center is an interesting statue of Ponce de León, which was cast out of English guns captured from Sir George Clifford. South of this plaza on Calle del Cristo, facing the Plazuela de las Monjas (little Plaza of the Nuns), is the dignified white cathedral. The Carmelite convent after which the plaza is named has been converted into a hotel, and back of the nuns' building there now stands a school, where, as I passed, I heard fresh young voices practicing English. Nearby are two fascinating short streets; the whole width of each is comprised of stairs.

Shaded by its lines of trees, the little street called Caleta de San Juan leads from the cathedral to the San Juan Gate. Near this gate, known also as the Water Gate, there was once a ships' landing; at that time it formed the main entrance to the city, and it was here that the galleons discharged their cargo. The street, built in 1635, runs between La Fortaleza and Casa Blanca at the foot of the little Plaza of the Nuns. Standing in Caleta de San Juan, one can vividly imagine the armored soldiers marching off the high-pooped ships, through the gate, past the Spanish residences, to hear Mass in the cathedral. Over the gate is an inscription in Latin: "Blessed is he who cometh in the name of the Lord." Outside the gate, and to the left as one faces the harbor, there is a bust of Queen Isabella. On the right, jutting from a section of curtain wall designed so as to conceal the gate from hostile eyes, stands a picturesque sentry box.

Unfortunately, the Santiago Gate, which once stood with moat and drawbridge below San Cristóbal, has been removed, as well as the San Justo Gate. Over the years a large group of squatters' huts gradually sprang up on the steeply sloping bank between the sea and the walls just below El Morro. Unfortunately, this area, called La Perla, remains a slum. The San José Gate opens onto La Perla and leads to the cemetery of San Juan. East of El Morro is the large fortress of San Cristóbal, which guards the approach from the mainland. This fortress, begun in 1631 and completed by 1771, was equipped to handle all military repairs. According to an old inventory it once contained 742 pieces of armor. The guns of San Cristóbal were so situated as to defend the city in all directions, and its chapel, fittingly enough, was dedicated to Santa Barbara—the patron saint of artillerymen. The walls that face present-day Santurce have been torn down, but the sentry boxes of San Cristóbal still stand and are as

6

Ceiling of San José Church

into a military museum, and was dedicated on November 19, 1962, the anniversary of the discovery of Puerto Rico. Among the exhibits are banners and armor used by the conquistadors, as well as period military uniforms that date from early Colonial times through those worn by the soldiers who fought against the Americans in 1898. There is also a photograph of the last Spanish governor, General Manuel Macías Casado. The chapel and kitchen are open to view, and in another room—notable for its tremendous black beams—a varied collection of historic ship models is on display.

On the corner of San José and Sol streets I had occasion to watch a group of workmen carefully converting an old palace into a home for Ricardo Alegría; the project was under his direction. The original edifice has six arches supporting the balcony and is notable for its fine stairway. There is a landing on the stairway on which old

Cristo de los Ponces (Christ of the Ponces), San José Church *Chapel of Santo Cristo de la Salud*

Delft stair tiles illustrate Biblical scenes. The tiles are in the form of circles inside squares, in alternating blue and mulberry brown.

Where else but in Old San Juan would you find people asking for cobblestones as souvenirs? They are all over Old San Juan, these blue cobbles of volcanic rock— polished by three hundred years of traffic—that were carried here long ago as ballast from the Canary Islands. During one of my jaunts along the gleaming cobblestones of Calle La Cruz, I came upon a very handsome building, which, I learned, is called Edificio Español, The Spanish Building. This building, three stories high, bears the coat of arms of Puerto Rico under its roof. What prompted me to investigate the interior court was a dado of fine Sevillian tiles—the first I had discovered on the island. They were used in great profusion throughout the patio; they served, among other things, as materials for a fountain and a seat. The windows about the patio displayed some fine wrought ironwork, and the patio itself held a splendid arbor.

26

Bar of the El Convento Hotel. The bar stools are reproductions of childrens' high chairs used by the Spanish Bourbon family.

House of Dos Zaguánes (Two Entrances)

What must have been a palace at one time is now an apartment building. It has not been modernized, and still retains its original charm.

Several interesting Colonial homes have *not* been restored and are not open for public inspection. The Casa de Dos Zaguánes (House of Two Entrances) was among the most beautiful of the eighteenth-century homes. It is located on the corner of Luna and San José streets and now serves as a dormitory for men. Behind the two doorways, two stairways, one above the other, lead to the upper stories. The building, with its beautiful patio, is scheduled for restoration. But I will remember it as it was, in all its decayed elegance.

Number 19 Tetuan Street, an old home of the Marqués de la Esperanza, contains a fine staircase and grilled window. Another eighteenth-century house is the Casa de Elzaburu, so named because the patriot and founder of El Ateneo, Manuel Elzaburu y Vizcarrondo, was born there on January 2, 1851.

Portrait of Don Juan de Arismendi (1760–1814), first bishop of Puerto Rico, by José Campeche

Our Lady of Mercy: oil by José Campeche in the Institute of Puerto Rican Culture

The only residence on exhibition at the present time is an eighteenth-century house called Calle del Cristo 255, or Casa del Libro, which was restored by the Economic Development Administration (more commonly known as Fomento). The house was then transferred to the Institute of Culture, and it now houses a library of more than 2,000 books from every century since the fifteenth, compiled for the purpose of raising the standard of printing in Puerto Rico. The late Dr. Elmer Adler, who until 1952 had been Curator of Graphic Arts of Princeton University, was chosen director of the Casa del Libro in 1955 and given liberal government appropriations. The Friends of Calle del Cristo 255 are custodians of an original royal order, signed by King Ferdinand and Queen Isabella, that assured provisions for a fleet in Andalucía at the time Christopher Columbus began his second journey to the New World. It was on this journey that Puerto Rico was discovered. The house is a narrow, E-shaped building with two patios. The arched doorways are topped

"El Velorio" (*"The Wake"*) *by Francisco Oller, in the new Art Museum of the University of Puerto Rico*

with open fanlight transoms, and each room still retains the original 200-year-old asubó ceiling beams.

On crowded San Justo Street is a restaurant, La Mallorquina, constructed in the early nineteenth century; it is still the most popular luncheon spot in Old San Juan. Standing at the open-air street side, one sees a long, dark wood bar and tables, once marble-topped, crowded with patrons enjoying *asopao* of shrimp and lobster. Unlike the celebrated Trece Monedas restaurant of Lima, Peru, which is housed in a sensitively restored and decorated Colonial residence, La Mallorquina has been a restaurant for 150 years, and has thus come by its antique atmosphere naturally.

On the corner of San Sebastian and Cristo streets stands *Obispado*, the Archbishop's Palace, a charming old building with thick walls, old wooden gratings and graceful arches. It contains what is probably the city's finest collection of portraits, many of them, needless to say, of bishops. The first archbishop's palace, next to the

29

cathedral cemetery, was burned by the Dutch in 1625. In 1733 Bishop Pizarro built the present palace on land purchased from Doña María de Amezquita y Ayala. The beautiful tiled stairway was built during a restoration directed by Bishop Fr. Manuel Ximénez.

Among the arts of Old San Juan, architecture is of chief interest; but certain painters have left works of historic importance. The Spanish painter Luis Paret y Alcázar, who arrived in the island in 1775 and stayed for three years, was considered by Osiris Delgado Mercado the best Spanish painter after Goya. None of his work remains in Puerto Rico except for a self-portrait in which he represented himself as a Puerto Rican countryman, or *jíbaro*. This portrait is in the collection of Don Acisclo Marxuach.

Puerto Rico's greatest painter, José Campeche—a pupil of Paret—was the third son of Tomás de Rivafrecha y Campeche, a liberated slave native to the island, and María Jordan of the Canary Islands. Two of José's five brothers, Miguel and Ignacio, were also painters; all three probably received their first instruction from their father, who was a gilder. José was undoubtedly influenced by Paret and by the engravings of notable European painters, which, in the absence of galleries, were studied by New World artists. For instance, as Delgado points out, the theme of Campeche's painting in San José Church, "The Shipwreck of Power," was probably derived from a picture by the French artist Simon Vouet which showed St. Nicholas saving a shipwrecked group.

Campeche's early renown was due primarily to his religious paintings, but Don Sebastian Gonzalez García, in recent commentaries on this painter's work, has drawn attention to the excellence of his portraiture. A unique Campeche painting hangs in the mayor's office in El Cabildo. It is the coat of arms granted by King Ferdinand in 1511 to the settlement of Caparra. The coat of arms contains a lamb bearing a flag with the device of John upon a red book, an *F*, an *I*, and the motto "Joannes est nomens Ejus." This painting is one of the city's great treasures, according to Doña Felisa Rincon de Gautier, who, in 1963, had held the office of Mayor of San Juan for seventeen years. Appropriately enough, the house in which Campeche lived at number 43 Cruz and San Sebastian streets, is now an art gallery.

Another well-known painter of Puerto Rico is the nineteenth-century artist Francisco Oller (1833–1917). Greatly influenced by Couture and Courbet, he traveled many times to Europe, and was successfully received in both France and Spain. Upon painting a portrait of Alfonso XII, he was given the title of Painter of

Our Lady of Belén (Bethlehem), in the Chapel of the same name in San José Church, the oldest foreign art work in Puerto Rico, is by or of the school of Roger Van der Weyden.

San Juan Bautista (Saint John the Baptist) by José Campeche

the Royal Court of Spain. Oller's masterpiece, "El Velorio" ("The Wake"), which shows many aspects of nineteenth-century life on the island, hangs in the new art museum of the University of Puerto Rico.

The literary life of early Puerto Rico was not very noteworthy. Madariaga, writing on this subject in *Rise of the Spanish Empire*, mentions but one writer, Bishop Balbuena, who, in 1603, wrote a famous poem on the great attractions of Mexico City. Madariaga describes him as "the man of letters, the wealthy and refined bishop of Puerto Rico in the seventeenth century."

Because most of the imported works of art were carried off by raiders, and because the land did not produce enough wealth to foster craft and art schools, holy images were produced by the humble *imageros*—the folk artists who carved and

31

San Raphael, Santo of the Institute de Cultura Puertorriqueña

Seated Madonna, Santo of the Institute de Cultura Puertorriqueña

painted small images of saints, crucifixes and Madonnas. These figures, called *santos*, served an historic purpose in the conversion of the natives to Christianity.

Even though many monks of the great missionary orders learned the Indians' tongues, they still had need of visual aids in their efforts to convert the Indians from the old idolatry and nature worship. In parts of Latin America, savage Indians can still be found; in 1957 five Protestant missionaries were murdered by the Aushires of the Amazon basin. This hatred survives from the sixteenth century, when Spaniards tortured the Indians to learn the whereabouts of the emerald mines. Such Indians can be taught Christianity only with difficulty. In converting the partially civilized Incas, Aztecs, Mayas and Chibchas during the Colonial Period, the teachers of Catholicism were greatly assisted by the iconography of the saints. During this same period the religious festivals often attained a level of artistic excellence, for the figures, and the *andas* on which they were carried, are truly beautiful and moving in their religious significance. One of the early efforts of Operación Serenidad, a movement aimed, among other things, at preserving Puerto Rico's Spanish inheri-

32

The Three Kings, Santo of the Institute de Cultura Puertorriqueña

Santo of a Mercedarian Bishop from San German, of the end of the eighteenth century

tance, consisted of the organization of Nativity Festivals during Christmas season. Inés Mendoza de Muñoz Marín, the governor's wife, was largely responsible for this project, which dramatically utilized the historic *santos*.

Visitors to other countries will discover religious folk images similar to the *santos* of Puerto Rico. In Provence, France, they are called *santons*. In the southwestern United States, the Indians produced characteristic images that were also called *santos*; many of these are now safely housed in museums. (The collections at Colorado Springs and Denver are noteworthy.) In Quito, Ecuador, the mestizo craftsmen were so gifted that their figures attained the status of objects of art, and, as *esculturas*, were sold all over Latin America.

It is impossible to predict how long the carving of *santos* will remain a living folk art in the Americas. One of the last Puerto Rican *santeros* was Zoilo Cajigas Sotomayor of Aguada, who was ninety-eight years old when Mary Slusser, in 1953, included him in her article "Tropical Christmas."★ At Cuzco, local artisans bring

★December, 1953 issue of *Americas* Magazine.

33

Santo in the Instituto de Cultura

Modern Madona Santo

34

Caleta de San Juan, connecting Water Gate and the Cathedral

Bohío or native hut (called machuelo or heart of an onion) in Ponce, P.R.

their *santos* to a Christmas Eve "fair" held in the plaza in front of the cathedral, and every year large crowds come to see and buy their work. At Ayacucha, Peru, similar carved figures enclosed in boxes with doors, called "retablos," can still be found.

The *santos* of Puerto Rico are the island's chief collectible art items. Fine examples may be found in the collections of Dr. Fernando M. Monserrate, the Instituto de Cultura and the University of Puerto Rico.★

The preservation and restoration of historically significant structures and monuments in Old San Juan have been the subject of concern for many years. In 1930 the Senate of Puerto Rico approved a law creating La Junta Conservadora de Valores Historicas. The committee, meeting that same year, formed an ambitious plan for mapping and restoring the fifty blocks which the authorities wish to preserve as Old San Juan. However, in the following twenty-five years little actual work was done. In 1948 Mario J. Buschiazzo, consultant of the Junta de Planificación de Puerto Rico, recommended in his report, *Estudio sobre Monumentos Históricos de Puerto Rico*, that a commission of five or six members be appointed and provided with an office, a technical staff, and the authority to select priority projects and expend funds. The commission was established, but very little was achieved. The historic buildings

★ Reprints of a talk by Dr. Monserrate on the *santos* in New York's Cooper Union Museum can be obtained at the Fomento office in San Juan.

La Perla, slum district below El Morro

now included in the official list may not be subjected to repairs or restorations, or be destroyed in whole or in part, or be transferred without approval of the Institute's Comisión de Monumentos Históricos. The regulation has been extended to include all buildings in the City of San Juan, even those not declared historical monuments.★

★ In the report, *Renewal Possibilities of the Historic Triangle of the City of San Juan* (1955), written for the Municipal Housing Authority of the Capitol of Puerto Rico by consultants Nathaniel S. Keith and Carl Feiss of Washington, D. C., the problem is stated in two parts. The first concerns slum clearance in La Perla, the slum area below El Morro, and in the La Puntilla areas. The second part constitutes an acceptance of the Buschiazzo plan for the conservation and restoration of the Historic Triangle. This latter area—which occupies no more than eight per cent of the present city of San Juan—constitutes what is known as Old San Juan. The report proposes La Perla as a fine site for a public park, hotels, and apartment houses. In addition, it recommends greater open space for parking and recreation within the triangle, and especially in residential areas, where a Georgetown-type renewal program is feasible. Among other improvements needed are new sewerage facilities, the underground relocation of overhead utility lines, development of major thoroughfares in the northern and southern boundaries of the Historic Triangle, along with development of Boulevard Norzagaray. Expanding of the business and commercial base of the Historic Triangle and the curbing of on-street parking are also needed.

36

Buildings restored are exempt from taxation for ten years, and the government bank loans money on such works. These buildings are also exempt from the rent-control law. Thus far these measures have insured considerable preservation of the Colonial section of the city, and have promoted a good deal of solid study and planning for future restorations. Governor Muñoz Marín has secured funds for and supported legislation favoring restoration projects. However, much credit for carrying out the projects in correct historical style must go to the Alegría brothers, Ricardo, director of the Instituto de Cultura Puertorriqueña, and José, a decorator and businessman. They have had much to do in encouraging others to restore and preserve the old buildings of San Juan. The restoration of Old San Juan is also part of Operación Serenidad, another of its aims being the preservation of a Puerto Rican cultural identity.

Most cities are forever changing, but prolonged colonization and lack of money kept Old San Juan in a static condition, and thus a great many of its old buildings have survived. After Puerto Rico became a commonwealth (and was fortunate enough to have Muñoz Marín for governor), an enlightened policy of respect for its historic buildings was developed. During the past three years this policy has come to impressive fruition.

The Cathedral, dedicated to San Ildefonso—Plaza Mayor (main square)

38

Chapter 2

MÉRIDA, YUCATÁN
The White City

As THE plane descends to the airport, Mérida—called La Blanca because of its cleanliness—gleams whitely against the straggly growth of the surrounding lowland. Like most of Yucatán, Mérida was relatively isolated from the rest of Mexico until 1960, when both railway and modern highway connections were completed. As a result, this pleasant, friendly capital still wears its modern improvements so lightly that one can savor the aristocratic Spanish Colonial flavor of the city founded in 1542. The houses in the old sections, abutting cleanly swept, narrow streets, display doorways and wrought-iron window casements reminiscent of Cádiz. Here and there primitive mahogany gratings fashioned from the native wood of the peninsula stand guard between householder and stranger. Past and present meet in the numerous charming plazas which, whether small or large, are adorned with statues, semitropical trees and flowers. Each day these plazas teem with colorful companies of Mérida's 160,000 people, including innumerable bright-eyed little boys whose importunate, "por favor, señor," must be answered, as my husband discovered, not only with a peso, but with the opportunity to polish proudly the señor's shoes.

Churches begun by the conquistadors raise their bell towers, or *espadañas*, in dignified grandeur, and the façade of the founder's house still fronts the main plaza. Streets are lively with traffic, picturesquely and excitingly complicated by a thousand horse-drawn carriages, which gather around the plazas waiting for fares and cause whirlpools of confusion when automobile collides with horse. Students pour through the doors of the relatively young university. One wonders what will happen now that the highway between Mérida and Mexico City is improved and an even greater influx of travelers arrives to augment the throng.

On the fringes of the city are the rectangular palm- or grass-thatched houses of the Indians, beautifully constructed by their owners without the use of nails—a method employed by the ancient Mayas, as stone carvings on one of the old Mayan ruins testify. The sapling sidings are tied securely with liana vines and, in some houses, are plastered with a mixture of chopped grass and red clay or black mud, polished with a bottle, and sometimes whitewashed with lime. As many as 10,000 palm leaves are used for one roof. The custom of sleeping in hammocks, which Columbus observed in San Salvador, still persists with rich and poor Indians alike. Hammocks range in price from twenty-five to 400 pesos, and styles include accommodations for matrimonial couples or whole families. Wood is scarce, and cooking, as in the past, is done over charcoal.

Against the rectangles and gentle curves that mark the skyline of Spanish Colonial Mérida, some thousands of windmills from Chicago rear their incongruous, galvanized-iron heads.★ A small water utility supplies the Mérida Hotel and a few government buildings, but the windmills pump up the city's major supply from the water absorbed by the limestone some twenty feet below the soil. Except for Lake Petén, Yucatán has almost no surface rivers or lakes, and therefore must depend on cisterns that store the rainfall, or on underground waters which appear, as at Chichén Itzá and Valladolid, in the form of ponds, or *cenotes*. The scarcity of water in the long dry season has historically been a problem in Yucatán; long ago, storage ponds, like enormous sunken jars, were constructed by the Indians against the time of drouth. In some places during the dry season the Indians had to descend deep into the earth, climbing up and down on swinging ladders and carrying lighted torches to guide them to the deep recesses of subterranean rivers. Some authorities conjecture that the desertion of the great Mayan cities was caused by failure of the water supply. Certainly one reason for the sacrifice of maidens to the gods at Chichén Itzá was the diminishing pools; the practice was, of course, intended to avert the inevitable catastrophe.

An extended visit to Mérida is rewarding not only because of the city's well-preserved Spanish Colonial features, but also because of its proximity to two out-

★Estimated at more than 6,600 by Hijuelos.

Native house under construction outside of Mérida

Ladder descending to well used during dry season. Illustration by Fred Catherwood in Stephens Incidents of Travel in Yucatán

Native hut at Uxmal

A view of one of the Mayan ceremonial mounds at Uxmal, Yucatán (50 miles from Mérida)

View of Mayan ceremonial mound

42

standing pre-Columbian ceremonial cities, Chichén Itzá and Uxmal. To explore the area without some acquaintance with its history would amount to eating the egg without salt.

The history of Mérida has a somewhat provincial flavor. For the traveler, some five or six names and the persons and events associated with them, will be enough to people the old streets and fill the liana vines with shadows. There are the Montejos —father, son and cousin, respectively called the Adelantado, Montejo the Younger, and Montejo the Nephew—who, between 1527 and 1542, contributed their efforts to the conquest of Mexico by reducing the Mayas of northern Yucatán to the acceptance of Spanish rule. There is the Maya, Cacique Tutul Xiu, who made the final gesture of surrender at T'ho, memorialized by the painting in the cathedral at Mérida. There is the contradictory Bishop Diego Landa, whose fanatical zeal in 1562 destroyed the written Mayan records of their own history and priestly culture along with thousands of Indian lives. At the same time, his scholarly instincts prompted him, in his own writings, to preserve descriptions of the culture and the vigesimal system, and to record the Mayan hieroglyphs, while his missionary ardor converted innumerable souls. Others of historical importance are John Stephens, the young New Jersey lawyer-explorer who verified the legends and disclosed the Mayan ruins to the nineteenth century, and Edward Herbert Thompson, whose inspired hunch led him to uncover the secrets of the sacred well at Chichén Itzá.

In 1527, at the age of thirty-five, Don Francisco Montejo, of Salamanca, Spain, set sail at the head of his own expedition to undertake the "pacification and conquest of the islands [sic] Cozumel and Yucatán." He had been twice before to Yucatán since its discovery ten years before by Francisco Hernandez de Córdova, the first time as a captain in the expedition of Juan de Grivalva and later in the company of Hernando Cortés. (Though Cortés was at that time only *Alcalde* (Mayor) of Santiago de Cuba, he, of course, was destined to become captain and conqueror of Mexico.) After both trips, Montejo returned to Spain as official commissioner to make reports. On his second trip he received from Charles V a new coat of arms and his own commission, dated December 8, 1526, giving to him and his heirs the rank of governor and captain-general. His privileges were numerous: he was to pay to the Crown only one-tenth of the gold from any mines to be developed; no export duties were imposed on him; large tracts of land were granted to him, along with permission to take rebellious Indians as slaves (even in 1842 Stephens found the Indians still suspicious lest they be enslaved by the white visitors). It was further specified that no

Mayan family in the Plaza Mayor with the Municipal Palace in the rear. The women wear their huipiles and Santa María shawls.

Caleza or surrey outside of the Cathedral (note the brass horse's head on the spring)

lawyers were to be admitted to the colony—a curious concession and a mark of royal confidence, since lawyers were usually sent as the king's representatives to check on the *encomenderos'* treatment of the Indians—and that one-tenth of any revenue was to be expended on churches and their ornamentation. All told, the venture held the hope of rich returns on an initial investment of 2,000 ducats (which Montejo had supplied by the sale of his wife's estate); but there was also the risk of financial loss and frightful death, as he well knew from his earlier experience.

The Adelantado Francisco de Montejo, who had received from the king an order permitting him to conquer Yucatán, ranks among the great conquistadors, even though he is not so well known as Cortés, Pizarro, Balboa and Alvarado. Less distinguished than they as a military figure, he was an outstanding administrator, colonizer and negotiator with the Indians. During the twenty-year conquest of Yucatán he crossed and re-crossed the territory, seeking a permanent base for operations (these he would often name Salamanca after his birthplace) which he was continually forced to abandon. Always short of food and water, he carried on heroically and was saved many times by a friendly, rich supplier for Cuba, Juan de Lerma. But the Mayas refused to be conquered and, in 1534, after the second attempt failed, the Spaniards retreated to Santa María de la Victoria, Tabasco. Later attempts were hampered by the desertion of many Spaniards who, disappointed by the poverty of

44

Yucatán, went on to Peru, the land of gold. The Adelantado retired with his faithful lieutenant, Davila, to Mexico City, where he had a house and holdings. Montejo the Younger stayed in Tabasco until, in 1540, he was commissioned by his father to undertake the final conquest of Yucatán from the base of Salamanca de Campeche.

The Adelantado, who was then in Chiapas, helped by gathering funds, recruiting soldiers and making basic policies. His instructions to his son, in brief, were as follows:*

You must strive to see that your people live and act as true Christians.

You should depart from Champoton and go to Campeche and present your commission and inquire if the natives have any grievances such as being made slaves against their will. Let them understand that for services of supplying food for two years they will be relieved of all labor.

Go to Campeche, taking lords from Champoton to speak to those of Canu, telling them of the intention of the Spaniards to colonize and instruct the natives in Christian faith and taking care in the Province of Ah Canul that the soldiery do not maltreat the Indians of the province. The lords of Champoton are then to return.

In the Ah Canul seek out the lord Nachan Chan, always a friend of the Christians and commend him for his good works. Ask whether they wish to make war and if they do what the consequences will be.

Arrive at the town of T'ho, establish a cabildo and strive to make peace. [This took some doing.]

Establish the land around T'ho in *encomiendas*, making divisions of land and natives among at least one hundred citizens but leaving some *repartimientos* as His Majesty sees fit to distribute.

Strive to see that all of the citizens build houses and establish farms and crops.

Open roads to Campeche, as well as to the sea and to principal towns. Place the will of God, service to His Majesty and welfare of the land above all else.

This was dated 1540, Chiapas. The Adelantado held for himself the province of Tutul Xiu, and the towns of Campeche and Champoton.

Satisfactory expeditions against Campeche in 1540, under Don Francisco the Younger, and in 1541 with a cousin, Captain Francisco Montejo, led to a joining of forces in 1542 for the successful effort to capture the Indian town of T'ho.

In the great fight for T'ho, 60,000 Indians opposed 200 Spaniards, but the latter, some of whom were mounted, prevailed and afterwards established their city on the ruins of the Indian town. The Spaniards called the new city Mérida, because on the

*See Robert S. Chamberlain's *Conquest and Colonization of Yucatán*, an excellent story of the conquest based largely on the *Historia General y Natural de las Indias, islas y tierra firma del mar oceano* of Gonzalo Fernandez de Oviedo y Valdes. Oviedo's work, published in Madrid in 1855, drew much from the accounts of Alonzo Luján, a noble caballero of the Order of Santiago, who took part in the conquest.

site of T'ho they found buildings of stone and lime worked with mouldings similar to those built by the Romans in the Mérida of Spain.

Later, during the stubbornly resisted conquest of Uaymil-Chetumal in northern Yucatán, Alonzo Pacheco, the elder Montejo's lieutenant, committed horrible atrocities against the Indians, sending dogs after those who fled to the bush, and torturing the women and children. Because of this and of their general desire to be free, the Indians organized the great revolt of 1547–48. This unsuccessful revolt was the last great uprising of the Indians against the Spaniards.

The only known account of the events at T'ho was written by a Spanish historian, Fray Diego Lopez Cogolludo, in a book published in 1658 called the *Historia de Yucatán*—a volume which might as appropriately have been called the "History of the Franciscan Friars." This book was an object of great reverence among the Indians, because it contained an impressive story of "the ambassadors" told in bloody detail. The story informs us that Francisco Montejo, after his arrival at T'ho, was approached by a large band of Indians. The group was headed by the Cacique Tutul Xiu, a lineal descendant of the lord who ruled over the Mayas in the days of their ascendency. The Cacique came in peace and as a gesture of surrender asked the Adelantado to go through the Christian ceremonies for him. He even kneeled to kiss the cross. Later Tutul Xiu sent ambassadors to the Mayan lords of Zotuta to inform them that he had decided to make peace with the Spaniards who, it was certain, had come to stay. The Cacique's ambassadors came before the chief lord of the district of Zotuta, Nachi Cocom, but he requested that they wait five days for an answer. On the pretext of a boar hunt, the ambassadors were lured into a dense forest and feasted for three days. Thereupon, the chief lord had their throats slit, sparing only one who, with his eyes put out, was sent back to Tutul Xiu as a reproach for cowardly submission to the Spaniards.

John Stephens, in the 1843 account of his experiences, relates that he saw, in the Casa Real at Mani, a treasured copy of Cogolludo's book, carefully wrapped up, and in it an illustration depicting the murder of the ambassadors, together with the original of the illustration—an old oil painting on cotton cloth. The design showed a coat of arms bordered by the heads of the murdered ambassadors, one of them with an arrow in his temple. In the center was a sapote tree growing out of a box, representing the tree at Zotuta under which the murder was committed.

The Franciscan friars were the first of the old orders to enter Yucatán, and their writings have been of considerable value in tracing the history of the country. It was

46

Ceiling and organ loft of the Cathedral. (Photo courtesy of the Crescencio Carrillo y Ancona Library)

a Franciscan friar, Jacobo de Testera, who, along with four assistants, accompanied Montejo's first expedition to convert the Indians. Their modest success was undermined by a company of thirty mercenary Spaniards; the latter, who traded images for slaves, so aroused the Indians that the friars were driven away. Friar Luis de Villalpanda, a graduate of Salamanca University, was the first to learn the Mayan language. He became the guardian of the Itzmal convent in 1550.

By far the most important of the missionary brothers in Yucatán was Diego Landa, who was born in Cifuentes, Guadalajara, Spain, in 1524, and came to the peninsula in 1549. In 1573, after many years of evangelical activity, he was appointed second bishop of Yucatán with headquarters in Mérida. With all his brilliance, he lacked prudence and had acquired the reputation of both saint and devil. It was he who was responsible, in great measure, for the auto da fé of 1562 in Mani to punish

47

the Mayas who practiced their native religion. It was estimated that 4,500 Mayas were tortured, eighty-five, wearing the garment of penitent culprits of the Inquisition (*sambenitos*), were burned, and 6,330 were fined. During this period, too, all of the native Mayan manuscripts were destroyed. The bishop was recalled to Spain for these excesses, where he was tried but exonerated.

Later, in 1566, while still in Spain, Bishop Landa wrote his invaluable source book, *Relation of Things of Yucatán*, dealing with the Mayan culture and including his explanation of the hieroglyphs of their vigesimal calendar. The book, discovered in the Royal Library of Madrid in 1863, established the author as the leading authority on the ancient Maya. The discovery of Landa's explanation of the hieroglyphs was to Mayan antiquity what the discovery of the Rosetta stone was to the study of ancient Egypt.

Mérida becomes more interesting the more one knows about it. As the only real city in Yucatán, it is the seat of the state's industries and contains three-fourths of the state's professional men and landed proprietors. It has always been the stronghold of the established aristocracy of Spanish descent. Mérida, in sum, is the operational headquarters for all of Yucatán and has been since its founding. Old Campeche and modern Progresso are its two ports.

One very pleasant way to see the famous architectural examples of the Spanish Colonial era in Mérida is to travel behind a pony-sized horse in a surrey—perhaps one which has two brass horses' heads on the springs and leather work decorated by brass nail heads. These surreys are a later edition of the *coche calesa* seen by Stephens in 1842.

We go first to the cathedral, a severe and majestic building★ which displays a mixture of styles—Moorish in the towers and Renaissance in the main body. Services there were inaugurated in 1598, and on December 12, 1763, at the time of the completion of the second tower, the edifice was dedicated to San Ildefonso.

This is one of the most impressive cathedrals in Latin America. The niches on both sides of the main door of the façade contain statues in stone of St. Peter and St. Paul. Unfortunately, the sculptured coat of arms of Castile and León over the door has been covered by a carved plaster national seal. George Kubler has thus described the Cathedral of Mérida: "The main façade betrays the hand of a military engineer in the abrupt geometry of towers and curtain-wall flanking a tall arched form. The contrast between the portal ornament and the cliff-like façade wall is blunt. The

★See description in *Catálogo de Construcciones Religiosas de Estado de Yucatán*.

Montejo Palace in the Plaza Mayor, built by the Indians from Mani in 1551.

Christ of the Blisters. A copy of the one formerly in the Cathedral. From the collection of Señora Teresa Herrero de Barbachano, Mexico D. F. (The original was destroyed on September 24, 1915.)

Seventeenth-century carving of Christ from Yucatán. It is in the private chapel of the 200-year-old house of Señor and Señora Manuel Barbachano in Mexico D. F.

façade is like the entrance to a walled city."★ The view in this book is from the main plaza, but to me the most thrilling aspect is from the side street, where, looking up the walls of both towers, one recalls the straight simplicity of certain Renaissance buildings in Italy, such as the Monastery of San Gimignano near Florence.

The cathedral is almost wholly the work of Juan Miguel de Agüero who, after working on the fortifications of San Cristóbal in Havana, secured King Philip the Second's permission to proceed in 1587 to Mérida and work on the cathedral. Bishop Toral collected the first stone in 1560, but the cathedral was not officially started, in accordance with the Bull of Pope Pius IV, until December 16, 1561. Of the 300,000 pesos supplied, one-third came from the Royal Treasury, one-third from the encomenderos, and one-third was extracted by Indian labor without cost. Agüero found the chapels and other parts in such bad condition that a suit was

★*Art and Architecture in Spain and Portugal*, p. 66. On page 67 Kubler gives a cross-section and plan.

50

brought against the heirs of Francisco Claros, an engineer who had worked on the cathedral previously. The columns, cornices, arches, coffered ceilings and other building details sculptured in stone were designed and built by Agüero, and his name is on the buttressed dome, the first to be built in Mexico. The square stones of the interior columns, like the stones of the exterior, were taken from the Mayan ruins. In 1600, after eleven years of work, Agüero received a memorial of merit from the king, and he and his sons were given payment and land by Montejo the Younger, son of the conqueror of Yucatán. "The nature of the architectural style of the Gulf and Caribbean settlements during the sixteenth century," George Kubler writes, "is exemplified by the Cathedral in Mérida, Yucatán—an aisled hall church in double proportion like the Cathedral of Santo Domingo. . . . Some of the workmen who made that cathedral also made that of Mérida."

In 1915, acts of revolutionary violence in Mérida caused the loss of the priceless old altars, figures and retables of the cathedral and other churches. Among the objects lost was the historic "Christ of the Blisters" ("Cristo de las Ampollas"). The original image was sculptured in the Mayan town of Ichmul from the wood of a tree which the Indians reported to have seen in flames at night. Fire destroyed the church in which this figure was first venerated, but the figure, blackened and blistered, was found among the embers and brought to the cathedral in 1645. Now that the original has been destroyed by vandals, a reproduction continues to be honored each year between September 28 and October 13.*

In the interior of the cathedral, over a side door, is a painting which depicts the visit of the Mayan leader, Tutul Xiu, to Conquistador Montejo. The background of the picture shows the ancient city of T'ho, on the ruins of which Mérida was built. The picture would seem to be relatively modern. At the left of this hangs a large, well-framed painting of the Immaculate Conception with St. Dominic and St. Francis kneeling on either side. This painting, one of the few in Mérida, is probably about 150 years old. It is of typical Renaissance style and, although darkened by age, it retains its beauty.

Originally, the archbishop's palace was attached to the cathedral. In 1915 the two buildings were separated by a street called the Passage of the Revolution. The residency now belongs to the federal government and serves as headquarters for the

---

*Pictures of the original may be obtained in the cathedral, and a very interesting reproduction is owned by Teresa Herrera de Barbachano of Mexico City. This same collection contains a primitive Indian carving of a seventeenth-century Christ, used before the family altar.

army. The part which faces 58th Street was once the Seminario Conciliar, the first seminary in Yucatán, and the door now marked 501-C was its main entrance. This stone doorway is still well preserved; it is identifiable by the episcopal coat of arms at the top, and the images of the Virgin of the Rosary and San Ildefonso, both patrons of the seminary, on the sides.

Our next stop by surrey is the Montejo Palace, where a Granadine façade is all that remains of one of the most famous conquistador residences in Latin America. Pál Kelemen, in his excellent book on the highlights of Latin America, *Baroque and Rococo in Latin America*, gives the history and description of this façade:

Civil architecture from this period also foreshadowed the originality and the great regional variety of the later centuries here. The Casa de Montejo which stands on the main plaza in Mérida, Yucatán, at an angle from the Cathedral, was built in 1549, only seven years after the founding of the town. It was ordered by Francisco Montejo the Younger for the use of his conquistador father. Stones from the wrecked Maya edifices were used in the construction and it was built after a Spanish design by an Indian master mason with Indian labor from Mani. Its peculiar combination of styles is distinctly regional.

The lower section with its panelled jambs, fluted columns and portrait medallions is Plateresque in effect, whereas the upper section recalls the Gothic. The gigantic halberdiers stand as atlantes, their feet on human heads—a symbol of the subjugation of the natives. Wild men, dressed in skins and carrying clubs guard the sides, a crouching figure upholds the corbeled balcony, and a variety of figural motifs, vines and mythical animals are spread all over the composition. The building extends to the right and has four large grilled windows, also adorned in monumental fashion.

This house was occupied by the old conquistador for only a short time before he was dislodged from office; he returned to Spain to protest his dismissal and died there in 1553. The son then lived in it from that time and until 1914 it had twenty-one owners.

Today the Montejo Palace is restored as a private residence. In the upper part of the still beautiful portico stand the busts of Montejo el Adelantado, his wife, Doña Beatriz Alvarez de Herrera, to the right and his daughter, Catalina de Montejo, to the left. In the lower part are the faces of the Spanish monarchs: first Emperor Charles V with his wife Isabel and, just below, Philip II and his wife, Isabel of Valois.

It is interesting to observe that the subjugation of the natives depicted in the Montejo façade is also symbolized by a figure—that of San Gabriel with his foot on a Mayan slave—which stands to the left of the main altar of the Church of Lourdes in Mérida.

The Executive Palace, which holds the governor's office, is located on the northeast corner of the main plaza. Its cornerstone was laid in 1883; but the Spanish

Corner of the Dummy (Monifato)   *Corner of the Elephant at 46th and 65th streets*

Colonial Palace of the Captains General of Yucatán once stood on this same site. On the west side of this plaza, the Municipal Building, containing plaques that commemorate historical events, is distinguished by its Colonial-style porches.

Across from the cathedral is an old building, built in 1625, which the Church has used at various times as a hospital for mental cases (under the supervision of the Juaninos Brothers), as a Catholic school and as the Bishop's Palace. Until recently it housed the Federal Museum of Archeology—a collection containing fine Mayan stone carvings, if little Spanish Colonial art. Adjoining and sharing a small patio was the Yucatecan Library, Crescencio Carrillo y Ancona, with its 10,000 volumes. A plaque on the wall of the patio honors the memory of John L. Stephens, the inspired archeologist and nineteenth-century reporter on pre-Columbian Mayan culture. Since 1959 the museum and library have shared a fine building on Paseo de Montejo, called the Museum of History and Mayan Archeology.

At one time street locations were designated by figures of animals, fruits or flowers placed on roof-top corners; one may still find the Corner of the Elephant, of the *Chac-mool* (the tiger of the Mayan ruins), of the *Monifato* (dummy) and of the Bull. Now, however, the streets are numbered, odd for those running north and south, even for those running east and west.

If the surrey turns down 61st Street one can see the Arco de Dragónes (Arch of the Dragoons), which is dated 1690. It is one of three remaining gates of a city wall which was to have protected the encomenderos from hostile Mayas; the wall, however, was never actually built. A second gate, the Arco del Puente, at 50th and 63rd streets, was so named because rains used to flood the corner, obliging pedestrians to cross the street on a wooden bridge. At 62nd and 67th streets, we find the Church of St. John the Baptist. Across from it is a park, once called San Juan but now named after a famous priest, Don Vicente María Velázquez, the originator of the San Juanistas (a group of early nineteenth-century patriots working in Yucatán for Mexican independence). Velázquez Park is a beautiful, small green spot with a delightful fountain in the center and a view on the left of the third old city gate, the Arco de San Juan. The arches are all similar, each with pointed pylons on either side and characteristic insignia in open niches above the arches. The insigne in the Arch of St. John is a figure of this same saint; that in the Arch of the Bridge is a stone cross; in the Arch of the Dragoons, a human figure. There were formerly seven arches.

A block to the west of Velázquez Park is a small church called La Candelaria (Our Lady of the Candle), constructed in 1609. The simple and beautiful interior, which escaped revolutionary despoliation, retains its original retable with gold leaf and oil paintings. An unusual feature is the wrought-iron pulpit.

Proceeding cloppety-clop out to La Mejorada Church at 52nd and 59th streets, we stop to observe the open niches and bells of the bell wall, or *espadaña* of the upper façade. Opposite is the beautiful building, completed in 1694, which was once the Franciscan Convent of Mejorada. After the year 1821, when its founders were expelled from Yucatán, it was converted to many uses and now serves as quarters for families of soldiers stationed in the nearby armory.

A second headquarters for surreys is the Plaza Cepeda Peraza, so named for the governor whose statue was erected in it in 1896. It was once known as the Plaza de Jesús. Another small plaza nearby is that of the Mother, close to the Jesús or Tercera Orden Church. The figure standing in it is a replica of a statue of motherhood in the Luxembourg Museum of Paris, carved by Francis Lenoir. The Mérida copy was carved by Lenoir's son. On May 10, Mother's Day, the statue is covered with flowers.

Church of San Juan Bautista (John the Baptist)

San Juan Gate

Arch of the Bridge (Arco del Puente), 1690, on 50th and 63rd streets

The University of Yucatán, on 57th and 60th streets, was built on the site of the School of St. Peter, founded by the Jesuits in 1618, and administered by them until their expulsion in 1767. The name was later changed to Instituto Literario del Estado. In 1938 the building, built around an open courtyard, was renovated and the institution became the University of Yucatán. It has schools of law, medicine, dentistry, chemistry and engineering.

Las Monjas Convent is located a block west of Plaza Grande, at the corner of 63rd and 64th streets. This convent, the cathedral and the Montejo façade are the three most architecturally distinguished buildings in the city. The convent, inaugurated in 1595, was occupied by the Conceptionist nuns, who maintained the chapel and a school until their exclaustration in October, 1867, under the governorship of General Cepeda Peraza. Only the chapel is now used. The Colonial arches, high up on the building and formerly used for observation, are still in good condition. They are the most beautiful feature of the old convent.

As one travels by calesa from the Plaza Grande to Santa Lucía Park, one follows an historic route; for at the end, within the churchyard of the Church of Santa Lucía, lies the cemetery of the cathedral. The little church of Santa Lucía was finished in 1575 and from 1580 to 1620 was used exclusively by mulattoes and colored slaves. In front of this church (built by Encomendero don Pedro García with his private funds) stands a figure of Cristo Obrero, the Working Christ, which was brought from Spain. The park adjoining is named for the same saint, and is also known as the Portales de Santa Lucía, because the columns of its arches still carry the hooks where the horses of travelers were tied.★

Of lesser note, yet interesting because of the use of the *cenote*, or underground river, is the restaurant Los Tulipanes (The Tulips). Here, legend has it, Mayan princesses and virgins once went bathing to purify their bodies and souls; today guests can do the same.

The historic private homes of Mérida, protected by governmental decree, are interesting, but they are accessible only through introductions and appointments. In these, besides fine doorways and, occasionally, balconies, there is an infinite variety of window casements with wrought-iron gratings, or *rejas*. These gratings are generally of two styles—ornate French and the more simple Spanish. Number 519 Calle 65 is a house which has been lived in continuously by the Mediz family for 200 years.† This is a typical, one-floor Spanish house whose rooms and covered corridors (the latter upheld by columns and arches) open onto the patio. There is a luxuriant growth of flowers and shrubs in the center of the patio. Much of the social life in this tropical climate is carried on outdoors in the corridors. The part of the exterior which faces the street contains a door and three typically Spanish casement windows; the latter, protected by wrought-iron gratings, reveal quaint openings in the interior shutters. Inside, the entrance is guarded by a magnificent wrought-iron grille. Between this and the outside door the coach was kept in Colonial times, while the horses were held in readiness in a rear patio. The main patio provides examples of the two sources of water used in Mérida today. In the center is a cistern which stores rain water caught from the roof. This water is pumped up by hand at a fountain as needed and, after being boiled, is used for drinking. A private windmill draws water from twenty feet underground for other household purposes.

The dining room contains many heirlooms. The white Limoges china, edged in gold, bears the family crest—three lions which signify, as the gracious daughter of

★The park has recently been converted into a playground.
†Its present owner is the lawyer and poet Señor Rafael Mediz Bolio.

57

University of Yucatán. Started by the Jesuits in 1618 as the College of Saint Peter, it was renovated in 1938 and renamed the University of Yucatán.

the house, Trinidad Mediz de Camino, explains, "I believe, I love, I hope." The antique family silver is rich with tradition, and there is still much handsome French Baccarat glassware, which was originally imported in sets containing twelve dozen of each type of glass. The library holds many rare volumes and family portraits. I was shown a miniature of the handsome Baron O'Horan, first president of the Republic of Guatemala and a great-great-grandfather of Rafael and Antonio Mediz Bolio. The Hospital O'Horan in Mérida is named in his memory.

Within walking distance are two other historically interesting dwellings. At Number 489 Calle 62 is the Portico de la Casa (Portico House) where, years ago, Don Estanislao José Martinez del Puerto y Solis de Montejo lived. This gentleman was perpetual alderman by grace of His Catholic Majesty. The doorway of this house, with escutcheon and helmet carved above it, has two small doors cut into the great main door. The typical flattened pointed arches are similar to those in the shutters of the Mediz house. At 59th and 58th streets is the Hotel Itzá, Mérida's oldest hotel, which, in addition to Colonial arcades and patio, boasts a library and Mayan museum.

The Spaniard's casa is indeed his castle, and the opportunity to enter the gates as a guest is to be treasured. To a considerate and courtly young host, Fernando Barbachano, Jr., and his charming wife, Maruja, we owed the experience of a true Spanish dinner. The main course, which followed delicious Mexican daiquiris and soup, was a dish of venison with sauce. Yucatán is rightly called The Land of the Turkey and the Deer. We learned that the hunters we had recently seen on the way to Chichén Itzá provide regular supplies of small native deer. A separate course of a paste of black beans was followed by a fascinating dessert, "Spanish Egg," a mixture of eggs and sugar beaten together until it was stiff enough to be sliced, and served with raisin sauce. This was followed by two kinds of tamarind paste, one prepared with refined white sugar, and the other with coarse brown native sugar. Coffee such as we never find in our North American supermarkets was the unforgettable finale.

To Señor Barbachano, the elder, I owe a pleasant bit of folklore—the origin of the word "cocktail," used now universally to designate an apéritif. In the old days in Campeche, visitors to the waterfront used to stir their rum drink with a small stick having a bit of feather at the end. This in time was called a cocktail, and gradually the name came to refer to the drink itself. (Others, no doubt, have different derivations for this universally used word.)

The years between the discovery and conquest of Yucatán by the Western World and the reawakening of interest there, through the cultural disclosures of the nineteenth century, were marked by no more than average interest. The Church had almost as much authority as the Civil Government, and conflicts of varying intensity were inevitable. The Indians at times proved rebellious; hostile nature produced droughts and famine; political developments in general reflected Spain's home problems.★

The relationships of the Holy Orders with the secular clergy were frequently strained. Early in 1700, the Church and State became so hostile over a supposed violation of the sanctity of the Church that a governor was excommunicated by the bishop and two political leaders were assassinated. In the early eighteenth century, Franciscan leaders aspiring to political power brought the order into such disrepute that the brotherhood was required to hold its services under the priest in the Church of Jesús María, instead of in its own monastery; only the dispatching of a Visitador from Spain improved the situation. In 1767 the Jesuits were expelled from Mérida and Campeche. In 1820 the anticlerical Marshal, Don Juan Echeverry Manrique de Lara, enforcing the law of Cortés that there be but one monastery in each population center, ordered the expulsion of the Franciscans and the retention of La Mejorada. As a result, the beautiful Franciscan monastery was sacked and priceless collections of art, reliquaries, books, translations and original memoirs were scattered or destroyed.

The *mita* system relaxed briefly from 1725 to 1731 on the installation of a new governor, Don Antonio de Figueroa y Selva; but the relaxation was promptly blamed for a devastating famine that occurred from 1725 to 1727. The famine, which caused a partial exodus to New Spain, Cuba and Puerto Rico, was alleviated by the distribution of imported food from the public granary. The system was resumed by special mandate of the king, but with specific protections for the Indians. Work was to be expected of all Indians equally; there would be no idle Indians; there was to be time for rest, personal work, religious instruction and recovery from illness; Indians were to receive payment in money and cotton. An interesting commentary on the application of the *mita* system to church work is afforded by Joaquin Vedoza in his *Letter on the Service Which the Indians Give in Yucatán to the Parish Priests and Religious Doctrines*, which states that by 1721 there had been 76,415 churches built to the True God in America.

★The untranslated *Historia de Yucatán Durante La Dominacion Español*, by Juan Francisco Solis, circa 1913, is the recognized authority on this local history.

Casa Mediz, Calle 65, showing doorway and two Spanish windows *Las Monjas (the Nuns' Convent)*

An uprising in the town of Cisteil in November, 1761, resulted in a battle between some 2,000 Spaniards mobilized by the new governor, Don José Crespo y Honorato, and uncounted Indians under the native *cacique*, Can Ek. Some 600 Indians were killed, and 500 were captured in flight. The prisoners were tried in Mérida. Two hundred of them were given two hundred lashes each and had their right ears cut off. The rest were condemned to public work for a certain time. Can Ek had his flesh torn with pincers and his body was burned in the Plaza Grande of Mérida. Eight of his aides were hanged. General Don Cristóbal Calderon de la Helguera and his men, having put down the rebellion, returned to Mérida on December 10, 1761. Among other rewards, he received from the king the title Sergeant Major of the Plaza of Campeche. Disciplinary measures were taken against the Indians; they were prohibited from carrying arms and from traveling without passports. Whipping in public and other punishments were reinstated. Order was restored.

Education of the natives was undertaken by the Church, but, during the seventeenth century, efforts failed for lack of interest. Primary schools for the Indians were again attempted in the eighteenth century and, in these, reading, writing, moral doctrine, music, singing and the Mayan language were taught with success. In the city of Mérida itself, schools and colleges were instituted under the tutelage of the Catholic Church. One of these, the Seminario Conciliar of Ildefonso, was almost

Patio of Casa Mediz showing old wheel pump   *Street scene in Mérida showing French window grill*

entirely the result of the efforts of one man, the beloved Bishop Fr. Ignacio de Padilla y Estrada. These institutions taught Latin, philosophy, theology, rhetoric, music and singing. Although many of the upper classes went to Mexico or Spain for further study, the local colleges developed their share of illustrious men, including Bishop Don Gaspar de Quemes (1651–1726), and Don Juan José de Vertiz, a viceroy at Buenos Aires (1789). In 1767, through the expulsion of the Jesuits, a grave loss to education occurred with the compulsory closing of the colleges of San Javier and San Pedro in Mérida, and San José in Campeche. After the Independence, the University of Mérida was established on the site of the San Pedro College.

The movement for independence, it may be said, sprang from the seeds of philosophical debate in the College of San Pedro, and was nurtured in the salons of Doña Josepha, proponent of absolute partition, and of Doña Joaquina Peón, the advocate of moderation. In Mérida, young men under the leadership of Father P. Velázquez, Chaplain of the Church of San Juan Bautista, formed the "Sanjuanista," an organization devoted to furthering the cause of constitutional government. The sentiment was part of the growing desire for independence in all parts of Mexico. To a degree, it also reflected developments on the continent. By 1812 Spain had achieved a constitutional monarchy, and a directive was issued by the Spanish Regency which established a constitutional government for Mexico. Under this

62

the Colonials, no longer obliged to pay their tenth to the king, paid only parochial tithes. This was rescinded in 1814 by King Ferdinand VII, who abolished the Constitution, punished his political enemies and resumed collections of profits and royal tithes from the Colonials. However, the imposts on commerce which had been lifted by decree of the governor in 1813, in order to remedy the poverty resulting from heavy duties, were not reinstated, and ships of all nations, friends and neutrals, continued to enjoy freedom of entry.

It seems remarkable that in his six-hundred-page volume on the Colonial era, Molino Solis does not mention the Mayan ruins, in spite of the fact that the cathedral was built of stones from these ruins and that Chichén Itzá lay astride the main road between Mérida and Valladolid (once the second city of Yucatán). It may have been that he took for granted the knowledge of the Mayan Indians, who are still in preponderance, who still speak Mayan, and who eat and live much the same as their ancient ancestors.

The great ruins of Chichén Itzá and Uxmal, reached by car in a few hours from Mérida, have fascinated sightseers from all over the world. These well-preserved ruins, belonging primarily to the later empire of the Toltec incursion on the Mayas, or the historic period of 975–1200, had been heard of by the conquistadors, but were later rediscovered by John Lloyd Stephens when he went as United States Chargé d'Affaires to Central America in 1839. He had read an account concerning military levies among natives by a Captain Antonio del Río, who reported seeing remains of ancient buildings in Central America and Yucatán. Stephens (1805–1852), who was a lawyer, had studied archeological remains in Palestine, Egypt and Mesopotamia. In a spirit of adventure, having secured an appointment as special envoy of the United States to Central America, he set out for Copán, Honduras, on an expedition which resulted in his first book, *Incidents of Travel in Central America, Chiapas and Yucatán*. The publication in 1841 of this book, eloquently illustrated by Frederick Catherwood, aroused considerable interest. Although F. de Waldeck had published *Voyage pittoresque et archéologique dans la Province d'Yucatán* four years previously in France, Stephens is credited generally with the effective rediscovery of the Mayan ruins. In his first book he reports his colorful initial purchase of ancient real estate. Having dressed in his official formal coat (but with dirty white pants) and patent leather hat to impress his audience, he bought the ruins of Copán, Guatemala, from the alleged owner, Don José María, for fifty dollars. He then held a celebration and passed out cigars.

Portal of the House No. 489 on 62nd Street. It was formerly the residence of Don José Solis de Montejo. (Photo courtesy of the Crescencio Carrillo y Ancona Library, Mérida)

Chapel of Itzimna, Mérida

A second trip, devoted wholly to Yucatán, was begun by Stephens on October 9, 1841. Again he was accompanied by Frederick Catherwood as draughtsman, and for the first time by Dr. Cabot of Boston. The two-volume account of this second trip was published in London in 1843. The book, *Incidents of Travel in Yucatán*, is a colorful account of people, places and events as well as of archeological explorations.

The party arrived in Mérida, burdened with paraphernalia and daguerreotype apparatus, at the end of the festival of San Cristóbal. Depositing their baggage, they quickly joined the crowd, following it from the brightly lighted church to a large hall. There they were astonished to see some 2,000 persons of all ages and conditions playing a game called La Loteria with grains of corn on sheets of paper—an ancestor perhaps of "bingo."

The next day found them in the Plaza of San Cristóbal watching a bullfight, noting with concern the vicious ways in which the bull was maddened, first by being cruelly knotted to a post, then by having a figure of fireworks set off on his back. The next bull was hauled into the ring by a rope through his nose. On the last day of the fiesta a procession threaded through the streets, headed by three priests supporting a large silver cross ten feet high, followed by an Indian band, and next by a party of Indians bearing upon their shoulders a barrow which supported another large silver cross, at the foot of which sat the figure of Mary Magdalene dressed in red with the image of the dead Christ across her lap. Shortly afterwards they started upon their epochal investigations of Mayan ruins.

The second volume of *Travel in Yucatán* contains an Indian map which shows the locations of villages and churches centering upon Mani. On this map, nearby Uxmal is marked as a ruin instead of a church, indicating the possibility that the Mayan religion was still practiced there at the time of the sketch. The map was from an old book, dated 1557, written in the old Mayan language, which could no longer be read by the nineteenth-century Indians. In 1556, Uxmal was evidently an aboriginal town occupied by Indians.

At Peto (which, like Mérida, has figures on buildings to distinguish streets), Don Pio Peréz gave Stephens a copy of a manuscript containing 4,000 Mayan words, an almanac and a fragment of a Mayan manuscript written by an Indian from memory entitled *Principal Epochs of the Ancient History of Yucatán*. This manuscript assigned the dates A. D. 360–432 to the founding of Chichén Itzá.★

★Etymologically, the name combines the forms *chi* (mouth), *chen* (well), with *Itzá*, the name of the tribe which allegedly founded the city.

Mayan stone carving of about 1100 or 1200 A.D. The cape might be of feathers and the figure might be of a male or female young person; possibly a god.

Church of San Cristóbal

The last stop of Stephens' second trip, before returning to Mérida, brought him to Chichén Itzá on the royal road to Valladolid. These ruins had been visited in 1840 by Baron Frederichstahl, who first brought them to the notice of the public. The Baron's route had been recommended to him by Stephens after the latter's return from the 1839 explorations among the ruins of Yucatán. Stephens, Catherwood and Cabot stayed at the historic hacienda belonging to Don Juan Sosa. The house, made of stones taken from the Mayan ruins, had been lived in since 1641.

Stephens' book about his experiences in Yucatán, so delightfully written, has lost none of its fascination, and Catherwood's drawings, in addition to their scientific accuracy, are remarkable for their excellent draughtsmanship. Their book is still an important source for the historical background of Mérida and Yucatán.★

Edward Herbert Thompson, the next distinguished enthusiast of Mayan archeology after Stephens, first went to Yucatán in 1885 at the age of twenty-five, the youngest man in the United States consular service. In a French translation of the book written in 1566 by Bishop Diego de Landa, archbishop of Yucatán, and unearthed in the Royal Library of Madrid in 1863, Thompson had discovered the story of the Sacred Well, the *cenote* of Chichén Itzá. In an account by Don Diego Sarmiento de Figueroa (the sixteenth-century Alcalde of Madrid), he had also read about the lords and priests who threw maidens and children into the well that they might speak with the spirits, plead for good fortune, and, on being hauled to the surface, reveal future events. Observing the faint indication of a path leading from El Castillo, the castle of Chichén Itzá, Thompson followed it and made the exciting discovery of a *cenote* which he suspected was the Sacred Well.

In 1894, Thompson bought the plantation containing the Chichén ruins and occupied the Sosa hacienda nearby. As preparation for proving his thesis, he returned to the States for instruction in underwater diving. Later, with two Greek divers, and the assistance of the Peabody Institute of Boston, Thompson went back to the Sacred Well supplied with dredges and other equipment.

In *God, Graves and Scholars*, C. W. Ceram tells the enthralling story of how Thompson, in the company of apprehensive and fascinated natives, finally dredged up his exciting treasures: carved jade, a carved turquoise bowl bearing the figure of

★Lord Kingsborough of Regency, England, between 1830 and 1848 wrote his *Antiquities of Mexico* in nine volumes, which sold for 175 pounds. He set forth his views that the ancient peoples of Mexico were descendants of the lost tribes of Israel. His reproductions of the known Mexican codices are the only ones in existence, and his material is of inestimable value. It is told that he spent his whole substance upon the publication of his books and, being unable to pay for the last volumes, was thrown into debtors' prison where he died.

Santo—eighteenth-century St. Anthony. From the collection of Señor Guy Puerto

San Isidro dressed as an Indian. Formerly in the church at Chichén Itzá. Collection of Señora Fernando Barbachano

a man with a planting stick and dog, symbolic figures beaten on gold, copper disks, masses of copal incense, skeleton remains, darts of obsidian, and gold objects engraved in repoussé. Most of the objects had been ceremonially broken. The bones were human, and thus the myth of a sacrificial well was proved true. Much of the collection was deposited with the Harvard Peabody Museum—a wise precaution considering the subsequent destruction by fire of the local hacienda, the laboratory, the valuable library and the artifacts during the political upheavals between 1910 and 1930.

After fifty years of archeological digging and twenty-four years in Yucatán as consul investigating the Mayan ruins, Thompson died in 1935, having spent most of his substance in his work. His holdings had been confiscated by the Mexican

70

government for default of payment for treasures discovered and removed. The plantations surrounding the ruins were later purchased by Señor Fernando Barbachano, and the hacienda, which had been restored by the Carnegie Institute of Washington, was remodeled in 1958 into a hostelry for persons visiting the ruins. It serves as an auxiliary to the beautiful Mayaland Lodge, with its authentic grass-thatched houses. The Mexican government retains possession of the ruins.

Today, tourist travel to the ruins, centering on Mérida, provides one of Yucatán's largest sources of income. With airplanes, and now, train and highway connections to Mexico, Mérida is readily accessible. Formerly it was relatively isolated; its poor land afforded no such great wealth as flows into Lima and Cuzco from their mines. It was for these reasons that Mérida had so few great art treasures brought in from abroad, and that no school developed artists as in Quito and Cuzco. The architecture was mostly Renaissance, and for that reason the façade of the Montejo Palace, with its Indian workmanship, is outstanding. Even that, however, was not distinctly Mayan; in general the influence was either French or Spanish. The anti-church insurrections of 1915 caused the destruction of what church art existed. Consequently the art interest in Mérida rests mainly in the architecture, the museums and the Mayan sculptures wrested from the ruins. But these attractions are indeed worthy of discriminating consideration.

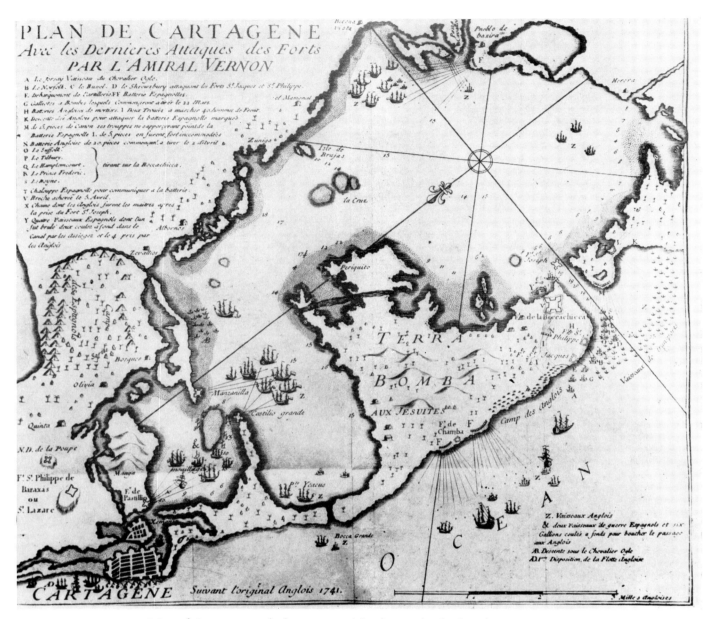

Map of Cartagena with ships arranged for the attack of Admiral Vernon—1741

Chapter 3

CARTAGENA
The Heroic City

CARTAGENA, southwest of Mérida across the Caribbean Sea, is a famous old Colombian seaport with the finest walls and fortifications remaining in the Western Hemisphere. It is the only walled city in South America; the history of its walls is the story of the city itself.

The city stands beside a sandy beach at the northeast end of the Bay of Cartagena. So large is this bay that in Colonial days it was said that all the fleets in the world could find anchorage here. There were two entrances from the Caribbean to the bay: Boca Chica (Little Mouth) seven miles from the city, and Boca Grande (Large Mouth) closer to it. The latter is situated between the city proper and the Island of Tierra Bomba which forms one side of the bay. The other side was formed by the islands of Manga and Manzanilla. Boca Chica is a narrower passage between the farther western end of Tierra Bomba and the mainland. To the southeast are lakes and swamps, to the southwest, the Island of Manga. Dominating the whole terrain is the mountain La Popa, crowned by a convent.

The most memorable view of the city is from the doorway of Old San Francisco Church in the adjoining suburb of Getsemani. Ahead is the Gate of the Bridge's Mouth (La Puerta de la Boca del Puente), so-called because it stood before a bridge connecting Cartagena and Getsemani over water which was filled in when the Plaza of the Martyrs was built. That spacious plaza can be seen on the right. On the left is the large, lively market; this is bordered by the slip of water lined with sailing boats that bring in fish and other merchandise. Beyond the sails one can see the historic wall of the redoubt of San Ignacio; near it the church of San Pedro Claver projects its two towers.

Cartagena was founded by Don Pedro de Heredia, a gentleman who was forced to leave Madrid as a result of a duel. The story goes that he went to live with an uncle in Haiti but the quiet agricultural life there palled upon him. He then took the rank of lieutenant and was named provisional governor of Santa Marta at the mouth of the Magdalena River. After the arrival of the titular governor he returned to Spain. There he was named Adelantado, or Governor, of the Province of Nueva Andalucía, a political division extending from the Gulf of Aruba to the banks of the Magdalena. With his permit in his hand, Don Pedro returned to America and arrived at the Bay of Cartagena on January 10, 1533, with one hundred twenty men of war and twenty-two horses. They landed on the sandy beach of what is now the walled suburb of Getsemani. There they established the colony at the foot of the enormous bay. It was later moved to the adjacent small island of Calamar, an Indian village where Cartagena was founded. Cartagena derived its name from New Carthage, Spain, which was founded in 227 A. D. and which provided the Carthaginians and Romans with much gold and silver from its mines, just as its namesake in South America later did for itself and the mother country.

The city progressed rapidly on the site of the Indian village located on the ocean beach, the population living mainly in *bohíos*, the Indian-type houses built of straw and cane. Later, under Governor Pedro Fernandez de Busto (1571–1585 tenure), the houses of straw were replaced by those of imported stone, the cathedral was begun and the streets were paved.

In 1534 Cartagena was made the seat of a bishopric and by 1573 there were four hundred Spanish families there. In 1607 the number had doubled, not including a large migrant population. (In 1950 the population was 114,830.)

The landing site, the island of Getsemani, was owned by a conquistador named Rodrigo Duran. Connected to Cartagena by a bridge, it was the first extension of the city and the site of the old Franciscan monastery. Juan de Castellanos, who wrote the *History of the New Kingdom of Granada*, voiced the opinion that the famous Dean Materano named the place Getsemani because, like the Mount of Olives from Jerusalem, it was cut off from the city.

When Cartagena was first founded, a serious objection was raised: the site had no source of drinking water. In fact, there never has been a natural well in the city.

74

Sailing ships in the slip between Cartagena and Getsemani

However, the port was so advantageous that the objection was overruled and in the next four hundred years water was obtained by collecting rain water in ponds, later in cisterns built into the walls. An aqueduct to bring water from the Turbaco hills was planned but was never built. Since 1906 water has been piped into Cartagena from Gambote along the canal.

For interior transportation in Philip the Second's time, this canal, called El Dique, was opened through the marshes to connect Cartagena with the western outlet of the Magdalena River, but it was allowed to silt up. (It has now been opened for steam navigation.)

It was necessary to have a protected port at which the king's treasure ships could stop, so Cartagena became the port of entry of the Spanish fleet which ended its run in Nombre de Dios and Porto Bello on the Isthmus of Panama. It was the first market of Spanish products in South America and the port of an immense and rich territory, drawing from Antioquia, Cali, Tunja, Bogotá and even Popayan and distant Quito. On each arrival of the fleet at Cartagena, *la feria de los galeones* (fleet fair) was held for the exchange of Spanish commodities with those of the colonists. Cartagena had many natural riches to export: fruits, the famous balsa wood of Tolu, gold from the rivers of the mountains and precious emeralds. From 1530 to 1570, pearls were taken from the island of Araya off the coast of Venezuela; the oyster beds were eventually depleted.

As the Pearl of the Indies, Cartagena had its disadvantages; it aroused the cupidity of pirates, kings, generals and admirals of France, England and even of Spain. As the Spaniards of Mérida had to fight against the Mayas, the Spaniards of Cartagena had to fight against pirates and corsairs, the latter sometimes raiding with the consent of their monarchs. In 1544 the French pirate, Robert Baal, sacked the city with the help of a Spanish pilot who wished to avenge himself on the governor. In 1585 the English corsair, Sir Francis Drake, with twenty-three ships and 2,500 marine infantrymen, took the city and pillaged it.

The first fortifications, to protect the Spaniards against the Indians, were constructed of stakes, but when the city's growing wealth attracted pirates, stone was brought over from the Island of Tierra Bomba. Eventually, over a period of two hundred years, a perfect system of fortifications and walls was in the building. Although these were first completed under Philip II, they were destroyed from time to time by the forces of nature and by pirates and had to be rebuilt.

Since the fortifications were so unique and distinguished, it is necessary to describe the three great sieges which dramatized their necessity: the sack by the Frenchman De Pointe in 1695; the glorious repulse of the siege conducted by the Englishman Admiral Vernon in 1741; and the eventually successful fight for independence which was signed at Boyacá in 1811. For good reasons Cartagena was called The Heroic City. Although the defeat and sack by De Pointe, as by Baal and Drake before him, showed that the city's strength had been weakened by the exactions of "fifths" by the Spanish Crown and the large requisitions by the churches, and that its morale had been affected by the cruelties of the Inquisition, its history was made glorious by the defense against Admiral Vernon. The city's history gained additional lustre by its ability to withstand such terrible sieges as that of Don Pablo Morillo in 1815.

Entrance gate to San Sebastian Fortress on Manga Island, called Pastellito or Little Pie when a fortress. It is now a seafood restaurant (La Popa in the distance).

At that time the people held out for one hundred and twenty days and presented to the conqueror such emaciated remnants of citizenry that even he was moved to compassion. We begin with the sack of Cartagena by De Pointe.

One hundred and twelve years after Drake's depredations, Cartagena had again become such a rich prize that it inspired a naval expedition by the French with the approval of Louis XIV; Jean Bernard de Janes, Baron De Pointe, was named commander of a very large force.

In the *Historia de Cartagena*, written by Don Sanchez Jiménes, Governor of Fort San Luis of Boca Chica, there is the detailed story of the sack of Cartagena by the

View of the City of Cartagena from the wall

Historic coins minted by Admiral Vernon to commemorate a victory over Cartagena which he never achieved

French. It tells of the failure of Governor Don Diego de los Rios to heed the many warnings and send help to the garrison. Boca Chica was taken by the French in a land assault and later, after San Felipe had fallen, De Pointe first took Getsemani and then walled Cartagena itself. Earlier, a great number of women of quality and priests had left the city, taking family valuables, but although De Pointe allowed the Spaniards to keep one-tenth of their gold, the churches were despoiled of their wealth, even to the bells and frames of the sacred pictures.

Later, after the French squadron had departed, the pirates, displeased by being awarded only their tenths, returned to the city and extracted from the population a million and a half pesos in gold, silver and jewels which had been sold back by the French. In the chapel of the Santo Domingo Church the marauders set fire to barrels of powder and caused great damage. Had they not heard of a squadron of the Spanish king coming to bring help, they would not have so hurriedly departed before burning the Tribunal of the Inquisition or completely destroying the city. It was deplorable that not enough Spaniards were left in the city to defend it against the pirates.

Because the plundering of the city, chiefly by Drake and De Pointe, denuded it of its artistic treasures of the sixteenth and seventeenth centuries, its churches lack the precious artistic heritage of Quito, Tunja, Lima and Cuzco. In 1695, for example, the sepulchre of solid silver, weighing eight thousand ounces, which was used in the liturgical ceremonies of the Holy Burial, was removed from the Monastery of San Agustín by the Frenchmen of De Pointe. The sepulchre was later returned by King Louis XIV, but without the golden clocks. Its final misfortune came when it was melted down by the patriots during the siege of Morillo to buy food and munitions.

The city and its walls were badly damaged by the assault of the French and it took many years for it to recover. In 1737, with tension increasing between England and Spain over English trading rights, Don Blas de Leso started working on defenses against the expected attack. Two years later, the English declared war. The brilliant Don Sebastian de Eslava was made viceroy of the New Kingdom of Granada and with Admiral Don Blas de Leso provided the leadership which resulted in Vernon's defeat.

The story of Vernon's disastrous expedition is also told in *Historia de Cartagena*. The work includes original accounts of the siege by the Spanish hero Don Blas, the Cartagenian governor Sebastian de Eslava, the Honorable Edward Vernon, the English captain M. Cooper, Dr. Tobias Smollett and others. The siege lasted from January until May of 1741, at which time the British retired, defeated by the spirited defense of Governor Eslava and Blas de Leso. Don Blas's seventeen-day defense of the Fortress of San Felipe de Barajas led to the defeat of the English.★

Sixty-eight years later the city of Quito declared for independence; all of New Granada became restless and the lower classes openly rebellious. Changes of government in Spain, with the decrees of each superseding those of the last, had made the local governments in America feel strongly that they were too large to be manipulated by parties far away. The Spaniards in Spain, and probably the Colonials too, rioted for the restoration of Ferdinand VII who was a Bourbon. He was not restored until 1813; the Napoleonic monarchy lasted until 1811. Ferdinand, who was very reactionary, proved a great disappointment; he revoked the Constitution of 1812 and the Colonial ordinances.

When the Spanish lost Santa Fé de Bogotá to the insurgents in 1813, the Governor of Tunja, Don José Mario Castillo, in accord with the Congress of all of the provinces of New Granada, proposed the establishment of a single central government. On January 23, 1815, the Government of the Union moved from Tunja to Bogotá and, although a civilian, Manuel Castillo, brother of Don José, was made military head of the forces of Cartagena. When Bolívar entered Colombia from Venezuela the leadership was divided. This proved to be unfortunate because the two became mortal enemies, mostly on account of Bolívar's disastrous expedition into Venezuela against Castillo's advice. There was also much dissension among the patriot leaders inside Cartagena. During the disputes between Castillo and Bolívar all of the lower Magdalena River was lost to the Union. Field Marshal Don Pablo Morillo of Spain encircled Cartagena with Royalist Venezuelans and 8,000 soldiers sent over by Ferdinand VII, blockading the port and forcing corsairs supplying the patriots to seek refuge in other ports.

The whole story of the one-hundred-fourteen-day siege by the Royalists is truly moving and tragic. Well did Cartagena again deserve the title "The Heroic City." The factions of the patriots continued fighting among themselves. From August 22 until September 22, 1815, only five boats with food were able to reach the city and none after that. By the end of October the patriots were forced to eat horses, burros, dogs, cats, rats and leather. Morillo tried to force the passage of La Boquilla between the sea and Lake Tesca but was repulsed by Captain Don Rafael Tono (at the trials he was saved by Governor Montalvo). Some seafood was coming from Boca

---

★Blas de Leso, Marqués de Ovieco, General of the Spanish Fleet from 1687 until 1741, died September 7, 1741, from wounds received during Vernon's siege.

Castillo de San Felipe de Barajas, a fortress which was one of the greatest Spain built in the Americas. It was recently restored. A building from 1730–1757.

Chica, so Morillo burned all towns on Tierra Bomba, including the hospital of Cano de Loro, killing the sick and well whom he had captured.

On November 22, Governor Amador separated himself from Union command and during the last days of November 2,000 persons left the walls of the city to surrender by different routes. By December 4, three hundred persons had died on the streets. Then Morillo sent a communication offering clemency of the king for surrender. On December 5, evacuation by sea was begun in ships of corsairs. General Castillo was warned that he could not emigrate because he would be assassinated on shipboard. He took refuge in the convent of Santa Teresa where he was later captured. In all, 7,300 of the population of 15,000 died of hunger; 4,700 more were executed. Of the garrison of San Felipe Fortress, once numbering five hundred, only thirty-seven were left. Morillo lost 1,800 Europeans and 1,200 Venezuelans; 3,000 fell ill.

Cartagena never surrendered, but when the king heard of its occupation he ordered thanksgiving Masses to celebrate the happy event and Morillo was made Count of Cartagena. The Tribunal of the Inquisition returned from Santa Marta and the old order was re-established with Colonel Don Gabriel de Torres y Velasco named governor of the city and the province.

Castillo de San Fernando at Boca Chica, at the harbor entrance to the Bay of Cartagena

On January 10, 1816, a war council was set up with thirty-five persons and twelve witnesses; on February 19, the sentence for nine persons to be put to death on the gallows was pronounced by the judge. The head of Ribón was to be fixed to a pole and exhibited in Mompos. Nine revolutionaries were sentenced: Manuel del Castillo; Dr. Miguel Dias Granados, member of the Supreme Council of Justice to declare independence who was captured in Veraguas; José María García de Toledo, governor and leader of the aristocratic party of patriots who conceived the plan for independence by an electoral college; Pantaleon Germán Ribón, mayor of Mompos; Dr. Antonio José de Ayos, president of the electoral college who revised its constitution, captured with Castillo; Martin José Amador, patrician member of the senate who was elected governor in 1814, captured at Veraguas; Manuel Anguiana, a citizen sixty years old who was caught in his own house; José María Portocarrero, a citizen who assisted in running the blockade and was captured when sent to Santa Fé to ask for aid; and Colonel Santiaga Stuart, an Irishman who had restrained the patriot Bermudez from killing prisoners and royalists.

Bolívar fled to Los Cayos, Haiti, and from there continued the war against Spain. The brother patriots Piñeres did not follow Bolívar. The bloodthirsty radical Bermudez escaped to Cayos de San Luis from Margarita Island.

On February 24, 1817, the martyrs were shot in the back (with the exception of Stuart, who refused to turn his back); they had been tied to black poles at the left of

82

Boca de Puente, against the wall of San Pedro Apóstol. The sentence had been commuted from hanging by Governor Montalvo.

Cartagena was recaptured by the patriots in 1821, and in 1823 Colonel Manuel Marcelino Nuñez returned to his native city and was made mayor. Under his administration the martyrs were buried in a wall on Manga Island, but the burial place has disappeared. Statues commemorating them have now been placed in Centenario Plaza near the place of their execution.

Fortifications, Engineers

The Italian, Bautista Antonelli, one of Philip II's foremost military engineers, came first to South America to construct a fort on the Straits of Magellan. A few years later he made a journey of reconnaissance through the Caribbean area. In 1588 he undertook the building of the fort of San Juan, Puerto Rico, the defenses of Santo Domingo and Morro Castle of Havana; his greatest achievement, the enormous fortifications of the Colombian port of Cartagena, was completed by his son, Juan Bautista Antonelli, and a score of assistants. Today the remains of this costly construction, comprising three separate forts, represent one of the finest examples of Spanish Renaissance military architecture in Latin America.*

These fortifications had not been built when Drake came with twenty ships and 3,000 men in 1585 and sacked the city. The people were thoroughly demoralized after the sack and two hundred and fifty citizens left the city. He had been master of the city just three months before the celebrated engineer, Bautista Antonelli, and the governor of Cuba, Juan de Tejeda, embarked for the Indies with an armada carrying the king's directions to study plans for the fortifications of the whole Caribbean area.† With their arrival began the decisive phase in the planning of forts and walls which occupied generations of engineers and lasted through the entire Colonial Period.

In the Bay of Cartagena the design by Philip II's great engineer was based upon three forts: San Sebastian on Manga Island, Castillo Grande (or Santa Cruz) at Boca Grande, and Manzanillo on the island of that name. (San Sebastian is now a seafood restaurant.)

After inspecting Nombre de Dios and Porto Bello, Antonelli returned to Cartagena and devised wooden fortifications including a bridge to the suburb of Getsemani. He advised the importation from Guinea of two hundred Negroes with their wives to establish a colony near the work on the Island of Carex, where there were plantations of corn and yucca. From Cartagena, Antonelli went to Nombre de Dios,

*Robert Smith, in *Latin American Republics*.
†Bautista Antonelli was a member of an illustrious family of Italian engineers whose origin was Rumanian.

Havana, Santo Domingo and Puerto Rico, after which he returned to Spain to draw plans for all of these ports. In 1594 he returned to Cartagena and on this second visit made plans for encircling the city with a wall and bulwarks, which, as carried out by other engineers, have been kept to the present day.★ The original plan was executed in wood by Antonelli, but permanent stone construction followed under Governor Acuna. Getsemani was not developed until later but a lock was placed in such a way that the swamp, La Cienega, could be inundated if necessary. The wharf there, built by Alonzo de Montalban, was insufficient and La Cienega was later filled in to make what is now the Plaza of the Martyrs. This was the work of Fernandez de Busto, who initiated many of the improvements in the latter part of the sixteenth century, among them the storing of water, which had been a problem since the foundation of the city. His system of storing water in the walls lasted for four hundred years.

Looking at the plan by Antonelli in Marco Dorta's book, *Cartagena de Indias*, I see that his Plaza Mayor is now called Plaza Bolívar; the cathedral plans have undergone changes but the Plazoleto de Santo Domingo is easily identified. Plaza Real, now Plaza Colón, or Yerba, was the place of intense activity and festivity because of its proximity to the shipping.

Marco Dorta describes the works of various engineers, their trips to Spain to make reports to the Council of the Indies, and the continual work of strengthening the walls and forts. Inspections were carried on continually. The engineers, in order, were Antonelli, Senior; De Roda; Antonelli, Junior, in the sixteenth century; Somovilla and Don José de Lara in the seventeenth century; Juan de Herrera, Mac-Evan and Antonio Arevalo in the eighteenth century.

When Antonelli the elder went to Spain, never to return to Cartagena, his son went to Havana in search of his cousin, Cristóbal De Roda, who was directing the building of the Fortress of El Morro. He followed De Roda to Cartagena but also acted as engineer in Araya and Cumana, Venezuela, besides building works against the Dutch invasions in small islands in the Antilles. After the death of De Roda in 1631, the royal building in Cartagena was under the direction of Antonelli, Jr. The last work of his forty years of service under Philips II, III and IV, before his death in 1649, was the San Luis Fortress of Boca Chica.

Juan de Somovilla succeeded Antonelli, Jr., after a long list of services in other

★Lamentably, three blocks of the beautiful walls were demolished to make way for some modern building in 1920.

Castillo de San Fernando at Boca Chica, showing fort opposite. At one time a chain was drawn between the two forts at night to keep out pirates.

Los Arcos (arches) or Las Bovedas Barracks beneath the City Wall, with ramp in the foreground

Boca de la Puente (Mouth of the Bridge or Gate of the Half Moon), Cartagena. Only the center opening is old; the two side passages were opened to make way for modern traffic. The clock tower was added later.

85

Moorish Tower of the Cathedral taken from a window of the Inquisition Building

lands in America. Having been sent to Cartagena in 1624 to serve under De Roda, he carried on the work while Antonelli was in Araya and Cumana. He was made Captain of Artillery and in 1640 salvaged two Portuguese warships which were grounded while trying to negotiate the channel of Boca Grande.*

In 1647, a platform had been constructed on Mount Lazaro which accommodated twelve pieces of artillery, and in 1657 Governor Don Pedro Zapata had the Fort of San Felipe de Barajas built there. San Felipe dominated the walls of La Puerta Media Luna and hence there was danger if an enemy should occupy it. Later, Zapata raised money from the inhabitants and gave 3,000 pesos of his own in order to build a small fort with nine cannon. For this there is a plaque in San Felipe, dated 1657, honoring Zapata. In the eighteenth century the Spaniards completed the work of the fortress, converting it into the most important fortification which Spain built in the Indies.

The death of Louis XIV of France in 1715 caused a radical change in the situation in the Indies. The French were converted into allies and while in 1697 De Pointe sacked the city, only five years later a French squadron under Jean-Baptiste Ducasse (of unhappy memory—he had been leader of the buccaneers) entered the harbor and protected the fleet of Tierra Firme (Colombia) after five days of fighting a much stronger British armada.

After the completion (one of several) of the walls of Cartagena under Francisco de Murga, the encirclement of Getsemani was undertaken. Fuerte Reducto was built on Getsemani to protect the bay side. Puerta de la Media Luna (Gate of the Half Moon, so named because of its shape; also called Gate of the Bridge) was built with batteries on either side to connect Getsemani with Cartagena under the engineer Juan Herrera y Sotomayor. He was the first of a line of brilliant engineers serving Cartagena in the eighteenth century. This gate had been begun originally as a civil military piece of architecture, but after five years the octagonal towers, one above the other ending in a capital, were built. Four town clocks were placed in the lower tower; in the beginning there were two arched doorways but later another was added to take care of the increasing traffic. Herrera also strengthened the Fort of San Sebastian del Pastelillo (the "Little Pie," evidently so named because of its shape),

*In 1656, an admiral's ship in an armada headed for Spain from Havana was lost in the channel of the Bahamas with 5,000,000 pesos in gold and silver besides sugar, dyes, wood and grain. When the news reached Cartagena the governor organized an expedition for salvage, naming Somovilla as head. They managed to retrieve 75,000 pesos in bars of silver which he handed over on the Canary Islands, receiving in reward a lifetime pension.

now a two-hundred-year-old landmark on the site of the first fortification, El Boquerón.

Under Herrera, for a quarter of a century, works of the utmost importance were undertaken, such as that on the walls of the Marina where the furious winds in 1716 had destroyed houses and a good part of the Convent of Santa Clara.

Herrera merits a brief sketch. In his twenties he had been quartered in the Alcazar of Toledo under his father as a lieutenant. He was granted a coat of arms from His Majesty in 1681 and began his services in America as Lieutenant of Cavalry in Buenos Aires. He later constructed the Fortress of Valparaiso, Chile, after which he went to Cartagena to work under Governor Pimienta. There he was named Engineer Director and Castellano of San Felipe. Herrera's plan for building continuous walls between the redoubts from Santo Domingo to Santa Catalina was accepted and he began that great work. During the five possible working months, pilings were placed along the beach to protect the building of the rubble-filled stone containers which made up the low walls. Because all the bastions were named for saints, the citizens' souls, as well as the King's exchequer, were tried by the damage done to the bulwarks when patrons failed to protect them from the tremendous seasonal storms. (The latter often won out over more celestial influences.)

Under Herrera the decision was made in 1702 to keep Boca Chica open and to close Boca Grande. Since the ships of the Portuguese navy had been shipwrecked there, an accumulation of sand around the wrecks had formed a barrier difficult to pass. A junta, formed of the governor, engineers and generals of the Armada of Tierra Firme, studied the question of whether to open the channel or leave it closed and strengthen Boca Chica. The decision being in favor of the latter course, the Fortress of San Luis was built on one side of the channel of Boca Chica on Tierra Bomba and Fort San José was built on the small island of Baru. In 1734, Engineer Director Lorenzo de Solis suggested a plan for closing Boca Grande by sinking small boats loaded with coral rock a little below the surface of the water to form a jetty across which sand would build up. At great cost this was carried out by slaves to protect the population against piratical attacks. This dike of Boca Grande was opened by storms in 1739 and years passed before Arevalo closed it in 1788 with six hundred workers at a cost of a million and a half pesos. It is still under water beyond the point of land occupied by the Caribe Hotel, but is negotiated by small boats.

A few months after Admiral Vernon retreated in 1741 from his siege, Don Bautista Mac-Evan was named Director Engineer of the fortifications of Cartagena.

Main altar of San Pedro Claver showing the Saint's casket · *Restored main altar of the Cathedral*

The most brilliant stage in their history began and the work was carried on almost without rest. It is said that King Carlos III, gazing from the window of his palace in Madrid, expected to see the silhouette of these forts on the horizon—because of their cost they should have reached the clouds. The fortresses of San Fernando and San José were built up at Boca Chica. Working as supervising director under Mac-Evan was Antonio Arevalo. San Fernando replaced the Fortress of San Luis which had been ruined by Admiral Vernon. (My husband and I visited this fort in 1957 on our boat trip out to Boca Chica. We were interested in the old fortress but most of the passengers were intent on swimming at a nearby beach.)

Arevalo's last work was on the walls of the city: widening, making ramps and esplanades and improving the troop quarters. The last task was the building of the vaults fronted by passageways with forty-seven arches; these permitted the troops to go from door to door out of the rain. These arches, called Las Bovedas, were bombproof quarters for troops. In 1795, Arevalo finished the piece of wall between the bulwarks of Santa Clara and Santa Catalina which had been open for about one hundred years. The Avenida Santander of today is built over Arevalo's breakwater which, in the course of time, was covered with sand.

Jesuit Cloister connected with Church of San Pedro Claver *Cloister of Santo Domingo Convent*

Arevalo was of noble birth. After service in Spain he embarked in 1742 to join Mac-Evan in Puerto Rico. He was commander of expeditions to Darien and Rio de la Hacha to pacify the Indians. As a reward he was made Lieutenant General and sought the governorship of Cartagena but only achieved that office late in life, when he occupied the post temporarily during the illness of Governor Don Roque de Quirago. Arevalo died on April 9, 1800, at the age of eighty-five, having worked the last forty years of the eighteenth century. Thus ended the two hundred years of construction on the walls. Marco Dorta says of Arevalo: "The walls of Cartagena are the pages of his biography." He was the last of the great colonial engineers.

In 1735 two members of the Academy of Science of France, Spanish naval officers Don Jorge Juan and Don Antonio de Ulloa, arrived in Cartagena on a scientific mission which resulted in a physical, political and ethnological study included in their report, *Relación de Viaje al America Meridional*. These representatives of the Spanish king complimented Cartagena on the architecture of the churches and commented on the balconies and gratings of wood (more practical than iron in that climate). They noted that the population contained about 8,000 Spaniards, that the majority

90

of the population was composed of Negroes, mestizos, mulattoes and quinterones, and that there were no Indians. The city was by that time impoverished as a result of the repeated sackings.

In spite of the fact that the interiors of the churches have lost most of their original artistic treasures, their history and architecture make them of great value to the city.

It is interesting that the churches of Cartagena contain no examples of Plateresque or Churrigueresque styles of architecture but adhere to severe Renaissance and Baroque. Much Moorish influence is present in arches and interiors but the fine old retables have been replaced by modern ones. The originals may be seen in Quito, Tunja and Peru.

The cathedral occupies first rank among ecclesiastical buildings and should be first in our discussion of churches. Cartagena's first cathedral was started in 1535 on what is now the site of the Church of San Juan de Dios; built of cane and straw, it was later burned. In 1565 an official document ordered that the cathedral be built of stone with the cost to be divided among the Crown, the Indians and the encomenderos. However, construction was not begun until between 1577 and 1579, according to the plan of the master builder, Simon González. ★ The main part was finished by 1584, but at this point Drake appeared. In order to frighten the citizens and extract ransom he destroyed three columns and four arches of the cathedral. After these were repaired another catastrophe occurred in 1600 when one side and the major nave collapsed without impulse from either earthquake or hurricane. The broken nave was covered with straw so that people had to stay away in the rainy season. The square tower was built in 1661 and the building completed five years later with a beautiful Sagrario Chapel in carved and gilded wood. Unhappily, this was later destroyed.

The cathedral is similar in style to Andalusian churches of the Renaissance, having a major chapel or altar in the center and one on each side forming a cross. The interior arches and walls were covered with stucco and painted to imitate marble. The floor is of real marble. The pulpit of colored marbles from a Florentine workshop of the seventeenth century was presented to the cathedral by Bishop Diaz de Lamadrid, although a legend claims that the pulpit was destined for Lima. In the sacristy there is a portrait of Bishop Lamadrid (the thirty-ninth bishop) painted by a painter of Cartagena, Pablo Caballero, in 1790. The rich custodia which had been a gift of this bishop was pledged by patriots in 1815 to a merchant of Jamaica, prob-

★Simon González also directed the work on the Convent of San Diego, and direction in the construction of the convents of Santa Clara, San Francisco and La Popa is also attributed to him.

ably in exchange for food. In 1912 Bishop Pedro Brioschi changed the old square tower to the present one of Moorish type, painted pink and white, with spire and arched windows. The taste that would dictate such a mixture of styles is perhaps disputable, but the view of the tower from the flat roof of the Inquisition Palace is arresting. The ancient stone saints which formerly adorned the façade were later put in niches of the surrounding wall, but due to deterioration they have been replaced by modern replicas.

Mounting the wharf-side ramp to the wall of the city, one encounters the citadel of San Ignacio, which gave its name to the nearby Jesuit church (later called San Pedro Claver). The plan that Jorge and Ulloa made of Cartagena in 1735 showed this new church of the Society of Jesus dedicated to that saint. The first church had been built in 1603; the beautiful adjoining cloisters served as the school of the Jesuits. These were considered the finest cloisters in Colombia. Because the city wall was built on twenty feet of the Jesuits' land, a dispute arose which lasted about fifty years; in the end the wall was rebuilt beyond the church property. Part of the college was built onto the wall and is still intact, although somewhat obstructed from view. The present church was decided upon in 1695 and was probably constructed in the early eighteenth century. It is one of the finest the Jesuits left in Colombia and was typical of those patterned on the one designed in Rome by the architect Vignola. The severity of its interior, its simple but monumental impact, is in contrast to that of La Compañía in Quito, with its Moorish interlacing in gold and red. But here too the façade is Baroque—the richest and most impressive of any in the city. The new dome of the Church of San Pedro Claver, replacing the old one, was built in 1921 by the French architect Gaston le Large. After King Carlos III caused the expulsion of the Jesuits in 1767, the church was occupied by the Order of San Juan de Dios, but it is now restored to the Jesuits who have named it San Pedro Claver after the "slave of the slaves." This Saint's life has become one of the great legends of Cartagena.

San Pedro, who arrived in Cartagena in 1610, was so known because he took great compassion on the poor slaves who came into port in crowded ships. He went down to the wharf to meet them, saw that the sick were cared for in hospitals and, in general, showed himself a friend of the slaves. Between 1654 and 1659 at least 300,000 Negro slaves passed through the port of Cartagena. Leprosy became widespread and Bishop Pedro Claver devoted the remaining years of his life to serving in the leper hospital and in charitable work. He died in a room of the Jesuit Cloisters on September 8, 1654, near a small chapel which he had used. He became the patron saint of the

Baroque side altar of Santo Domingo Church

Detail over the entrance of Santo Domingo Convent

Republic. In 1885 he was canonized by Pope Leo XIII. His bones lie in a glass casket below the main altar of the church with his carved image above.

Leaving the Church of San Pedro Claver and proceeding along the top of the wall to the ocean side we come at the middle of that exposure to the bastion of Santo

Domingo and the church of that saint. Santo Domingo is a fortified church, Mexican style; its apse, abutting on the beach, was fortified in connection with the wall and in its history took much punishment from both pirates and the elements. Marqués de Villalta spent 15,000 pesos for the series of arches and vaults, and to repair the damage done by corsairs. The first part to be built of straw was the monastery, under Fray José de Robes, in 1551. The stone church was begun in 1577 and the building continued in five stages until it was finished about 1695 according to the original plan. The second tower is still lacking, however, and the existing tower is not in line with the church façade but follows the line of the monastery built in 1603. Legend holds that the tower was twisted by the Devil. On the street side the Herrerian portico reflects the style of the Spanish Renaissance and is very impressive. In the interior to the right of the main altar is a very interesting Baroque retable of 1807, the work of the native sculptor Hermenegildo José Ayala. Above this altar is the fine old carved figure of the Holy Christ of the Expiration. Above other side altars are the figures of the Madona Inmaculada and La Virgen del Tránsito with the costly crown that is one of Cartagena's chief treasures. Dominican establishments always display a dog somewhere in the decoration; true to tradition the doorway of the convent is surmounted by two barking dogs.* The symbols refer to the dream of Saint Dominic's mother, as explained in the chapter on Quito.

Another distinguished church sighted from farther along the wall is that of Santo Toribio. It was commenced in 1666, with gifts from the inhabitants and the ecclesiastical authorities, in the Plaza del Jagueyes (Reservoirs). The king had given 3,000 pesos when the cornerstone was laid. The church was finished by Bishop Don Gregorio de Molleda in 1732 and consecrated in 1736 in the name of Santo Toribio Alfonso Mogrobexo. The church has a single nave with a fine main altar; its most distinguished feature is the Moorish ceiling with raised interlacing designs called *artesonada*. The façade is similar to that of the Church of the Third Order (Iglesia de la Orden Tercera) and is divided into two parts. The lower half holds the arched doorway flanked by two pillars supporting a cornice, a niche with a figure, and finial; the upper half is composed of a square containing two arched windows suggesting a Moorish *alfiz*. A plaque on one of the supporting columns inside the church states that on April 27, 1741 (the Feast of Saint Toribio), when the church was full during a holy Mass, a cannon ball from Admiral Vernon's fleet came through the

---

*During a recent visit to Vicenza, Italy, I enquired about the dog in the Santa Corona Church and was shown that it was incorporated into a stained-glass window behind the main altar.

window and fell harmlessly among the people, leaving only a mark on the floor. Among the treasures of the church are a ciborium of gold set with emeralds, dated 1761, a tabernacle of wood covered with velvet and trimmed with silver, and a gold reliquary of San José.

East of Santo Domingo and equally exposed on the Marina is the Convent of Santa Clara after which another bastion was named. Destroyed in part by storms in the eighteenth century and changed to conform to its present purpose as a Hospital of Charity, it still retains the old church, the keeper's lodge, and the principal cloister with arches over the columns similar to other cloisters in Cartagena. The church is of one nave and still preserves its original retable in Churrigueresque style; its statues are the best in the city. There is also a fine pulpit of the seventeenth century, a statue of the patron, Santa Clara, carved in wood and polychromed, and a baptismal font of stone from Tierra Bomba surmounted by a folkish figure of Saint Michael. A screen of Venetian blinds at one end protects the choir from view. Also preserved is the chair of the abbess, of Colonial work.

The façade of the church has a bell wall (*espadaña*) and a Renaissance doorway. For its original contribution, the Convent of Santa Clara was left a legacy of 1,500 pesos by Catalina de Cabrera to be used for the Order of San Francisco. The sum was insufficient to build the convent, but when Pedro Osorio offered to pay the royal treasury 10,000 pesos if a vacant encomienda of Indians was granted to the convent, the king acknowledged the gift and in 1621 the convent was finished. A stone commemorated the benefactor, Don Pedro Osorio.

Other convents, San Francisco, La Merced, San Agustín, San Diego and Santa Teresa, no longer perform their religious functions. The Monastery of San Francisco, which was begun in 1582 in the suburb of Getsemani, is now used for secular purposes. The coral rock façade of the church still exists but the interior has been converted into a movie theatre. The Convent of San Agustín was founded in 1580 by Fray Geronimo Quevara and is now occupied by the University of Cartagena. Only the old convent and cloisters are original, and these have been modernized.

The Convent of La Merced, built in 1625, has also been modernized: the cloisters have been incorporated into the Palace of Justice, and the walls of the church are used for the Teatro Heredia. What is now the jail utilizes the walls of the old San Diego Convent which was consecrated in 1625 but was later destroyed by an explosion. The Convent of Santa Teresa is presently a police headquarters, but the old church has been opened recently for worship using only the old walls and the roof.

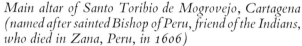

Main altar of Santo Toribio de Mogrovejo, Cartagena (named after sainted Bishop of Peru, friend of the Indians, who died in Zana, Peru, in 1606)

Baroque portal of the House of the Inquisition, Cartagena

A relic in Getsemani marks the site of what was once the hospital of Espiritu Santo. Five *religiosos* under Padre Francisco Hernandez of the San Juan de Dios congregation arrived in Cartagena in 1596 with a directive to build a hospital. In 1603 the Juaniños founded one in Getsemani under the advocation of the Holy Ghost. This was done by surrendering the property of San Sebastian to the brothers. The building was on the site of the primitive cathedral. In 1665 the Church of San Roque united with the Hospital of Espiritu Santo after which the street was named. It is a typical Getsemani street—one-story houses with windows protected by wooden gratings and shaded by tiles. The door of the residence of the Brothers of San Juan de Dios, according to Marco Dorta, is the most interesting in the city. It is flanked by two columns above which is a frieze with a niche in the center and on either side two conical finials. Inside is a fine example of a *tinajero*, or water cupboard, a niche for storing water jars. In the eighteenth century the hospital was occupied by the Semi-

97

Moorish (artesonada) ceiling of the Church of Santo Toribio de Mogrovejo

nary of San Carlos. All that is left today is the doorway of the church, which, however, is of architectural interest.

The Hospital of San Lazaro formerly stood outside of the walls, at the foot of Mount Lazaro below the Fortress of San Felipe de Barajas. Farther still from the city, in a wild retreat on top of La Popa Mountain (a former refuge of runaway slaves), the Augustinian Recoletos founded a monastery. In 1608 Fray Vicente Mallol, as first authority of the Province of Our Lady of Grace for the Augustinian Recoletos, asked Governor Diego de Velasco for a license to start a convent on La Popa. A congregation of prelates of Bogotá confirmed the foundation and named Fray Alonzo de la Cruz Paredes as Superior. According to the historian Zamora, Fray Alonzo had heard a supernatural voice ordering him to Cartagena to found a house on a mount outside of the walls near the city. There was no other but La Popa.

The Recoleto house was preferred as a place for fasting during Lent and was the center for pious pilgrimages. In connection with the convent a church was built and dedicated to La Madona de la Candelaria. The dressed and crowned image of La Candelaria, Virgen de La Popa, was the patron saint of Cartagena, and most popular among people of the sea. A lantern, lighted by the monks at night, served as a guide for ships seeking port. When the fleets arrived, soldiers and sailors climbed the mountain to give thanks to the Virgin for their safe arrival and to ask protection for the return journey. The church also contains images of San Blas and San Agustín made by a native carver. They were used in the performance of the Mass and to teach the precepts of the Church to farmers, workers and slaves.

A story by Eustorgio Martinez Fardo, called "Jealousy of a Slave," describes a fantastic pilgrimage to the church just mentioned:

The sun rose radiantly on the 2nd of February and the hill of La Popa was at the same time a splendor of radiant jewels shining on the breasts of hundreds of Negro slaves, who ascended singing up the sacred summit. It was the end of the eighteenth century.

The Spanish nobility had the custom of celebrating in this way a kind of "out-bidding" by showing their slaves as the most richly bejewelled. Fundamentally this typical custom was no more than a simple pretext for exhibiting, each rich family, their best jewels to the envy of their rivals. It was spectacular vanity in which it was made known that the old family descending from the illustrious *condes* of Fuente Seca y Villar, or the inheritants of the great gentlemen of Rumazo y Torres of Castillo still kept the rich diadems of gold of their ancestors or the fabulous rings of their grandparents, which had been envied by the most haughty dames of the Court of Spain or the Castilian *condales* of Seville and Toledo. The typical Negress, similarly and for her part, emulated her mistress.

The story goes that in ascending the hill the bejewelled slaves made themselves in the aggressive form of an arrow. Their native African songs contained a mixture of ritual allusions and allusions to offensive personalities (like the calypsos of Trinidad). And, naturally in the quarrels that were provoked, it did not fail to happen that there was a loss of rich garments and jewels of the masters, a loss for which the Negro paid with heavy work or reduction of rations.

On this day the sound of tambours and the rustic flutes of the pilgrims of color, whose entirety, no one knew why, they called "meetings," filled all of the crest and the defiles of La Popa, in the cold morning of the 2nd of February of our story. Each *cabildo*, then presided over by a chief or a chieftainess, intoned a distinct song, melancholy and accentuated profoundly by that slow groan peculiar to the sounds of Africa. Possibly anyone who attended these parades of rich splendor might detect, below the superficial courtesy of the ostentation, the infinite sadness of a race. This golden chain of captives was, in truth, fantastic, because below the golden finery they could not hide the stamp of servitude.

Arcaded ruins of the ancient Monastery of La Popa

Suddenly, in the midst of the singing, at the bottom of the hill, colored by a thousand tones and polychrome of the rare clothes of the slaves, a fracas commenced. Simon Casiano of the surname, pro-slavery, of the family Orellana de Azua, a well set-up man of the Coast of Gold, had seen on his approach the most juicy young woman slave of the brilliant caravan fighting tooth and nail with Sebastian, another Negro of the "Meeting of Mandingas." Simon Casiano's devotions were already working toward the day of matrimony with this Cimmarona; but, since among the slaves the masters of the house extended their social prejudices to not permitting a Negro of "house and family" to marry a Negress who was a runaway slave or the daughter of one, Casiano had not been able to contract marriage.

Like an avalanche stones came skipping down the declivity and fell between his intended and his odious rival, flooring them both and rolling them scratched into the brambles. And what followed after that was a real Moorish festival on the edge of the dark continent. All the Negroes, some more and some less, came to blows and entered into the hurly-burly. The chroniclers of the epoch, in their relations of this episode referred to the plain of the ascent as turned into a rivulet of gold and precious stones, in which the nobility of Cartagena lost thousands on thousands of Castilian pesos because "there were people—they say—who busy themselves with the question of who are Negroes and are not Negroes and push themselves to the point of quarrel by robbing all."

Passing from fiction to description, let us continue with a brief discussion of the old civil buildings and houses of Cartagena. Entering from the Plaza of the Martyrs through the Puerta de la Media Luna we find the busy Plaza de Yerba, surrounded by arcaded buildings and warehouses.

The Colonial buildings still standing are the Cabildo, or Government House, and the Casa Real, which is the custom house. La Casa de Moneda, established in 1630 by Captain Alonzo de Yerba to coin money by royal decree, was occupied as a home by Rafael de Zubiria until it burned in 1947.

La Casa Real, or La Cantaduria, is still the custom house as it was originally. It was designed by the engineer Cristóbal de Roda, who served Cartagena from 1609 until 1631. Located as it is in Plaza de Yerba, La Cantaduria was built of brick with stone lintels and arches similar to those of the cloisters of the period. The roof is tile and the wooden balconies are apparently those originally built.

The second plan for the Cabildo, now called Palacio de Gobierno, was sent to His Majesty in 1677. The original Cabildo, with its double galleries open on the square, has been enlarged, but the lower floor still contains the offices of notaries just as in the olden days. The building also houses the government officials.

The House of the Inquisition, situated in the Plaza Bolívar on property which the Holy Office had acquired in 1630, is the finest example of civil architecture in Cartagena. Especially distinguished is the Baroque doorway. The date of erection, 1770, is recorded on the shell above the portico which also shows a cross, the coat of arms of the Inquisition, which held office in the city until 1811. Its activities, which included more civil investigations than burnings, were among the causes of the emancipation. During the restoration of 1957, a workman showed the author a rusty chain he had dug up in an adjoining cell—an object attesting to the sinister side of the In-

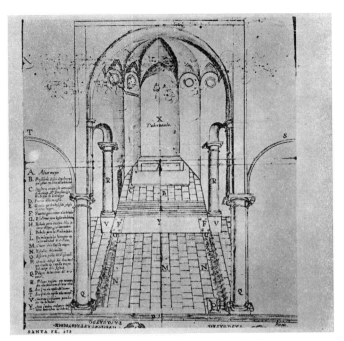

Cathedral (1666) from the Archives of the Indies   *Sketches of the Aduana (Royal House),* (1575)*

quisition. On the side of the Calle de Inquisición was a small aperture covered by a strong grating. This once served as a letter-drop into which the denunciations were placed, some of which led to large and small prosecutions—much in the Giaconda manner. The interior of the patio, with its galleries and arches above and below, is beautiful. From the Hall of the Inquisition one can get a charming view of old roofs and the Moorish tower of the cathedral. During the Festival of May 8–28, 1959, an exhibition of contemporary paintings from fifteen Latin American countries was held in this assembly hall. A nice transition.

Most of the Colonial residences within the walls of Cartagena have either been demolished or converted for business purposes. The streets were similar to those of all of the coast cities of the Antilles and the Gulf of Mexico from Cumana to Vera Cruz. The houses were generally of one or two stories. In Getsemani—out of the commercial section—they were generally of one story, such as the residence of Don Gonzalo de Herrera, Marqués de Villata, the cornice of whose house preserves his coat of arms. The balconies of Cartagena are of wood and in Getsemani one often sees the *ventana de panza*, or "belly type." The best example of this, on Espiritu Santo street, is the only house with a pair of low windows on either side. Unfortunately,

*It was built at the beginning of 1621 by de Roda and contained the custom house, the treasury, the auditor's office, a warehouse, food exchange and the living quarters of the royal officials.

Señora Rosa María de Ochoa Covo beside the well of the Casa del Marques de Valdehoyos

Casa del Marqués de Valdehoyos, patio view, still occupied by descendants of Captain Rafael Tono of Independence fame

it is now badly restored and used as a school. In 1586 Philip II dictated an order prohibiting balconies or anything hung outside projecting from the walls, but the edict was never followed. Besides the *tinajero*, something like a dresser with a wooden grating door, a typical feature of the larger houses is the *mirador* on the roof from which one could gain a view of the sea or bay. The combination of the house and shop is similar to that found in Cádiz with which colonial Cartagena had relations. The cloister-like patios were closed on only three sides to make it possible to catch the breeze. Because of heavy rains, the balconies and miradors were always covered with tile roofs. In most two-story Colonial houses the lower part was used for business and the upper part for living.

The best preserved typical example of a Cartagena mansion is located on Calle de la Factoría, not far from the wall. At the end of the seventeenth century it was the residence of the wealthy Marques de Valdehoyos, who in that epoch had the concession of importing slaves. The salon of this house had a Mudéjar ceiling similar to that of the Church of Santo Toribio, but it has been hidden by modern plaster except in one corner. In the entrace hall is the stone block for dismounting riders. The exterior of the house is simple, with balconied windows and a door with a fine knocker. But inside the vestibule one sees three stories showing corridors with turned railings upheld by jutting beams. One side is closed by wooden screens under the arches. On the fourth side is an open space for a garden containing a pool with steps

103

Plaza of the Seven Martyrs—Outside of the Old Walls and across from the Public Market

Church of San Pedro Claver, viewed from the waterfront

Aisle of the fascinating Cartagena Market Bird-Cage Walk

formerly used by the family for bathing. A wall separates the pool from the well which supplies it. The third floor of the house was once surmounted by a mirador which was destroyed by a storm. Our chapter contains a picture of Señora Maria de Ochoa (whose maiden name was Rosa María Covo Tono) seated beside the ancient well.

The Tono family, descendants of the Marqueses de Arellano, lived here, as did Captain Don Rafael Tono, of Independence fame. During my visit in 1958 there was a ship in the harbor named after this hero. At that time the owner of the house was Doña Lucía Tono Macía, aged ninety. She has since died, leaving her historic home to relatives. A charming Moorish-type house built on Manga Island is now occupied by descendants of Captain Rafael Tono. It was built by Don Victor Manuel Covo Iglesias, whose architect came from Spain, bringing with him the beautiful tiles used in the Alhambra-like interior. Most of the modern houses are built either on Manga or on the Peninsula of Boca Grande.

We have discussed walls, churches and homes but have said very little about the inhabitants of Cartagena. The best place to see them in all their varying tones and habiliments is the market on the wharf; it is hard to choose between what is more interesting, the native products or the natives. While sipping a glass of expresso coffee, one of the excellent products of the state, the eye is drawn to the brilliant flower stalls and the flower vendors. The inhabitants do not wear hats like those worn in the *altiplano* of the Andes. This is a tropical country and the clothes are nondescript. The only characteristic headgear is the straw sombrero of the cowboy in from his ranch. This has a black straw design. He wears boots, too. Antique spurs are collectors' items today.

Cartagena is a delightful city to visit, if one can avoid the rainy season and enjoy the tropical climate (average eighty-two degrees), as do people from Bogotá who descend from their cool height to go swimming in the ocean. Cartagena still maintains a great deal of Spanish and Moorish atmosphere. For those who read Spanish there is a wealth of old documents and maps, to be found both locally and scattered in other countries, which explain the origin of this "old country" charm. Fortunately, there remain the churches, balconies, forts and walls to give visible testimony.

In its beautiful setting at the edge of the immense bay lies this city through which once passed much of the wealth of the New World. Scarred by pirate raids and bitter sieges, it has a rugged, heroic history. Having learned of its tumultuous past, one can better appreciate the present significance of South America's surviving walled town.

Famous gold Rosario Chapel of Santo Domingo, Tunja

Chapter 4

TUNJA
The Emblazoned City

Tunja, Colombia, is one of the few cities in South America in which one can intimately feel and touch the sixteenth century, the Century of the Conquest. No other city, to my knowledge, presents a more numerous or better aggregation of Spanish Colonial buildings. Because of this and because it is so little known, it is my fourth treasure city.

Though Tunja is only about one hundred miles northwest of Bogotá, a Milwaukee travel agency could not inform me how to get there. In Bogotá, however, I found that there were four means of reaching it: train, *autocarril* (gasoline railway), bus and limousine, ranging in fare from one dollar to thirty dollars. I chose the *autocarril* (fare one dollar), which took us through many communities where hatted and beshawled Indians collected at stopping places. Along the way we were interrogated in broken English by what we learned was a Tunja police inspector; he had once visited San Francisco and was very curious about our reasons for visiting his city. Eventually we arrived in Tunja, 9,000 feet up in the Andean foothills, a flourishing city of 50,000, which most North Americans have never heard of. In the next four days we found only two persons who spoke English. However, my limited Spanish met with courteous attention everywhere, and consequently we greatly enjoyed our stay in a city indelibly marked by Spain—a city quite unaccustomed to tourists. (It was the late art historian of Michigan State University, Dr. Martín Soria, who had recommended the visit.)

Portrait of Capitán Gonzalo Suárez Rendón in the Club Boyacá, Tunja

In 1538 three leaders of distant civilizations arrived at the same point in the Andean altiplano: Gonzalo Jimenez de Quesada, Sebastian de Belalcazar, and Nicolas de Federmann. Together they founded the capital of the New Kingdom of Granada, Santa Fé de Bogotá, now called simply Bogotá.

Belalcazar then organized an expedition under Captain Gonzalo Suárez Rendón, charging him with the commission to erect a new city in the vicinity of Zaque. A site at the Chibcha city of Hunza was chosen, and on August 6, 1539, on the Day of the Transfiguration, Suárez Rendón became the founder of the city of Tunja. A Spanish nobleman of Málaga, he had assisted at the coronation of Charles V and had fought at Pavia against Francis I before coming to the New World. Nobility of blood, distinction of person, and a kind, equable personality make him one of the most interesting figures of the conquest in Colombia, and he gathered around him the most distinguished men from the three expeditions. He married Doña Mencia de Figueroa and never afterwards lived in any city but the one he had founded.

In less than seventy-five years Tunja became a beautiful city with 432 houses, ten richly appointed churches, fountains for every part of the city, paved streets and a public spirit reflecting the culture and dynamism of the founders and their sons. The Chibcha Indians were peaceable, and the entire city became a large factory, with thousands of natives carrying wood to the immense furnaces that fired pottery and tiles for the new town.

Conquistador Don Juan de Castellanos worked conscientiously to record the facts pertaining to the city and its founders, and his *Elegías de Varones Ilustres de Indias* is one of the best sixteenth-century source books of the conquest.

The design of the plaza mayor, or the principal plaza, was prescribed in 1610 by a master plan sent out by the Council of the Indies in Seville to all overseas possessions. *
The plaza, 174 paces square, was the site of the city hall, the jail, and the chief church. The municipal palace of today was built on the site of the original municipal building, in front of which, in 1663, bullfights were held to celebrate the birth of the royal heir of Spain, Carlos José. There was a fountain in the middle of the plaza which served the convents of San Francisco, Santa Clara and Santo Domingo. This fountain, made in 1573, was surmounted by "el mono de la pila," a man with a face resembling a monkey and a hand over his mouth to denote silence. This was removed

---

*Ulises Rojas, in the introduction to his *Coats of Arms and Ancient Inscriptions of the City of Tunja*, writes: "The archives which the city possesses, composed of more than 1,500 volumes of the colonial epoch, are almost never consulted and their richness is incalculable. Enough to say that in Colombia there is no colonial city that, like Tunja, conserves in the original the act of foundation and all the proceedings of the mayor and municipal government up to the epoch of the Independence, and after that."

to make way for a statue of Bolívar in 1891, and a replica of "el mono" was given to the Museum of Tunja. In 1925 the present equestrian statue of the Liberator by Andelini was ordered, and the first statue of Bolívar was removed to a site near the Bridge of Boyacá. At the time of the fourth centennial the plaza was paved in stones with the design of the city's coat of arms.

The escutcheon of Don Juan Rodríguez de Morales was on the Colonial house of Carrera 4 a, Número 3–83. Don Juan was born in Tunja in 1560, son of Don Francisco de Morales, a conquistador who accompanied Quesada in the conquest of the New Kingdom and who then followed Rendón to Tunja; there he was allotted the encomienda of Soraca which his son inherited. The son's house was torn down at the time of the fourth centennial to make way for the Centenario Hotel, and at that time the *escudo* was transferred to an angle of the façade of the new structure.

It may be indelicate to mention, but to keep warm in the Centenario Hotel at night I needed—besides the two regular blankets and a hot water bottle—long underwear, nightgown, sweater, leather jacket, coat, and a fur cape over my feet which were already sheathed in woolen sweat socks borrowed from my photographer. The Indian maid, who brought orange juice and hot coffee to the room at seven o'clock in the morning, was amused to see this array of covering. In extenuation I might mention that a pane was out of the window and, being a tenderfoot, I was somewhat affected by the city's 9,000-foot elevation. On the first morning, having been thawed by the sun shining through holes in the clouds, I went on a tour of the sights of Tunja which included the churches, colleges, parks, the market and the Pozo de Donato beyond the Normal School. The Pozo de Donato was a sacred pool of the Chibcha Indians into which they threw gold and emeralds as appeasement to their gods. It was eighty meters deep. In 1733 a Spaniard named Donato spent a great deal of money attempting to empty the pond and find the treasure. His only success was to inspire a proverb; even today, when something is lost in Tunja, one hears "it fell into the Pozo de Donato." Efforts were also made to find treasure in 1880 and 1908, but without success.

Among other records, there is preserved a map of Tunja, dating from the year 1623, which gives the original layout of the city and all of its houses. Many of these houses have survived the centuries and still proudly proclaim their lineage through the heraldic devices of old Spain. Indeed, Tunja is called The Emblazoned City because so many of the founding fathers and their wives who were of noble birth had their coats of arms carved in stone over the doorways of their homes. There are at

Tunja's finest doorway—entrance to Santa Clara Convent, with coat of arms of Governor D. Bernardino de Mujica Guevara

Portal of Casa Vargas, home of a conquistador. Note the carved stone Coat of Arms.

least twenty such escutcheons of which the original history is known. These coats of arms are so characteristic of Tunja that some description of their detail is merited.

Many are the quarterings of the old Spanish nobility, but they were also granted by the king to conquistadors in reward for their part in the conquest, the patent conferring on them the rank of *caballero*. These latter did not have the helmet, which would have denoted nobility, above the escudo.

There were four Spanish military orders—Alcántara, Santiago, Montesa and Calatrava—which had been founded in Spain by various kings in commemoration of certain battles. These had distinctive insignia to add to their coats of arms. The sign of the order of Santiago was a red sword in the form of a cross, that of Calatrava a red cross, of Alcántara a green cross, and that of Montesa a very plain red cross. A crown usually indicated the title of Marquis, but in the case of Bravo Maldonado, the crown showed that he was a descendant of old caballeros with the appellation of Suarez. He was an *hijodalgo* (son of a noble), a term later shortened to *hidalgo*.★ The house in which Capitán García Arias Maldonado lived is at Calle 6 a, Número 3 E. Above the doorway is his coat of arms, quartered by a cross. In the upper right-hand quarter there is a pear tree without leaves, which is one of the insignia of the Military Order of Alcántara. Below that is a castle with three towers. To the left, above, is a fleur-de-lis and below that a lion rampant. Named perpetual magistrate of the city, Maldonado joined with his intimate friend Capitán Suárez Rendón in August, 1541, to take possession of the high post of Justicia Mayor and Capitán General of Tunja. He acted as sponsor of Suárez Rendón. He married Doña Catalina de Pineda and was encomendero of the nearby village of Tinjaca. From the revenue he derived from the village, he and his family built up Tunja's richest art treasure, the Chapel of Our Madonna of the Rosary (El Rosario) in the Church of Santo Domingo. When García Arias Maldonado died in 1568, he left a great part of his worldly goods to the chapel as an endowment for its chaplain. The chapel is so beautiful that there is a proverb which states: "It alone is worth a trip from Europe." I found it to be one of the most precious art gems of my seven cities, uncluttered by cheap candles and paper flowers.

A square stone in the wall of the central nave of Santo Domingo has this inscrip-

★Later in the Colonial Period, when the Spanish Treasury became depleted, it was possible to buy a title and coat of arms. Philip II presented only five titles without purchase, one a marquisate to Francisco Pizarro who was without estate. The decline of the Spanish Empire financially was not obvious until after the death of Philip in 1598. But the practice of selling patents of nobility was common over much of Europe, especially in France under Louis XIV and Louis XV, and in England under James I and his successors.

tion: "This is the chapel and tomb of Capitán García Arias Maldonado and his sons and descendants. He died in the year 1568." The stone has a lion rampant engraved in the middle with a skull and cross bones on either side, and the legend, "Cuan Amarga es tu memoria al hombre que tiene paz" ("How full of sorrow is your memory of the man who has attained peace").

Another Maldonado, Don Antonio Bravo, was born in Tunja in about 1571. His father, Don Pedro Bravo de Molina, was married in Spain to Doña Ana Maldonado and later emigrated to Tunja, which became his base for establishing the encomiendas of Tutasa and Topaga. He died in the latter village in 1575, leaving the properties in trust to his son. When Antonio Bravo Maldonado grew up he became a member of the municipal council and at one time was put in jail with other councilmen for protesting the imposition of excise taxes. Don Antonio's house in Tunja retains today its beautiful stone entrance marked 7–15 Carrera 4. Above the door are three escudos, each surrounded by a cordon ending in a rosette. Since the cordon was used exclusively for bachelors and widows, it was deduced that the blazons were ordered after the death of Don Antonio by his widow. Because the five fleurs-de-lis on the two outside escudos, one of which showed a ladder scaling a castle, were also on the doorway of Holguín Maldonado (Carrera 4, Número 7–81), it is further believed that the five fleurs-de-lis must have been the old Maldonado insigne. The beautifully restored Colonial mansion of Don Diego Holguín Maldonado now houses one of the finest membership clubs, the Club Boyacá, which was very hospitable to my photographer and me.

After several hours of strenuous photographing at the Museo Casa Vargas we returned to the Centenario Hotel and found it cold and "temperance." Having seen the nearby Club Boyacá the day before, when the hotel manager had driven us on a tour of the city, I had the inspiration of attempting to gain entry although I had never made it a habit to ring the doorbells of strange clubs or crash parties. I told John, my photographer, to put on a clean shirt; I put on my mink cape and the two of us sallied forth. At the club entrance we met a handsome member who was about to enter, and I asked if it would be possible for us to obtain a warming drink. He graciously invited us in, and we passed through an elegant patio lined with dark beams into the panelled bar. There we seated ourselves and placed an order with a white-coated waiter while our sponsor went in search of an English-speaking friend. The friend turned out to be a distinguished young judge, Jaime Ruiz Ojeda. I explained why we were visiting Tunja, and we engaged in a very interesting conversa-

A section of the restored frescoed ceiling of Casa Vargas

Frescoed ceiling of Casa Vargas showing Minerva

Other Pompeiian-type decorations of a ceiling in Casa Vargas with cartouche of Joseph

Elephant panel of the frescoed ceiling of Casa Vargas

tion. After awhile the judge explained he must leave to keep an appointment, but not before he had offered us all privileges of the club and told us of the portrait of the city's founder, Suárez Rendón, in an upper room. The next day we returned and took the photograph which appears in this book. Judge Ojeda later sent me the book by Ulises Rojas, to which I have already referred, entitled (in translation) *Coats of Arms and Ancient Inscriptions of the City of Tunja*, written for the celebration of Tunja's Fourth Centennial in 1939. It proved to be an invaluable reference book for its descriptions of the city's coats of arms.

At Calle 6 at Número 2–20 there lived and wrote one of Tunja's most illustrious men, the Don Johan (Juan) de Castellanos mentioned earlier; besides *Los Varones*, he also wrote a history of the conquest of the New Kingdom of Granada in verse. His title was "Benefactor," for it was under his leadership that the building of the cathedral was completed. The house he lived in on the northeast corner of the cathedral square, next to that of Suárez Rendón, had been bequeathed to him by Domingo de Aguirre, who also endowed him with the chaplaincy of the cathedral. A recent marble plaque over the door of the house carries the inscription: "A la memoria de Juan de Castellanos ilustre conquistador-cronista-poeta-cura de Tunja—Alanis 1522–Tunja 1606." ★ A bronze bust stands in front of the house he occupied on the Plaza de Bolívar; over the house of Rendón, Carrera 3, Número 6–68, an inscription reads (in translation): "The congress of young university students and citizens of Boyacá to the noble city of Tunja on the 4th Centennial of its founding, 1539–1939, in honor of its illustrious sons Gonzalo Suárez Rendón and Juan de Castellanos."

Among the most interesting of the coats of arms of the New Kingdom of Granada is that of the Castillos, Marqueses de Surba. His coat of arms was placed over the entrance of the Hacienda de Bonza in 1910. It showed the crown of a marquisate and the initials I.H.S. Below was a blazon quartered by a sword cross with one quarter holding a castle, a tree and a lion rampant, the second quarter a chessman, the third quarter thirteen roundels and the fourth three soldiers. The chess board in heraldry is one of the oldest insignia used and denotes a field of battle. The use of the human figure represents the men who took part in battle or tournament. The trunk of the family tree in new Spain was the lawyer Don Francisco Ventura de Castillo y Toledo, who was born in 1630 in the kingdom of Toledo, Spain. He graduated as a Bachelor of Laws from the University of Salamanca, and in 1660 the

---

★"To the memory of Juan de Castellanos illustrious conquistador, chronicler, poet, curate of Tunja—Born in Alanis (Spain) 1522—died in Tunja 1606." (The latter date should be 1607.)

Bedroom with lavabo and brazier in the Casa Vargas

king named him Lieutenant General of the Province of Tunja; it was there that he married Doña Maria de Guevara Niño y Rojas. Among other descendants of this marriage was Doña Francisca Josefa de Castillo y Guevara, the celebrated nun of Santa Clara, Tunja's immortal poet, and the author of *Afectos y Sentimientos Espirituales.*

Don Pedro Antonio de Castillo y Guevara, who was baptized in Tunja in 1673, inherited the property of San Lorenzo de Bonza founded by his great-grandfather in a fertile valley near Tunja. In 1790 a large seignorial mansion, Hacienda de Bonza, was built as a summer home by Don Joaquín del Castillo, and here Francisca spent many

Retablo of Saint Anthony on the balcony of the Casa Vargas

Colonial chair of the Casa Vargas. The tooling may show seated portrait of the owner.

days of her childhood. The same escudo, engraved on a silver pitcher of the rich table setting of the marqueses, was still preserved by the family Penuela del Castillo in 1959.

At Carrera 5, Número 7–63, stands the Casa del Gobernador Don Bernadino de Mujica Guevara who occupied it in 1597. In my opinion it has the most beautiful doorway in Tunja. The hearts in the escudo are the insigne of the Guevara family. At one time the martyr of the Independence, Doctor Don José Cayetano Vasquez, lived here; but since 1875 the house has been occupied by the Convent of Santa Clara and the famous doorway is the entrance to the chapel. The Liberator, Bolívar, stayed in this house on the 5th of August, 1819.

Over the stone doorway at Carrera 5, Número 4–51, is a coat of arms of the Military Order of Calatrava bordered with eight crosses of San Andrés and with a helmet above, both of which denote a caballero of noble lineage. According to the map of Tunja this was the house of Don Bartolomé de Alarcon who in 1610 was seventy years old and a very distinguished man. The escudo belonged either to him or to one of his descendants. Other caballeros of the order of Calatrava were Capitán Francisco de Torres Barrera, corregidor and chief justice of the city from 1634

118

Chicha cup of Chibcha pottery in Casa Vargas *Kitchen in Casa Vargas*

to 1639, and Don Miguel Montalvo de Luna, who held the same offices from 1681 to 1683.

The house of Capitán Antonio Ruiz Mancipe (Calle 6a, Número 5–13) was left by him to the legitimate descendants of his daughter, Francisca Ruiz, as patrons of the Mancipe Chapel in the cathedral. Francisca married Don Cristóbal de Riano, and it was on that account that in the old map of Tunja this house figured as the property of the Riano family. It is a well-constructed house with stone arches and columns of excellent workmanship, one bearing the date 1597. One column shows the ornaments of an old caballero—the helmet, sword, spurs, coat of arms, gloves, lance and also cornucopias of flowers.

It is impossible to describe all of the houses and escudos of the sixteenth-century caballeros, but we must not omit the houses of the Rojas and of the Niños. The house of the Rojas is situated on Carrera 3a, Número 8–05, and today serves as the San Antonio asylum for poor girls. The Rojas coat of arms shows a helmet with plumes and five stars symbolizing light, truth and patriotism; its five bars represent straps which held swords or crossed the shoulders. Capitán Martín de Rojas was perpetual

Cathedral on Bolívar Plaza

alderman of Tunja; in 1594 he was the oldest man in the city. When the president of the New Kingdom issued the order imposing taxes in behalf of the king, Don Martín presented a paper, signed by thirteen members of the council, containing a protest. When they refused to withdraw it, the president took Don Martín to Bogotá as a prisoner, along with Antonio de Mancipe, Diego de Vargas, Juan Chacón de Porras and Antonio Maldonado. The tribute was imposed, nevertheless, and the aldermen submitted, but Tunja was forever proud of the fact that this was the first protest in America against taxes imposed by Spain.

When a king of Spain was crowned there were always elaborate fêtes arranged to celebrate the event in the colonies. For instance, when another Rojas, Don Geronimo de Rojas, *Alferez real*, or royal agent, arrived at the fiesta in Tunja to proclaim the ascent to the throne of Philip III on the 16th of May, 1599, he came on a gaily caparisoned bay horse covered with a cloth of red silk sprinkled with gold and pearls. He himself was arrayed splendidly in a surtout of red velvet slashed and lined with a white silver material, the whole embroidered in silver and gold. On either side of his surtout four slashes were joined on top by a rosette, in the middle of which was a medallion with seven emeralds. The breeches were similarly embroidered and the large sleeves were slashed and sprinkled with gold brooches and pearls. Sword and dagger were ornamented; the boots were white. His hat of red satin was sprinkled with rich pearls and small medallions of gold and emeralds, and the hat band carried a large medallion and was adorned at intervals with gold lions and emeralds. Footmen and pages in livery followed. Such was the luxury of the period.

On the corner of the Plaza de Bolívar, Número 6–15, Carrera 49, is the house of Don Juan Agustín Niño y Alvarez, whose arms display five fleurs-de-lis and two branches of laurel. Don Juan was born in Tunja of noble parentage and his only son, Doctor Don Juan Nepomuceno Niño, held high office in the independence movement. Because of his campaigns he was imprisoned by the Spanish regime of terror against the patriots, and on the 29th of November, 1816, he faced the firing squad before a wall in the Bosque de Republica; with him were Doctor Cayetano Vasquez, Coronel José Ramón Lineros and eight others. A descendant of the martyr, Doctor Aquilino Niño, illustrious canon of the cathedral, a poet and literate, died in Tunja in 1927.

Of the many reasons for choosing Tunja as an interesting example of a Spanish Colonial city, the most persuasive, perhaps, is that it preserves as a museum a rare, and possibly unique example of an original conquistador's house with authentic furnishings. This was the home of the king's notary, Don Juan de Vargas, on Calle 7a, Número 2–50. The house has two stories, an early Renaissance doorway with the Vargas coat of arms and, in the rear, a porch on columns overlooking a walled patio of true Spanish style. The living quarters on the second floor consist of two salons (one of which was the office), a bedroom and a kitchen. The servants were housed in an adjoining wing. The most remarkable features are the frescoes in the salons. I saw nothing of the sixteenth century in Lima, Cuzco or Quito to compare in interest and rarity with these frescoes in Tunja. Incorporated in them are grotesques; Christian symbols of Mary, Christ and Joseph; coats of arms of the Vargas family and of Tunja; the pagan god, Jupiter, between the goddesses Minerva and Diana; and a rhinoceros, an elephant and a lion. The Tunja Vargas frescoes were probably painted between 1587 and 1590. The ingenuity of the painting led Dr. Luis Acuna, former Director of the Museum of Colonial Art of Bogotá, to believe that the painter was a Creole (Spaniard born in South America), a mestizo, or an Indian working from the ideas of the owner, Juan de Vargas, and his good friend, the poet and clergyman Juan de Castellanos. On the ceiling of the two salons the unknown Tunja painter used many inspirations, Italian, Flemish, Dutch and German, drawing them all from an extraordinary source, the chapel of François I at Fontainebleau.

In 1535 François I of France gave a commission to two Italian artists, Rosso Rossi and Primaticcio, for the decoration of this chapel. Nowhere, following the Italian Renaissance, had there been painting so free of ecclesiastical influence as in these masterful designs which, in general, were inspired by Pompeian painting. In the main salon of the Casa Vargas one finds grotesques and Roman gods taken from drawings on the walls of the Fontainebleau chapel. These grotesques and pagan gods were copied from drawings made by the Dutch artist Thiry, who had painted at Fontainebleau with Rosso and Primaticcio. On the ceilings at Tunja the painter had also employed many motifs from the drawings of the Dutchman Wredeman de Vries. The animals used were symbolic: the elephant was a symbol of wisdom and of the Christian gentleman, and in the blazon of Vargas the elephant was shown in conflict with the choleric rhinoceros. The date of the painting is deduced from the fact that the rhinoceros must have been taken from a book by the Flemish writer Juan de Arfe, published in Seville in 1585, the third volume of which treated the heights and forms of animals. The drawing of the rhino in the book had been made by Albrecht Dürer in 1515, after the first rhinoceros had been brought to the King of Portugal from India in 1513.

Main altar of the Cathedral dedicated to Nuestra Señora de Guadalupe

Altar in the Cathedral with figure of San Rafael

Tunja: The Emblazoned City

To quote Dr. Soria in describing the frescoes of Casa Vargas: "Thus we have a work of art in a direct line from the Greek Olympus, Pompeii, Fontainebleau and Tunja, a pearl of colonial New Granada."*

Before eventually yielding in primacy to Bogotá, Tunja was the cultural center of Colombia, with several churches which were among the most important in the New Kingdom. The Spaniard, religious in temperament, constantly implored the protection of God in his conquest of the warlike Indians. The beautiful churches and chapels and retables were accordingly erected by the conquerors in thanks for their preservation and, perhaps, as Ulises Rojas says, to expiate the violent seizure of the natural riches of the country and to answer the censures of the missionaries at the exploitation of the Indians.

Pál Kelemen describes the exteriors of the churches of Tunja as "frozen Renaissance"—that is, lacking in the ebullience of the Baroque. But the interiors of these churches, undoubtedly following the patterns established in Quito, are rich in carving and gold, with a blending of styles which were predominantly Mudéjar and Baroque. These interiors are enhanced by the excellent craftsmanship and originality of the Chibchas, who had been skilled workers in gold long before the Spaniards arrived. Mario J. Buschiazzo says: "The architecture of Tunja is of extraordinary artistic value. Few cities in America have more or better quantity of buildings of the Colonial epoch, some with characteristics of pure Spanish."

The most outstanding churches are the Cathedral of Nuestra Señora de Guadalupe with its Rendón and Mancipe chapels, Santo Domingo with Tunja's prize gem of art, the Rosario Chapel, the Church of San Francisco, and the chapel of the old convent of Santa Clara.

The cathedral stands majestically on the southeast corner of the Plaza de Bolívar. Its single tower is silhouetted against the generally cloudy sky. Its fine Renaissance portal rests on a platform. Abutting the church is the *Atarazano,* or parson's residence,†

*The restoration of Casa Vargas is of recent date. "The house of Juan de Vargas was almost in ruins on a visit in August of 1950 taken by my dear friend, Master Luis Alberto Acuna," writes Doctor Soria. As director of the Museum of Colonial Art of Bogotá, he was particularly aroused by this sad state of affairs and started a movement to save the priceless relic. Through dedicated effort he achieved the victory of having the house declared a national monument. It was accordingly acquired by the State and placed under the care of the Service of Archeology of the National Ethnological Institute. Its folklore section proceeded with a careful restoration of the house and frescoes, and in the end established a Living Museum of Colonial Art which was inaugurated on the 7th of August, 1953, the anniversary of the Battle of Boyacá, by His Excellency the President of the Republic, General Rojas Pinilla.

†The bishop lives three blocks from here in a stone, one-block building named Palacio Episcopal, which is a real palace, huge and richly decorated in Renaissance style with beautiful rose gardens.

with a Spanish balcony from which pronouncements were made. Don Juan de Castellanos, aided by the mayor and citizens, was responsible for the construction of the cathedral, which was completed in 1600. It replaced the first church which had been built by Rendón.

The façade was originally designed in 1598–1600 by Bartolomé Carrión of Spain and, although the exterior of the cathedral has been modified through the years, the façade remains relatively unchanged. The interior of the church is predominantly Gothic and Mudéjar. Today one can see, framed and flanked by paintings hung on one of the principal columns, the wooden cross which was used in the first Mass celebrated in the city by Padre Vicente de Requesada of the Order of St. Augustine. In the left nave, near the original location of the choir, with its carved stalls, is an elegant stone altar holding two coats of arms with eagles and an inscription which reads: "Here is interred Francisco de Estrada and his heirs, in the year of 1593." At the foot of this altar, below the pavement of slabs, is found the sepulchre of the benefactor, Don Juan de Castellanos, covered with a large square stone on which is engraved a Latin inscription. Translated, it reads: "After many things done, Juan de Castellanos lies beneath this stone. He was in this temple for many years Minister and Rector." This is followed by the words, in Spanish: "Su Patria Alanis."

Off the south nave is the Chapel of the Clergy, containing mystical paintings in frames, a beautiful colonial altar, and a pulpit. In this chapel is the entrance to the crypt which holds the remains of the founder, Suárez Rendón. The altars of Rendón and Mancipe are to the left of the main retable. The Rendón Chapel is especially distinguished by a beautiful altar and a renowned rosette ceiling. Opposite it is the statue of Rendón, in marble, placed there in 1939, with his coat of arms.* They are also the primitive arms of the Sarmiento family, which incorporate two towers with eagles on top, a band of gold with serpent heads, a border with thirteen roundels and the motto, "To conquer but never be conquered."

The oldest sculpture in the cathedral is an imported Crucifixion group of Vazquez, dated 1583.†

There have been many vicissitudes in the history of the Mancipe Chapel in the cathedral. The Chapel was decorated with its Moorish ceiling and paintings by Don

---

*Rendón's escudo was not carved over his doorway but it is known that his house was decorated by frescoes in color; the arms may have been included in them just as they were in the Casa Vargas.

†In the Church of San Lázaro are statues of St. John the Baptist and St. Blaise, some of the oldest and best sculpture in South America.

Chapel opposite the tomb of the city's founder, Suárez Rendón, in the Cathedral

San Francisco Church with a bust of Juan José Rendón of Independence fame

Nunnery in the garden behind San Francisco Church

Historic cross used in the first Mass said in Tunja Cathedral on the founding of the city

Pedro Ruiz García, owner of the rich encomienda of the village of Toca, after he had asked permission to build the chapel at his own expense in veneration of the Sainted Cross. But, unfortunately, he died when the roof was begun and the work had to be suspended. His wife, Isabel Mancipe, also died, leaving three sons: the eldest, heir to the encomienda, Don Antonio, who, while still young, had come to America with his parents from Puerto de Santa María in Spain, and Don Pedro and Don Juan, who were born in Tunja. In the village of Toca, Don Antonio met the beautiful daughter of his *mayordomo*, the Indian *cacique*. She had been baptized with the name of Antonia Linar. The two fell in love. On the death of his father, Antonio brought Antonia, by whom he had two daughters, to Tunja. Society murmured against this conduct, with the result that his right to the mayoralty and his right to inherit were denied and the rights assigned to the second son, Don Pedro Ruiz Mancipe, who had lived and married in Tunja.

Don Antonio did not agree to this determination and brought suit, before the Real Audiencia in Santa Fé de Bogotá, against his brother, promising to finish the Mancipe Chapel at his own expense if he won the suit. He did win and his brother retired to Garagoa. The chapel, called at that time the Chapel of Veracruz, was ac-

129

cordingly finished and richly decorated with images, missals, pictures and jewels which have disappeared in time, many of them removed on the order of a former governor of Boyacá who claimed to be a descendant of Don Antonio. Originally the portrait of Capitán Don Antonio Ruiz Mancipe, painted when he was fifty-six years old, hung in the chapel, but it was later removed to the chapter house next to the church. There is a crypt containing the remains of Don Pedro Ruiz García, his son, and other members of the family.

In the Mancipe Chapel today one finds only the beautiful *artesonado* ceiling done by Alonso de León, an altar, and two pictures painted by Angelino Romano Medoro, a sixteenth-century Italian painter. In 1588 this important artist had signed an "Annunciation" for the Santa Clara convent in Tunja, and ten years later he also painted the "Agony in the Garden" and "Descent from the Cross" for the cathedral.

The Church of Santo Domingo, although less prepossessing than the cathedral, is, in many features, equally distinguished. The Dominican fathers erected a convent in connection with the church which took from 1568 to 1600 to finish. The arches of the two-story cloister are particularly arresting. Marco Dorta says of the structure: "The cloister of San Domingo is, as is that of Santa Clara (Antigua), one of the most beautiful that the Mudéjar art of the Renaissance left in Colombia."

The famous chapel of the church of Nuestra Señora de Rosario (Our Lady of the Rosary) has reliefs above the altar and on either side of the Madonna, depicting the mysteries of the Rosary. They are separated by double, richly carved columns. The *camarin*, or niche, of the Virgin is encrusted with shell, porcelain and antique crystal. The Virgin, the work of Roque Amados, was brought from Spain by Don Felix del Castillo. Carved in the ceiling of the chapel are octagons with fruit, flowers and vegetables. The ceiling is also decorated with framed Delft ceramic dishes which were brought from Holland as ballast. The color of the chapel is gold on a red base, giving the same effect as the interior of La Compañía in Quito. At the foot of the gold proscenium arch is a plaster dog, the customary symbol of Santo Domingo. The picture of the pulpit in this book shows the same decorative motifs as those used in the chapel. Also in the church are oil paintings of Santa Catalina, Santo Domingo and San Francisco by Vasquez Ceballos.

The old convent of Santa Clara on Carrera 1a, well established by 1578, harbored the first order of nuns of Santa Clara in the New Kingdom of Granada. Here is still preserved the cell occupied by the abbotess and poet, Sister Francisca Josefa de Castillo y Guevara. Born in Tunja, this first religious writer in America stands

The decorated ceiling of the Chapel of Capitán Antonio Ruiz Mancipe

The Mudéjar ceilings of Colombia were copied from the house of Juan Diaz Jaramillo, el Rico, a conquistador who lived in Tolima in 1560. His house was flooded, but the ceiling was saved and later used for the ceiling of the Church of Conception de Bogotá. A school of artesonados Colombianos was started in Bogotá and workmen trained there made the Mudéjar ceilings in Santo Domingo and Santa Clara cloisters in Tunja. This one in the Mancipe Chapel of the Cathedral was commenced in 1569 and finished in 1590 by conquistador Don Pedro Ruiz García. It took many years and over 6,000 pesos to finish it.

Pulpit of Santo Domingo Church

in rank after Santa Teresa de Jesús. The proscenium arch of the chapel, with its columns, is decorated with the same flowers and vegetables and gilt over a red ground as the Rosario Chapel. The convent's most famous feature is the ceiling; on it, gilt octagons overlay exposed beams which display Mudéjar interlacing.

I tried for several days to see this ceiling in the absence of guides but failed, due to my confusion between the old and the present home of the Santa Clara nuns. I had sought permission from the invisible nun behind the revolving cupboard door of the present convent, but did not learn until too late that the famous chapel ceiling is in the *antiguo convento*, not the one now occupied by the nuns. The only contact with the nuns of Santa Clara was by means of this revolving cupboard. People brought cans and placed them inside, the door revolved and later the can appeared filled with corn. I placed there a written application for the privilege of photographing the ceiling of the church—"yes" or "no." The answer came back "yes," but no means were indicated. I never saw the ceiling which was in the old convent, and the bishop's permission was necessary to admit my photographer.

Another distinguished church is San Francisco, founded in 1572, which contains colonial altars of great artistic merit. The exterior is of simple Renaissance style. There is a small yard in front of which a bust of the Independence hero, Colonel Juan José Rendón, stands on a pedestal. Inside, the ceiling of the apse shows exposed beams with Mudéjar interlacing, similar to those of Santa Clara. Next door to San Francisco is the abbey, with an auditorium and colorful gardens. It is surrounded on two sides by tall, thick walls.

The Franciscan fathers also assisted in the foundation and organization of the secondary school, Colegio de Boyacá (Carrera 4a, Número 5–91), which was established by decree on May 17th, 1822, and expedited by the Vice President of the Republic, General Francisco de Paula Santander. The building has an old and a new part. The old part was built originally by the Jesuits and consists of two floors, the part on the lower east side having Mudéjar arches. The new section has an elegant doorway on Calle 6a.

The political history of Tunja has also inspired art and commentary. Around the city there was a cluster of provinces; in 1815 these united under a federal constitution whose president was Doctor Camilo Torres, a friend of Bolívar. Tunja was the main center of organization and supply for the Independence army and many of its best sons were killed in action or executed in the struggle against the tyranny of Spain. To thank the city for its services Bolívar gave it the title, "Taller de la Libertad"

Ceiling of Santo Domingo showing use of framed Delft plates for decorations

("Workshop of Liberty"). Ironically enough, the Emperor Charles V, three centuries before, had given it the title, "Very noble and very loyal City."

To write of Tunja without describing two of Bolívar's most decisive battles, which determined the fate of Colombia and, eventually, that of South America, would be like writing of Yorktown and omitting the surrender of Cornwallis.

Ten miles from Tunja, on the road to Santa Fé de Bogotá, is a small park with statues, columns and an elaborate memorial to Bolívar, all in memory of the two battles: the battle of Pantano de Vargas, July 25th, 1819; and the battle of the Bridge of Boyacá (over the once large but now small Teatinos River) on August 7th, 1819.

The hero of the first battle was Colonel Juan José Rendón, a native whose bust is found in front of the Church of San Francisco in Tunja and to whom the column at Vargas Place is dedicated. Bolívar had rallied the flagging spirits of the Venezuelan plainsmen in June, but at a point in this July battle, when he saw the royal cavalry regrouping, he said, "The battle is lost." Rendón asked: "How is it lost when neither I nor my troops have fought?" "Do what you can and save the country, Colonel!" Bolívar replied. Then Rendón, placing himself at the head of his squadron, waved his lance and cried, "Comrades! Those who are valiant follow me, because in this moment we triumph." After hard fighting, in which General Barreiro lost one thousand royalist troops and Bolívar five hundred, the battle of Pantano de Vargas was won by the patriots.* The Vargas cavalry charge was fantastic. A detachment of only thirty *llaneros*, headed by Rendón, smashed the brilliant Spanish cavalry, catching it by surprise. The *llaneros*, like the gauchos of Argentina, are incredibly skillful riders; in this battle they carried sharp lances three meters in length.

It happened that in the battle of the Bridge of Boyacá a break in the main Royalist force offered the patriots the chance for victory which they proceeded to exploit. After this battle, the volunteers of Tunja and Socorro dedicated themselves to taking prisoners, among them General José María Barreiro, his second in command, Colonel Francisco Jiménez, and many more top officers. The Patriot General Santander pursued the Royalists in the direction of Bogotá. Anzoategui stayed up all night recovering wounded, scattered arms and ammunition. Later, on the 11th of October, 1819, Barreiro and thirty-eight companions were shot by order of General Santander in Bogotá. The Liberator, Simon Bolívar, was the commanding general of the Patriot forces in both battles. His age at this time was thirty. Santander was twenty-seven

---

*This famous battle was fought in fields owned by José María Ruiz, the great-grandfather of my friend, Judge Jaime Ojeda.

years old, Anzoategui thirty-one, Obando thirty-one, Rendón twenty-nine and Paris twenty-four. It was truly a rebellion of the young.

In the battle of Pantano de Vargas, the Royalist forces numbered 3,800, opposing 2,500 Patriots.★ In the battle of the Bridge of Boyacá the forces of Ferdinand VII numbered 2,940, while Bolívar commanded 3,430.

These decisive battles in the fight by the Creole Patriots for liberation from Spanish rule engaged no large number of men, but great bravery and generalship were displayed. The hilly wooded park of Boyacá boasts more impressive monuments, in quality if not in number, than does the historic North American battlefield of Gettysburg. The battles might be described as only skirmishes, considering the number of men engaged, but politically they were highly important.

The outlying districts of Tunja contain many ancient memorials. These include the hewn columns of stone which were the work of the Chibcha Indians or their predecessors. Not much archeological investigation has been carried on to decipher the hieroglyphics or establish the dates of these ancient relics, but I understand that a probable date might be fixed at about 1,000 A.D.

★This included three hundred British Legionnaires under Colonel James Rook, who was killed and replaced by Colonel MacIntosh.

House and tile kiln on outskirts of Tunja

Among these pre-Columbian ruins in the vicinity of Tunja is an interesting example at Sogamoso; there, the Chibchas had built a temple of the sun decorated with gold, which was burned by the Spanish soldiers in 1537. The archeologist Silva Celis, investigating the site, located a cemetery where he found enough significant objects —ceramics, mummies and stones—to stock a museum in Sogamoso. The museum is visited daily by tourists interested in learning about the place where the Indians venerated the Sun King of the Firmament. In Ramiriqui, Virachacha, Tibana and Monquira are large stone columns which were cut out by the Indians for a sumptuous temple of the sun in Hunza (Tunja), but which were never transported there because of the arrival of the Spaniards.

At the confluence of the rivers Gameza and Sogamoso are large stones with carved pictures of frogs, monkeys and men, made five centuries before the conquest by aborigines of Cundinamarca; these record a cataclysm in which the water of Lake Fuquene precipitated into the bed of the Saravita River. In Tras del Alto, near the hermitage of San Lázaro and west of Tunja, is a large number of stones carved with hieroglyphics and colored; this was a place of pilgrimage for the Chibchas where they celebrated the sun with dancing and music.

137

Scene in the public market

The descendants of the Chibchas, both mixed and of pure lineage, can be seen in Tunja's large, flourishing market any day. Each is garbed according to his village tradition. These Indians and their forbears provided the labor to build the city.

Tunja, like each of our seven cities, is not without its local tales and legends. Her historic murder mystery is as gloomy as the somber hills where it was unfolded.

In 1571, in the Century of Gold, Doña Inés de Hinojosa, rich, beautiful and flirtatious, married Don Pedro de Avila, through family arrangement, in Carona, Venezuela. He squandered her money to such an extent that her affection dwindled and she became enamored of the handsome music and dancing teacher of her niece Juana. The romance flourished between Doña Inés and the teacher, Jorge Voto, to such an extent that they decided to murder her husband, and the assassination was so successful that the crime was never solved.

The three remaining characters in the story moved to Pamplona where Voto started a school of dancing, and there he and Inés were married. Suspicion arose, however, and it was then thought necessary to move to Tunja where they took a house on the street now called Calle del Árbol.

Jorge Voto continued his teaching in Tunja and also in Bogotá and upon that revenue the family lived. Time passed, and also their love. In a house near them, Vaca, the foundling son of Don Pedro Bravo de Rivera, encomendero of Chivata, came to live. As a result of this proximity Don Pedro often visited Doña Inés and later took a house next door, pretending to have taken a fancy to her niece, Doña Juana. In fact, Don Pedro told Voto that he wanted to marry Juana and asked Voto to accompany him to Bogotá to ask the Señor Archbishop to publish the banns. On this journey, with Voto and Don Pedro de Rivera, went his brother Hernan Bravo and the sacristan of the cathedral, Pedro of Hungary. The first attempt to murder Voto was at an inn but, that failing, he was later treated to a banquet after which Don Pedro invited him to call upon some women friends. Later in the evening on the way home, in a deep ravine in the Santa Lucía section of Bogotá, two hooded figures in white fell upon Jorge Voto and killed him.

When the body was brought back to Tunja it caused great excitement and suspicion. The disappearance of Doña Inés' first husband was brought back to mind and the knowledge of her romance with Don Pedro caused them to be brought to trial for the murder. The day after the murder, Pedro of Hungary, assisting the parish priest at Mass, was seen to have blood on his sleeve and he also became suspect. He escaped on horseback and was never seen again. President Venejo gave the sentence for the beheading of Don Pedro Bravo de Rivera after confiscating his possessions. Don Hernan Bravo was hung, as was Doña Inés, from the tree in front of her house. For this reason the space from the cathedral and the Lesser Seminary has been called Calle del Árbol (Street of the Tree). The patronage of the Chapel of the Mancipes, which entitled the possessors to a house left by Capitán Don Antonio de Mancipe as chaplain, was given in 1571 (there being no priests in the Mancipe family) to Juan Bravo de Guzmán, son of the disgraced Don Bravo de Rivera, who had paid with his life for his love of Doña Inés de Hinojosa.

Whether time will march gently or ruthlessly through the streets of Tunja remains to be seen. On my 1958 visit, a highway connecting the city to Bogotá was being built and is now finished. Judge Jaime Ruiz Ojeda, with whom I shared my concern, assured me that thus far there has been little damage to colonial Tunja, and that he did not believe future material progress would harm its picturesqueness and historic relics. I am inclined, however, to share the sentiments of the distinguished Franz Blom, explorer of San Cristóbal de Las Casas, Mexico, whom I heard say: "I hate progress. It means destruction." I have only one reservation in respect to Tunja: let progress, in the guise of *central heating*, be welcomed there!

View of Quito from Pichincha Volcano

Chapter 5

QUITO
The Queen of The Andes

CRADLED by the mountains and guarded in the distance by Cotopaxi, the Fujiyama of the Andes, the city of San Francisco de Quito, capital of Ecuador, lies at the foot of the volcanic hill, Pichincha. This sequestered setting is the home of a picturesque people and of a distinguished art and architecture, the legacy of three centuries of Spanish domination. Second in age to Cuzco among South American capitals, Quito is perhaps the oldest with an unbroken record of habitation. The highest capital in the world next to La Paz in Bolivia, Quito still enshrines its Spanish and Incan heritage. It is a city that offers enchantment and dramatic contrasts to the discerning traveler.

Although one of the most artistically important cities in this hemisphere, Quito remained one of the least known until the advent of the airplane made it accessible. Today, despite increasing evidences of our own age—airfields, skyscrapers and movie theatres—Quito carries on the tradition of a much older world. Majestic churches and convents, spacious plazas, red-tiled roofs and green domes gleaming in the sun, narrow cobbled streets, houses set on the hill in labyrinthine fashion—all these retain the Spanish accent. Happily, the mountain barriers have helped to preserve its culture; change is taking place, but not at such heartbreaking speed as in the Colombian capital, Santa Fé de Bogotá, where plazas are being torn up to make way for parking lots and speedways.

At the center of this city of a quarter of a million inhabitants lies the famed Independencia Plaza, so named because it contains a slender column, bordered by flowers and fountains, commemorating the liberators of 1809 and 1822. Palaces of Church and State and a great cathedral dignify the plaza. Yet, imposing as these structures are, its appeal rests in the human life that flows in and about it. The plaza provides a meeting place for all segments of Quito's rigidly classified society. Here the Indians habitually gather, and one may still see pigtailed men clad in scarlet or striped ponchos and women in multicolored skirts, even though the traditional dress of the Indians is steadily giving way to nondescript Western fashions. Almost continuous bartering takes place around the arcades and in the little shops, where Indian children tend babies while parents work at their trades.

The plaza fronting the Church of San Francisco is larger and even more populous than the Independencia. Cuenca Street, which leads to this square, is lined with food shops where strange cuts of meat on braziers emanate peculiar odors. Here too are dramatic contrasts; for between the simple shop fronts one catches a glimpse of lovely patios and discovers entrances to Spanish Colonial houses, massive wooden doors, barred windows and carved balconies. One wishes that some of the houses, dilapidated with age and neglect, might soon be restored. Until recently, Señor Victor Mena—descendant of an aristocratic Spanish family and owner of a notable collection of art works—lived in one of the finer old houses on this street. The Colonial Museum, housed in the beautiful Villacis mansion, is also located on this same street. Another busy plaza, Santo Domingo Square, contains a statue of Antonio José de Sucre (hero of the Battle of Pichincha) as well as the famous Arch of Santo Domingo over which the Rosario Chapel stands.

The climate of Quito is temperate and its air widely praised—a fact which may seem remarkable considering its proximity to the equator. However, this mountain city stands at an altitude of well over nine thousand feet—a situation that insures chilly nights and cool, though often sunny days.

The exact location of the equator was determined in the mid-eighteenth century by French scientists, but the pink granite monument which marks the line—about thirteen miles outside of Quito—was not unveiled until 1937. This monument commemorates the important scientific expedition under the leadership of Charles Marie de la Condamine, a French aristocrat, which was dispatched in 1736 by the French Academy.* Condamine was accompanied by nine other members of the

*The story of La Condamine's expedition is well told in Victor von Hagen's *South America Called Them* and in *Relación Historica de Viaje* by Don Jorge Juan and Don Antonio de Ulloa (1748, Madrid). Antonio de Ulloa's report, *Noticias Secretas de America*, was long unpublished because of its candid criticism of Colonial administration, but is now an important source book, having been discovered and published in London by David Barry in 1826.

Group of Indians of the Otovalo tribe

Academy, including a mathematician, an astronomer, a botanist, a naval officer, a physician, a technician, and a draftsman. This party was joined in Cartagena by two Spanish naval officers, Captain Jorge Juan y Santacilla and Captain Antonio de Ulloa, who were assigned by King Philip V to watch over Spain's interests. The expedition, proposing to test the then-disputed Newtonian theory of the curvature of the earth, made Quito its headquarters. Another member of the expedition was Pedro Vicente Maldonado y Sotomayor, a native Ecuadorian, who took part in the earth measurements and rendered invaluable aid to Condamine in a perilous descent of the Amazon. Later Maldonado was elected to the Académie des Sciences in Paris and was about to be given membership in the Royal Society in London when he died, prosaically, of the measles.

Although the beginnings of Quito are obscured in myth and legend, unwritten history and the records of archeology establish it as the site of a well-developed Indian

Indian woman with large wax candle

La Ronda

culture, even before its invasion, in 1487, by the Incas under Huayna-Capac. This extension of the Peruvian Empire lasted only about fifty years. The last Inca ruler before the Spanish conquest was Atahualpa; he had inherited the empire jointly with his brother, Huascar, the legitimate heir, whom he then defeated in battle. The fratricidal conflict made it comparatively easy for the Spanish conquistadors, Pedro de Alvarado and Sebastian Benalcazar, under orders from Francisco Pizarro, to seize the kingdom. Atahualpa was captured at Cajamarca, Peru. After his fabulous ransom of a room filled with gold had been paid almost in full (the llama train bearing the last of the treasure was on its way), he was given a mock trial and executed—"one of the most atrocious acts of perfidy," in the words of Prescott (in *The Conquest of Peru*), "in the annals of history." On the ruins of the conquered city, Quitu, San Francisco de Quito was founded in 1534, and became a Colonial capital for the three centuries of Spanish rule. In 1563, Philip II of Spain established it as a Royal Audiencia attached to the Viceroyalty of Peru.

The Spaniards were builders as well as conquerors. In the early years the main plaza was laid out and its four sides designated for the governor's palace, the bishop's palace, the office of the mayor, and the cathedral. On land allotted them, the Franciscan and Dominican orders erected their magnificent churches. Land within fifty yards of the cathedral was assigned to the Jesuits for La Compañía. La Merced, another beautiful church, was built a little farther away on Cuenca Street. Embedded in the walls of these Spanish buildings are carefully chiselled stones taken from the mighty temples of the Incas.

For centuries, the majestic beauty of the great churches of Quito challenged and influenced the architecture of the Andes, and even of Europe. The Royal Audiencia of Quito became not only the administrative center for the whole region but the spiritual and cultural center as well. Indeed, the city of Quito bears eloquent testimony to the wealth and power of the Roman Catholic Church in the Andes. Several of its fifty-seven churches challenge comparison with any on the continent; all of them enshrine treasures of priceless value. So intricate and profuse is the carving on both the exteriors and interiors of these great structures, so gloriously are the interiors adorned in red and gold, that the visitor often fails to appreciate the exquisite detail of the craftsmanship.

In Quito, as in Europe, a number of architectural styles are often represented in a single church. The first style, dating from the mid-sixteenth century, was the Plateresque—a Spanish variation of the early Renaissance—so called because the decoration resembled chased silver work. In the colonies this decoration was generally concentrated around entrances, leaving the walls plain. The Plateresque style—which, incidentally, does not occur in Italy—so defies definition that Wethey ignores the term in his book on Peruvian architecture. Plateresque was succeeded by the exuberant Renaissance style imported from Italy, its place of birth, and this was followed in turn by the Baroque which, marking a revolt against the classical forms, was to become particularly characteristic of Latin America. "It was," according to Pál Kelemen, "not merely an art style but a mode of living, the last grand spectacle of Feudalism." In the eighteenth century the style called Rococo modified and lightened the massive, heroic compositions of the Baroque period, giving emphasis to the vertical line and to delicacy of form and color.

Just as the Greek revival in the United States is not a soulless imitation of an old world style but mirrors North American spirit, so the Baroque and Rococo of Latin America reflect artistic impulses invigoratingly new and different from those of contemporary Europe. The Baroque style lent itself to the fusion of Indian and European art styles resulting in another, mestizo, marked by sincerity and power.*

To these styles was added the Mudéjar, a style incorporating Moorish designs that was used extensively throughout the colonies in the treatment of brick, wood and tile.

In discussing the essence of Baroque style which flowered so luxuriantly in South America and Mexico, Fray José Vargas points out that in Italy Benedetto Croce accepted the term Baroque, first used by scholars as a synonym for bad taste or artistic deformity, as denoting a contrast to the Classical style. Enrique Wofflin was the first to apply the word to literature, with the sense of exuberance, dynamic force, emotional penetration. He draws five distinctions between the Classical and the Baroque: the former is lineal rather than pictorial, superficial rather than profound, employs closed instead of open form, tends toward unity as opposed to dispersion and toward clarity rather than indefiniteness.

Vargas quotes Hatzfeld, who maintains that Spain has always been basically Baroque and that it was the historic center from which the Baroque spirit radiated throughout Europe. Certain Spanish writers identified themselves with *baroquismo*, among them Calderón, Cervantes, and Góngora. In the field of the fine arts in Quito, the sculptor Bernardo de Legarda represented the Baroque spirit much in the way

*Pál Kelemen, *Baroque and Rococo in Latin America*, Macmillan, 1951.

Beautiful façade of La Compañía with the huge Salomonic columns

Choir loft of La Compañía

that the painter Gorívar epitomized the spirit of the Classical Renaissance. Fray Vargas notes abundant examples of the Baroque style in Quito, including the retables of the lateral naves of La Compañía, the columns of the screen of the Sagrario, the columns of the retable of La Quinche, and the lateral retables of the Chapel of the Rosario in Santo Domingo Church.

Before discussing the various churches of Quito in detail, a word should be said about the best-known church architect, Rodríguez. To quote Padre Vargas, "In the XVIIth century Fray Antonio Rodríguez responded to the religious atmosphere of Quito to make the city a reliquary of art." The works of this architect included the Church of Santa Clara, noted for its elliptical dome, which was built by the Indians in 1657, La Sagrario, and the Church of the Virgin of Guadalupe at Guápulo. He also assisted in the construction of La Compañía, the cloisters of Santo Domingo, San Fernando College, and the University of Santo Tomás.

148

Organ in the choir loft with Moorish ceiling of La Compañía

The aggregation of the Franciscan structures started with the laying of the cornerstone of the Franciscan monastery on January 25, 1535, one month after the founding of the city by Fray Jodoco Ricke de Marselaer. This was the first major Franciscan monastery of South America. Although the name of the architect is lost, it
may well have been Fray Jodoco Ricke himself. The style suggests that of the severe
Escorial outside of Madrid, which was designed by Juan de Herrera, architect to
Philip II.

The Church of San Francisco was built of limestone and brick on the site of an
old Inca temple; when it had been completed, about the middle of the sixteenth century, the whole establishment, including monastery, chapels, and cloisters, occupied
four blocks. The severe but majestic Renaissance structure, with its rusticated façade,
noble parapet, and circular stairs, dominates a spacious cobbled square. The interior
is breathtakingly magnificent: arches heavily goldleafed and polychromed, a Mudé-

jar ceiling over the transepts, an elaborate choir dating from the last third of the sixteenth century, and side chapels lavishly endowed by wealthy conquistadors and Creoles. In addition to the beautiful pulpit and the golden retable with a silver altar frontal, there are countless works of art both in the church and in its museum.

Its Renaissance cloister, supported by one hundred and four Doric columns, has a marble fountain set off by beds of flowers; the flowers are tended by Padre Samuel Calvo, curator of the museum. In the early days, the Colegio de San Andrés was conducted in these cloisters. This institution trained the thousands of skilled artisans who not only built the churches of Quito but were also responsible for such master-pieces as the monstrance of San Francisco. This splendid monstrance contains no less than two thousand emeralds and six hundred pearls.

The Church of San Francisco is complemented by two smaller churches or chapels: Cantuña and San Bonaventura. Cantuña, to the south, has a large crucifix in front and is dedicated to Our Lady of Sorrows. It is known, however, by the name of the donor, Francisco Cantuña, a wealthy Indian, whose tomb within the chapel bears the date 1699. Its lovely retable is thought to be by Legarda. Once the head-quarters of the *cofradía* of painters, it contains a beautiful statue of St. Luke by Padre Carlos (1688), as well as works of Caspicara and Samaniego.

The terrible earthquake of April 26, 1775, which is said to have killed forty thousand people in Quito alone, severely damaged San Francisco, which had already suffered in the earthquakes of 1560 and 1662. The restoration, directed during the years 1792 to 1796 by Fray Francisco Javier de la Graña, was so careful and complete that the church remains one of the wonders of Latin America. The *Obrero Mayor* of the new arrangement of this celebrated church was Fray Mañuel de Almeida, as no-torious for the dissipations that preceded his conversion as he was renowned for the virtuous deeds which followed it. In 1792 Bishop José de la Madrid y Unda made a large donation for the main altar and for the purchase of one thousand yards of crim-son damask. In 1958 we saw some of this damask unrolled during a funeral, while the tessellated, horse-drawn hearse waited outside.

The towers of San Francisco, which were destroyed in the earthquake of 1868, have now been replaced, and no scars from the Independence uprisings of the nine-teenth century are visible.★

The Cathedral lacks the architectural distinction of a number of churches in

★The treasures contained in the church and friary are described in a brochure by Fray Benjamín Gento Sanz: *Guía del Convento de San Francisco*, Quito, 1949.

150

A confessional in La Compañía showing painting of one of the prophets by Goribar

The birth of the Virgin, 17th century painting, in La Compañía; Rosa of Lima at lower right side

Quito. Even its green-tiled domes are overshadowed by that of the adjoining Sagrario. The cathedral was begun in the mid-sixteenth century with the founding of the city. Having passed through various stages of adobe and stone, it was considered complete in 1570, under the second bishop of Quito, Fray Pedro de Pena. After extensive enlargement during the next hundred years, it was again consecrated in 1667, although work on it was continued until the nineteenth century. The tower is partly new and the Mudéjar ceiling no longer remains. The building is distinguished

Santo Domingo Church showing Marshal Sucre statue

outside by the Carondolet Arch, named for Baron Carondolet, once President of the Royal Audiencia, who had the arch built on the eve of Independence. The cathedral, which contains Samaniego's masterpiece, "The Assumption," is the final resting place of General Antonio José de Sucre.

The interior of the cathedral was greatly enriched in 1793 when a suit over the estate of a wealthy man was decided in its favor. At that time, the original retables were removed to smaller parishes and four figures attributed to Caspicara were acquired, including a "Santa Rosa de Lima" and a "Pietà." "The Holy Sheet," by the same artist, is inside a niche in the retable of a back altar, and there is also a Creole replica of Juan de Juni's "Sepulture of Christ." The main altar has a silver frontal dedicated to Santa Ana. An unusual feature is the Plateresque door of the sacristy on which three identical figures of Christ represent the Trinity. The image of San Francisco de Paula, kept in the cathedral, was made by Padre Carlos and is used for the festival of April 12.

The Sagrario Church, a separate sanctuary for the Holy Sacrament, communicates with the cathedral. Its construction was begun in 1699 and completed in 1706. The two masterpieces of this church are the pulpit and the beautiful *mampara*, or screen, which shows Oriental and Mudéjar influences. The Baroque angels on the ceiling, painted in 1717 by Francisco Alban (for one hundred pesos), represent the Old and New Testaments. The doors are Renaissance and the whole interior is refulgent with gold leaf.

The perfection of La Compañía, the church of the Society of Jesus, is revealed whether one faces the remarkable pillared façade or, gazing from the steps of San Francisco, beholds the roof and domes. The interior, dazzling but harmonious in its lavish blend of red and gold, contains a wealth of native art. The choir, the main retable by Legarda, the *mampara*, the pulpit, even the confessionals combine to make it, to my mind, the most beautiful church in the Western hemisphere.

The Jesuits began work on their church in 1605, the year of their establishment in Quito, using plans brought with them from Spain. The Baroque style, verging on the Churrigueresque, was influenced by the Gesù Church in Rome; but the style is refined in La Compañía. The architect, Fr. Venancio Gandolfo, came from Mantua, Italy, and had undoubtedly studied the Church of San Andrea in his native city. The latter church, designed by Alberti in the fifteenth century, and the earliest example of a cruciform church with a barrel roof, is very high and impressive, contains a beautiful central dome, and in the sixteenth century was covered with frescoes. In La

Compañía the ceilings are of Spanish Moresque interlacing designs. Particularly notable is the façade, which was finished in 1765 under the direction and from the designs of Padre Deubler; its unusual Salomonic columns rank as the most important sculpture in the city. The stone interior is stuccoed and gilded in a style that blends Hispano-Moresque with Persian and Arabic. Two retables were brought from Spain; the paintings are on canvas framed by polychromed stucco and wood. The sixteen figures of the prophets on the pilasters are by Goríbar.

Another beautiful church is La Merced. Although the Mercedarians were the second religious order to receive an allotment of land, their church was the last to be built. The first little church, begun by Captain Sandoval, who accompanied Cortés to Mexico in 1559, is still standing, but the second, which was completed in 1627, was destroyed by the earthquake of 1660 and not rebuilt until 1737. The present church, the third La Merced, has a lovely white and gold Mudéjar ceiling, a beautiful choir loft with twin organs, and distinguished cloisters. There is also a very fine pulpit and a Legarda retable.

San Agustín is called one of the martyr churches because of the great damage it suffered in the earthquakes of 1662 and 1775. It bears the following inscription: "On the 27th day of October in the year 1660 at nine o'clock in the morning the Volcano of the Pichincha Broke Out. On the Twenty Eighth of November 1662 the Earthquake occurred." Legend has it that in the seventeenth century pious Mariana de Jesús offered her life to God as a sacrifice if He would save the city from destruction, and for that service she was canonized.

The main church of San Agustín, originally designed in the Gothic style by Francisco Becerra who came from Mexico in 1575, now holds but slight interest. The lower cloister contains paintings of the life of San Agustín, referred to previously, although some of them have been removed. The beautiful chapter room, with a capacity of two hundred persons, is noted for its Mudéjar ceiling of wood and for furniture that is unique in the history of Renaissance ornamentation in Quito. It also has historic associations. To quote from *An Eulogy of Quito* by Miracle:

> The historic house of San Agustín, where, on August 16, 1609, the noblemen of Quito, presided over by the Marquis de Selva Alegre, constituted the supreme council for the defense of King Ferdinand VII against the tyrant of Europe, Napoleon, and took, in doing this, the first step towards the emancipation of that part of the former Spanish colonies.

Santo Domingo, another of the martyr churches, is on the Machangara River. The church faces a plaza containing a statue of General Sucre, hero of the Battle of

Interior of Rosario Chapel of Santo Domingo

Cloisters of La Merced

Pichincha. One of the busiest churches in the city, its masses are held every half hour. According to Miracle it has suffered more from the hands of restorers than from natural catastrophes. He puts it graphically:

This second martyred church owes its destruction more to the friars than to the Pichincha volcano. Becerra designed a church here similar to that of the Convent of San Francisco, with Moresque roofs and Baroque reredoses, but the excellent Italian Dominican friars brought over Barcia Morena ninety years ago who decided to paint it over like an operetta theater, and to raze its altars, its choir and its pulpit. Fortunately, they forgot the cupola of the transept. They also tore out the beautiful tiles which rivaled those which are the pride of the Dominican cloister in Lima.

However, the walled-up entrance with its mirror cross, and that brilliant gem of Quito art, the Chapel of the Rosary over the Arco de Santo Domingo, still remain. In this chapel the main retable is devoted to the figure of the Virgin of the Rosary, which was presented by Charles V. The chapel, filled with masterpieces, is in three parts, the third part consisting of the dressing room of the Virgin, in which her dresses, jewels, and ornaments were kept. The principal room, an ample hall for the public, is adorned with sculpture and paintings and is, according to Miracle, "a perfect specimen of this Quitonian Baroque in which the fundamental red kindles in the gold, and flames like a bonfire of religious fervency."

Early in the seventeenth century the Franciscans built a retreat called La Recoleta de San Diego on land donated by Don Marcos Plaza and his wife, Doña Beatriz de Cepeda. Fr. Antonio Rodríguez is said to have been the architect. The façade, of simple Renaissance style, contains studded doors; the whole is surrounded by high walls. It has an exquisite chalice-shaped pulpit, a fragment of Mudéjar ceiling left after the restoration in the seventeenth century, and some unique paintings which have fabrics sewn onto the canvas. The sacristy holds a crucifix said to be the one which spoke to Fray Almeida and turned him from his dissolute life. The Sisters of the Immaculate Conception of San Francisco now have charge of the shrine.

Quito has two chapels of particular interest. The Chapel of El Tejár is noted for a cloister that contains bull's-eye arches and twin lanterns over the roof. The first Mass in Quito for the Spanish Conquistadors was celebrated in the chapel of El Belén, the oldest in Quito.

The suburban church of Guápulo was built a short distance from Quito as a sanctuary to Our Lady of Guadalupe, the dark-skinned Virgin brought from Extremadura. This beautiful church was erected by the priest Herrera y Cevallos with

Twin organs in the choir loft, La Merced *Pulpit of La Merced*

alms collected on a 6,000-mile pilgrimage through South America. Although fires and earthquakes have destroyed much of the original decoration, its cupola, pulpit, and rose-colored vaults remain. The Indians now use it for festivities called *priostazgo*, and it is the focal point of processions in which they carry their patroness, Our Lady of Guápulo, surrounded by large colored wax candles.

The nunnery of La Concepción on the corner of the main plaza was built in 1635 when Philip IV sent a large contribution in behalf of its inmates, the daughters and granddaughters of the conquistadors. A fire in 1878 destroyed the valuable contents of the church, but its museum contains a few remains, including an Inmaculada with a chain extending from her hand.

The beautiful cloister of Santa Clara was built in 1596 by the Franciscan lay brother, Antonio Rodríguez, as a gift from Doña Francisca de la Cueva.

The church of Carmen Alto owes its erection to Mariana de Jesús, and is built on the site of her dwelling. A cult formed after her death in 1645 venerated her portrait, painted by Hernando de la Cruz, or one of its numerous replicas. She was canonized in 1950 as Santa de Mariana de Jesús, Azucena de Quito. Carmen Alto possesses a retable by Bernardo de Legarda, a fine pulpit, and two cedar doors carved with angels and coats of arms. In this church the trisagio (the angel chorus of "Holy, Holy, Holy") is sung on the fifteenth day of each month. Also in this church is an impressive life-size group of the twelve apostles around the Virgin's bed which had its origin in a Spanish mystery play.

Carmen Bajo's erection was paid for by the alms collected by Bishop Paredes de Armendariz. Both churches are maintained by the Carmelite Order, and both cherish the belief that Santa Teresa, the Spanish reformer of the Order, appeared miraculously in Quito at the home of her brother, Don Lorenzo Cepeda, in 1560, although, she did not found any of her "mother convents" while there. Carmen Bajo contains, in its large salon, a Bethlehem crib with enamel earthenware figures produced in the factory of Manuel Rodríguez de la Peña in the eighteenth century.

Dr. Martín Soria comments that Quito produced the most sensuous and humorlous pulpits in Latin America. Concepción, Santa Clara, San Francisco, La Compañía and La Merced churches offer fine examples.

I believe the architecture of two churches of Quito, San Francisco and La Compañía, ranks with that of the churches of Europe. Certainly in size and majesty they cannot compare with the great cathedrals of Europe—Toledo, Notre Dame, Chartres, Durham, or Cologne. Recurring earthquakes over the centuries necessitated constant rebuilding and precluded building structures of great height and mass. On the other hand, the façades of La Compañía and San Francisco can well hold their own among the world's architecture. The red and gold interiors, with their carved figures, their ceilings decorated in the Moorish style, and rich gold leaf that covers retables, altars, chapels and confessionals, surpass anything I have ever seen in Spain, France, Italy, England, or elsewhere. Though the earthquakes of Quito restricted the size of churches and towers, the spoliation of churches by war and revolution, so common in Europe, seems virtually unknown in mountainous Ecuador. Over the centuries the decoration has maintained its gleam and beauty.

The artisans who built the churches were natives—Indians and mestizos—but they worked under the skilled direction of Spanish friars who provided Old World models. Prominent among the friars was a man of Flemish birth, a cousin of Charles V, Fray Jodoco Ricke de Marselaer, who, attached to the San Francisco monastery from 1535 to 1569, devoted his considerable talents to furthering education in Quito. At the Colegio de St. Andres, which he founded, thousands of native workers were trained in the appreciation and technical skill needed to build and adorn those structures that still glorify God in Quito. The training was both extensive and practical. Fray Jodoco taught the Indians to plow, make roads, count, bind books, and write, as well as to paint, carve, and play musical instruments. Early in 1535 he was allotted Indian labor to build the Church of San Francisco.

The groups of artisans formed in Quito were modeled upon the medieval guilds of Europe and were known as *cofradías* (religious) or *hermandades* (civic). They included such assorted craftsmen as candlemakers, silk growers, gold and silversmiths, carpenters, tanners, fringe makers, leather workers, masons, bricklayers, as well as painters and schoolmasters. In practically every field the service of the Church came first, and Quito during the Colonial Period has appropriately been called a "veritable ecclesiastical studio."

The beauty of its Colonial products is poignantly suggested in this passage by Miracle.

In his pontifical exile of Faenza, surrounded by all the splendor of Italian art, the great Jesuit Father, Juan de Velasco, felt his mouth water when he remembered the wonders of art in his home town, Quito.

The Indians themselves, as well as the mestizos, having an extraordinary talent, together with a natural inclination, helped by a great constancy and patience. There is not an art they do not practice to perfection. The woven fabrics of various kinds, the rugs and carpets, embroideries rivaling those of Genoa, the finest laces, gold and silver trimmings—which were once fabricated in the town in its own factories capable of competing with the best ones in Milan, works in wrought iron, repoussé, carving, embossing, engraving—every kind of manufacture, ornaments, and curiosities, and above all the arts of painting, sculpturing and statuary have filled the American territories, and they have been seen with admiration in Europe.[*]

The painter's handbook for over a hundred years was *El arte de la pintura, su antigüedad y grandeza*, by Francisco Pacheco, first published in Seville in 1649. In it, Pacheco, himself a painter and an authority on religious iconography, set down not only the approved methods of painting and varnishing but the attributes of each saint, together with the proper attitudes and traditional insignia for their representation.

Although inspired by Spanish models, the style of painting and sculpture in Quito was distinctive. The goal was realism; the means of attaining it were carefully worked out. Life-like translucency was achieved for faces and hands by a process called *encarnación*, and verisimilitude was further attained by the insertion of such materials as hair, nails and glass eyes—all designed to heighten the emotional impact. Another

[*]Ernesto de la Orden Miracle, *An Eulogy of Quito*, Madrid, 1950.

160

Church of San Francisco

process called *estofado*, which was invented by a Spanish professor in the sixteenth century, enabled the painters, by tooling through paint, to adorn garments with elaborate rococo patterns worked on a gold or silver base. Statues were either of carved wood finished with *encarnación* and *estofado*, or were dressed in garments made from cloth that had been stiffened and moulded. Another method employed candlestick bodies dressed in real robes.

The Quito school of painting, long preëminent on the continent, produced masterpieces that have evoked world-wide admiration. Quito art is principally religious, and the prevalent theme of the seventeenth and eighteenth centuries is adora-

Pulpit of San Francisco Church with the "Rose of Lima" by Caspicara at left

Mudéjar ceiling of San Francisco Church

tion of the Virgin. Much of this is due to the pronouncement by Pope Alexander VII —some say at the instance of King Philip IV—that "the soul of María in the first instant of her creation was by special grace of God, and by virtue of the merits of Jesus Christ, Redeemer of the human race, preserved free from original sin." ★ This doctrine of the Immaculate Conception stimulated an enthusiastic adoration of the Virgin throughout the Roman Catholic Church. Sculpture and painting were put in unremitting service of this theme. This was particularly true in Spain, where the most notable of the artists devoted much of their work to the Inmaculada. Among these artists were Juan Martínez Montañes, Alonzo de Mena, Alonzo Caro Zurbarán and José de Ribera, and the most popular of all, Bartolomé Estéban Murillo. The last three were contemporaries of Miguel Santiago, the greatest of the Quito painters; but it was his representation of the Virgin, rather than those of his European contemporaries, that was to dominate the ecclesiastical art of Quito.

For the portrayal of the Virgin of the Immaculate Conception, the role in which

★In the *Bula Solicitudo Omnium Ecclesiarum* of 1666.

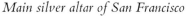
Main silver altar of San Francisco

"S. Pedro de Alcántara" by Padre Carlos. Detail from el Capilla de Cantuña

Mary was most cherished in Latin America, particularly by the Franciscans, Pacheco's explicit directions are singularly appealing. "She should be represented in the flower of youth," he wrote, "some twelve to fourteen years old, clad in white with a mantle of blue; she should be crowned with stars, under her feet the moon, and the rays of the sun should encircle her." Indeed, the correct portrayal of the Virgin was an art in itself.★

One of the most priceless art treasures of Quito is "La Inmaculada," of Legarda, over the main altar in the Franciscan church. It depicts the crowned Virgin with eyes cast down; her raised hand aims a spear at the dragon, symbol of carnal sin, at her feet. The pose of exquisite grace is characteristic of Legarda's sculpture. It is distinctive Creole art.

In 1760 the Virgin of the Immaculate Conception was declared the principal patroness of the Spanish possessions, although she had competitors in the Virgin of Guadalupe (the patroness of Mexico), and Santa Rosa de Lima. Certain times were

★This subject has been fully explored in *María en el Arte Ecuadoriana* by Padre José Vargas of Quito.

163

set apart in honor of the Virgin: August for the feast of the Assumption, October for Our Lady of the Rosary, December for the Immaculate Conception.

The statue of the Blessed Virgin occupied a central place in the great religious processions. These processions, conducted during the high festivals of the Church, performed a function similar to that of the medieval miracle plays, in that they were designed to entertain as well as to edify. The whole community, either as performers or spectators, took part in these colorful dramatic spectacles which continue, in modified form, down to our own day. Houses were decorated with banners, streets strewn with flowers, and elaborate arches erected for the occasions. At the head of the procession marched the crucifer, followed by the bearers of candles and torches (at night) and, on Corpus Christi, a jeweled monstrance enveloped in clouds of incense. Members of the *cofradías*, dressed in festive attire and carrying the insignia of their craft, marched in a body. They were joined by military and civil functionaries in full regalia, and, in more sober garb, the members of the monastic orders and the regular clergy. Music was provided by massed bands and choirs. Figures of the saints, some of them works of artistic excellence, were always carried in these processions. ★

Despite the profusion of art objects produced in Quito throughout the Colonial period, very little is known of the men who created them. Many of the artists, mestizo and Indian, were employed in the studios of a relatively few masters, and although they may have attained the same high standard of workmanship as their masters, their names are not recorded. The achievements of these native artists are the more remarkable in that they had no opportunities for travel and knew the masterpieces of Europe only through engravings, illustrated books and reproductions which often had to be smuggled past the Council of the Indies. The influence of certain Spanish masters—Ribera, Zurbarán, Morales, and Murillo—can be traced in their

---

★Among the saints represented were St. James the Apostle, St. Jerome, St. Christopher and St. Raphael. St. James the Apostle, or Santiago, was the patron saint of Spain; his name was the battle cry of the conquistadors. At least 155 cities in Spanish America bear the name Santiago. A military order was named for him, and 138 of its members accompanied Pizarro at one time or another. Santiago is depicted riding a white horse which is trampling a Moor.

St. Jerome, the patron of scholars, made the Latin translation of the Bible, known as the Vulgate. He is depicted with a cardinal's hat, the trumpet of the Last Judgment, and the lion from whose foot he is said to have extracted a thorn.

St. Christopher, the patron of travelers, is commonly shown with a staff in his hand and the Christ child on his shoulder. Sometimes the staff burgeons with leaves or flowers.

St. Raphael the Archangel, mentioned in the Apocrypha as accompanying Tobit on his journey, traditionally carries a rod, a fish, and sometimes a box of ointment.

"San Rafael" from Victor Mena collection　　　　　*"St. Martin Moresque" (dark) in the Alberto Mena collection*

work, but in diluted form. In his chapter on "Unknown Painters," Pál Kelemen writes, "The work of the colonial painter is permeated with devotion, intensity and a folkish stylization—and nearly always with a charming naïveté."

Ferdinand Perret, in his privately printed *Encyclopaedia of the Colonial Epoch of the Americas and the Philippine Islands* (Mexico, 1958), lists 178 artists of Ecuador about whom little or no material has as yet been published. In this chapter only a few of those artists have been included, primarily those whose works have been most widely collected. In the appraisal of the artists of Quito I have drawn largely from three books written by Fray José María Vargas, but especially from his *Los Maestros*

Virgin and Child by Caspicara, the Indian artist. A dark coat of paint simulates dark skin of the Indian. From the Gerhardt Bading collection in the Milwaukee Public Museum

del Arte Ecuatoriana. This author acknowledges his indebtedness to Carlos Barnos, who was born in Germany in 1879 and who learned the art of restoring from his father, a Viennese painter. Barnos' first position was with the museum of Amsterdam. He also dedicated himself to heraldry and illustration about which he wrote several books. After making several journeys to Italy, France and England, Barnos went to Quito in 1936 and set up a studio for restoring pictures; while there, a great many works of Colonial painters passed through his hands. He became the most authoritative critic of Colonial painting. He helped to organize the museum in San Francisco and was director of the collection of Victor Mena. In 1950 he went to the United States to become director of the museum of Houston, Texas, where he died in 1953.

In the sixteenth century the most important artist in Quito was Padre Pedro Bedón, who was born there, probably in 1555, of a Spanish father and a Creole mother. In 1577 he went to Lima and graduated in philosophy from the University of San Marcos; in 1584 he returned to Quito where, in 1857, he was named Lector of Arts and Theology and then Maestro in the convent of Quito. He is best known for his contributions to the Dominican *Brotherhood of the Rosary* which he helped establish.

Bedón made a famous title page for a book on the *cofradía* (1588) and also painted for the Dominican convent the celebrated "Our Lady of the Rosary," which bears the portraits of Saint Dominic and Saint Francis and has a dog, the symbol of Dominic, in the corner. The prevalence of a dog in the decoration of Dominican establishments is based on the legend that the mother of the saint dreamed she was to give birth to a dog, and was assured by her confessor that her son would be "as a dog in the House of the Lord."

Bedón was always concerned with the Indians, whose language he learned. In regard to the imposition of taxes in the province of Quito, Fray Bedón took the position that taxes, though they were just, should not be collected by force. For that opinion he was exiled to Colombia, where he painted refectories in Bogotá and in Tunja, and started building the Rosario Chapel in Santo Domingo Church in Tunja, a famous work of art. He was later recalled to Quito and started the Rosario Chapel in Santo Domingo of that city. Fray Juan Lopez, Bishop of Monopoli, who wrote a life of Padre Bedón, recalled that he preached emotionally and said that it was a shame that never in the Indies was the gospel preached in the mode and style of the disciples. Very famous paintings of Fray Bedón are "La Virgen de la Escalera" and "La Virgen de las Lajas." This last is in Colombia and is a famous object of pilgrimage.

Miguel de Santiago was the greatest of all South American artists according to testimony given by Fray José Vargas in his book *Los Maestros del Arte Ecuatoriana*. This great mestizo painter had a tragic life, for he lost his three sons, his wife, his daughter, and his son-in-law, who was his apprentice. This may have affected his style; yet his output was extensive. His first work was for the Augustinian friars; in 1656 he finished the life of Saint Augustine for the walls of their cloisters.

On December 13, 1629, Dr. Antonio Morga offered for sale forty objects of European art in Quito. As a result of this the artists of that city were familiarized with the European tradition, and, in fact, Santiago began his career by copying twenty-eight scenes of the life of Saint Augustine from engravings done by the Dutch artist, Childeric o Schelte Bolswert (1586–1659). In Cuzco, Basilio Pacheco copied these same prints for San Agustín Church.

These paintings of Santiago reveal a technique that is Italian rather than Spanish. Their colors are beautifully preserved to this day. His paintings, found in practically every church and convent in Quito, were widely dispersed throughout the Andean region as well; some of them even reached Rome. Like other artists of his school, Santiago strove for realism. The story is told that when he was painting his "Christ in Agony," he struck his model with a lance in order to obtain the right expression, and then had to seek refuge from authorities in a convent.

Miguel de Santiago spent the last quarter of the seventeenth century at Guápulo, living below a hill on the outskirts of Quito. Here, under the tutelage of the great architect Fray Antonio Rodríguez, he decorated the pilgrimage church of the Virgin of Guadalupe. These paintings depict miracles attributed to the saint, and in the pictures of the retables Santiago introduced a new element—the landscape of Ecuador. For the Convent of San Francisco, Santiago painted a series of pictures illustrating Christian doctrine, a work which presupposed a profound knowledge of Catholic dogma, in which he created or adapted various symbols: original forms for the Trinity, a peacock for pride, a hog for gluttony. In addition to the life of Saint Augustine and portraits of important personages of Quito, Santiago executed church figures in the cathedral, La Compañía, Santo Domingo and La Merced. The house of Miguel de Santiago had been a museum of art, and when he died, on December 31, 1705, he left his Spanish collection, consisting of fifteen portraits and fifty pictures, to his daughter Isabel and his nephew Agustín Ruíz. All others of his family were dead.

In general, religious pictures in the Colonies were not signed by the artists and,

Sacred Family by Bernardo Rodríguez, seventeenth century

"San Gabriel" by Miguel de Santiago, from Victor Mena collection

therefore, it has been questioned whether Nicolas Javier de Goríbar, pupil of Santiago, painted "The Prophets" of La Compañía and "The Companions" of San Francisco. Carlos Barnos was of the opinion that the artist of both series was the same. Padre Vargas gives a list of authorities, headed by Dr. Pablo Herrera in the early nineteenth century, who believed that Goríbar painted the prophets that adorn the pillars of La Compañía—a group which shows its artist to have possessed a thorough knowledge of history in addition to great artistry. However, he did sign certain pictures painted for Guápulo. His "Kings of Judah" are in the Museo Jijón y Caamaño in Quito, and the busts of apostles are in La Curia Metropolitana. As a painter Goríbar was excelled only by Miguel de Santiago.

Quito was blessed with three distinguished artists by the name of Rodríguez: the city's greatest architect, Fray Antonio Rodríguez; Diego Rodríguez, who painted a "Rose of Lima" for El Sagrario; and Bernardo Rodríguez, the half-brother of the painter Samaniego, who is believed to have painted the pictures in the nave of the cathedral. In 1783 Bernardo Rodríguez signed a picture, "Descent from the Cross," which is now in the Museo Jijón y Caamaño. The collection of Victor Mena

169

"Angel de la Guarda" by Caspicara, San Francisco Museum

"Virgin of Light," with a silver crown. This is considered by Victor Mena the most beautiful escultura of the XVIIIth century in Quito. The Virgin is offering a soul to the dragon, representing evil.

contains a "San Eloy," patron of silversmiths, with a portrait of don Vicente Lopez de Solis, who commissioned the painting in 1775, at its foot, and the San Francisco Museum exhibits a picture of "La Inmaculada" with the arms of Spain; both of these are by Bernardo Rodríguez.

Two other painters should be mentioned. José Olmos (Pampite) was a disciple of the seventeenth-century sculptor, Padre Carlos. Among his paintings is the

"Calvary" in the church of Carmen Bajo Moderno. Hernando de la Cruz (1591–1646)—the name was adopted by Don Fernando de Ribera when he entered the Jesuit order—led an adventurous life which took him from his native Panama to Quito, where he fought a duel and had to seek sanctuary. Many of his works are in the cloister of La Merced, but he left his master work, "Pious Mariana," to Carmen Alto (Antiguo).

The sculptor Legarda and the painter Manuel Samaniego y Jaramillo were the great artists of the eighteenth century in Quito, according to Vargas. Both penetrated to the core of the Baroque style. Samaniego was born in Quito before 1761. While very young he married Doña Manuela A. Jurado Lopez de Solís who was related to Quito's famous family of jewelers. In 1795 he was charged with the work of painting the main retable of Santa Clara, and there he met Doña Josefa Rosales Yepez. He had a daughter by her and, as a consequence, his wife brought a suit of adultery and kept her husband in jail from October to December, 1797. He died in 1824, but during his life he had enjoyed an excellent artistic reputation. As new themes he took "Divina Pastora" and "Tota Pulchra." He also interpreted the allegories of the seasons (as did Miguel de Santiago) and specialized in miniatures on glass and brass for retables. He used landscape in his pictures and was known for his brilliant palette. His madonnas were animated by suave, graceful femininity. His colors are soft and delicate, and the group scenes in the rococo manner attributed to him—"The Return from Egypt," "The Carpenter's Shop"—have a delightful narrative quality and were much sought after. Samaniego's pictures may be seen today in churches and private collections. He painted many portraits including those for the country house of the old Marqués de Selva Alegre. So numerous were Samaniego's disciples, that he might be said to have conducted a school of painting.

Sculpture in the Colonial Era required the combined talents of sculptor and painter, for the decoration of a figure was as essential as its form; in the technique of estofado statues were gessoed, painted, gilded and tooled so that the fabric of their clothing appeared sumptuous and colorful. Among the many sculptors whose creations have made the churches and museums of Quito glorious, two are preëminent: Bernardo de Legarda and Manuel Chili (the latter better known as Caspicara). For two hundred and fifty years the works of these masters and others, most of them nameless, who preceded and followed them, enriched not only Quito but the whole Andean region. A few examples reached Europe.

Legarda was a Creole sculptor of great talent and influence. We know that between 1748 and 1751 he was at work on the high altar of La Merced, but little else has been recorded about him. The beautiful statue on the main altar of San Francisco—the previously mentioned "La Inmaculada"—is his only signed work; but many others are attributed to him. He is probably the originator, certainly the favorite interpreter of the "Vision of the Fifth Seal," a somewhat unorthodox image of the Virgin of the Immaculate Conception, based on a passage in Revelations which was popular in the colonies.

From the year 1734, when he made "La Inmaculada" for the Church of San Francisco, until 1773 when he died, Legarda labored to make Inmaculadas large and small for the churches and houses of all the Audiencia of Quito. The dynamism which animated the victorious Virgin responded to the artistic spirit incarnate in the *Baroquismo Quiteno* of the eighteenth century. Legarda's Inmaculadas, more artistic than devout, lacked the ingenuity of the sixteenth century and the serenity of the seventeenth.

He had made the retables for Cantuña Chapel and for Santa Marta Church, for La Compañia and La Merced as well as the famous Salomonic columns of La Compañía. When he died, Legarda left a workshop equipped with anvils and tools for many crafts as testimony to his great versatility. His statuary could compete with the best of Europe. The retable of Carmen Moderno is considered his, as well as many other excellent works in churches, convents, and homes. A prolific artist, he had many apprentices working under him.

The celebrated Indian sculptor, Caspicara, producing his masterpieces in the Rococo period, a half century later than those of Legarda, maintained the same high standard. A signed work, the "Infant Christ" or "Baby God," contained in the Salguero collection, combines native strength with a delicacy of feeling suggestive of Donatello.

Other signed works of his in the Church of San Francisco are "La Virgen del Carmen," the "San José" over the altar which covers the tomb of Atahualpa's son (Don Francisco Auqui Inga), "San Juan Nepomuceno," and the famous "Santa Rosa" to the left of the pulpit.

His statues are almost all half life-size, and he is noted for his narrative group composition. In describing Caspicara's "Pietà" in the cathedral, Pál Kelemen refers to "his ability to convey the drama of a scene without hyperbole." Among Caspicara's groups and single figures are "El Cristo" in the chapel of Belén, "La Carmen Virgin" and "La Dolorosa" in the cathedral, and the "Santa Rosa de Lima" and the altar of St. Anthony in the Church of San Francisco.

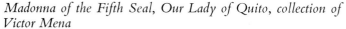
Madonna of the Fifth Seal, Our Lady of Quito, collection of Victor Mena

Jewelled "Piedad" calvario from collection of Victor Mena

Another sculptor who attained eminence was Padre Carlos, a contemporary of the painter Santiago, and an artist of considerable influence. Among his works are "San Juan Bautista" and "San Francisco de Paula" in the cathedral, and "San Diego" and "San Bernardino" in the San Francisco church; the well-known "San Pedro de Alcántara" in the Cantuña Chapel is attributed to him. A valuable jeweled "Crucifixion" of his is in the Victor Mena collection.

Though sculptors of Quito compare favorably with their European contemporaries, the art of Quito as a whole, according to Doctor Soria, should be considered a folk-art, expressive and interesting, but lacking depth of emotion. "Colonial art," he asserts, "preferred decorum to violence and sweetness to passion." Still, considering the isolation of the Colonial painters their achievements were remarkable. Their best works could be hung in any museum or gallery, even though they may fail to attain the highest standards of the great masters.

173

In his *Eulogy of Quito*, Orden Miracle makes clear the fact that the Colonial homes of the city as well as the churches owed their inspiration to Spain:

Ah, the noble houses of Santillana, the renaissance palaces of Salamanca and the baroque mansions of Andalucía! Their stamp was graven on the mind of the people of America who applied themselves to copying it with the riches of the *encomiendas*. Their idea was "Give me a patio, a little cloister—not one, but several patios."

The mansions of Quito are less pretentious than those of Tunja or Cuzco, and façades with coats of arms are not so easily found, for at the time of the Emancipation the resident nobility comprised only a viscount and seven marqueses. The residences were usually constructed of adobe made with *cangahua*, a natural Andean cement which could withstand earthquakes. Their most striking feature is a noble stone doorway framing a brass-studded door, topped with a massive lintel that often bears some religious emblem or a floral or geometrical design. The typical entrance hall, paved with pebbles or little bones, contains a good stone stairway, a fireplace or braziers, carved chairs, a religious picture, mirrors, devotional urns, and chests and *bargueños* for clothes. Today most of the houses and patios have been broken up, converted into shops and sadly altered; a few, particularly those in the Plaza de Santo Domingo, are worthy of restoration. ★

The handsome contemporary mansions of the Mena family (that of Alberto Mena has been bequeathed to the city) are virtual storehouses of Quitonian art. With no other introduction than a telephone call from the Majestic Hotel, I was fortunate enough to be received in them by the two brothers, Señors Alberto† and Victor Mena, who graciously permitted John Engel and myself to inspect and photograph their distinguished collections. In Don Alberto's home the large gallery on the second floor contains many fine examples of arms, paintings and *esculturas* (small polychromed figures). Off the master bedroom is an exquisite private altar of the kind often found in homes of this type. The home of Victor Mena is a veritable museum; its collection is remarkably well balanced and contains rare examples of sixteenth-century esculturas (these lack the glass eyes that were introduced in figures

---

★Each family mansion bore a distinctive name, some of which have a special appeal: e.g., Casa de las Flores y los Peces (House of the Flowers and the Fishes); Casa de las Seis Flores (House of the Six Flowers); Casa de las Columnas Salomonicas (House of the Salomonic Columns); Casa de Jesús María, a large, splendid house on the Plaza de Santo Domingo; Museo Jijón, which houses the collection of la Circasiana of don Jacinto Jijón; the house of the conquistador Sandoval, with richly blazoned portal, situated on Calle García Moreno in the Casa Reales district; and the Museo del Arte Colonial (Cuenca Calle), formerly Casa de Villacis, or the home of Francisco de Villacis, royal commisioner of the Quito district, who defrayed the expenses of the chapel in San Francisco (the house contains a portrait of him in the costume of the mid-seventeenth century).

†Since deceased.

Casa de los Flores y los Peces (House of the Flowers and the Fishes)

Private altar of Don Alberto Mena

after the seventeenth century). There are also works of almost every artist mentioned in this chapter. It was a deeply appreciated privilege to be received by these two eminent collectors.

Some of the finest mansions in Ecuador are found outside the city of Quito. In the Otavalo Valley, for instance, are large haciendas which have been there since early Colonial days. Here, where land is plentiful, the mansion house has been allowed to expand in the grand manner and often presents a prospect of sumptuous elegance. Above these spacious haciendas, which include most of the arable land in the valleys and sweep up the mountain slopes, are tiny patchwork plots of grain which belong to the small landholder. They intermingle with terraces built by the Incas, still in active use.

A trip of six hours by autocarril or four to five hours by automobile from Quito takes one to the picturesque village of Otavalo. Each Saturday and Sunday the pure-blooded Indians from the valley congregate here for the weekly market, which no visitor in the region should miss. These Indians are a handsome people; in their colorful traditional dress they provide a moving background for the neatly arranged rows

Portrait of Simon Bolívar in the collection of Alberto Mena

Gypsy dancer of carved wood. In Alberto Mena collection

of food and craft products. At this market the visitor can purchase products which in design and use claim a direct lineage from the earliest times. Cloth and belts, for instance, are still woven on the same type of looms which were used by the pre-Inca cultures. The designs are a curious mixture of Inca and pre-Inca patterns, flamboyant Colonial motifs, and figures from the latest comic books. The bulk of the Otavalo craft production is not for tourist trade but for local consumption, and the quantity and quality of these products are thus limited by the needs of the Indians themselves. Unfortunately, the craft heritage seems to be doomed by the advance of modern civilization. Craftsmen cannot compete in "slick finish" or in "quantity price" with commercial methods, and gradually the craft products are being replaced by factory goods.

In an effort to revive extinct designs and techniques and to preserve existing ones, an artist from Holland, Jan Schreuder, founded the Ecuadorian Art Center

176

in the Casa de Cultura a few years ago. Here he is successfully reviving the art of weaving by teaching improved techniques and providing adaptations of pre-Columbian designs. The Indians are evincing their native skill, but they are also becoming unionized and demanding such high wages that the products cannot be sold profitably. Mrs. Hilda Fisch, who established the attractive Folklore Center, finds that the hand-knotted rugs need to retail at such high prices that the market for them is extremely limited. It is possible that under these conditions and in spite of outside stimulation Ecuadorian hand products may not long survive.

In the atmosphere of the Colonial Period the primary motivation for artist and craftsman alike was to be found in religion. The early friars or padres instilled in Indian and mestizo not only craft knowledge but religious faith, and certainly it was the fervor of their devotion to Christ, the Blessed Virgin, and all the saints that inspired them in the building and adorning of the magnificent churches in Quito. The Roman Catholic Church in the sixteenth and seventeenth centuries was a vital force in all aspects of civilized life in Latin America, and though corruption and immorality were not lacking, the faith remained strong and secure.

A friend of Puritan spirit sitting beside me in La Compañía, where gold and crimson vie with each other for preëminence, exclaimed: "How ornate!" But to me it was a most glorious outpouring of the creative force that manifested itself in exquisite form, the radiant color, and the fascinating blend of motifs—Renaissance, Baroque, Mudéjar, Indian. Is it possible, in this machine age, for the Ecuadorian ever again to create such beauty or attain to such heights of creative expression?

I recalled one of the padres having said to me a few days earlier: "Religion is good, but art is another thing." At the time it seemed reasonable but now, remembering the splendor of art in Quito, I am not so sure.

LEYENDAS
(Legends and Stories)

The story that interested me most in connection with Quito concerns an expedition assembled there in January 1514, under the leadership of the governor, the dashing, young Gonzalo Pizarro, in search of El Dorado. Belief in a vast treasure in a sacred lake had inspired the expedition of Diego de Ordaz ten years earlier and was to inspire others, including that of Sir Walter Raleigh in 1595. The belief was based on reports of a ceremony held each year by the Guatavita Indians, during which their

"Flight of the Holy Family into Egypt." Figures from the collection of Victor Mena

king or chief priest covered his body with balsam oil, then with gold dust, and finally threw gold and emeralds into a lake in which he bathed to wash off the gold. However, the rite, if it was ever practiced, has long been discontinued, and since the fabulous treasure was never found, the name "El Dorado" has come to signify a hopeless quest as well as any place of fabulous riches.

The preparations made by Gonzalo for his expedition dwarfed those made by his older and more famous brother, Francisco Pizarro, in the conquest of Peru. The latter exploit had involved only 180 Spaniards and twenty-seven horses, whereas Gonzalo brought together 350 Spaniards in armor, half of them mounted, 4,000 Indians, a large herd of swine, and 2,000 trained dogs, most of which were later

178

eaten.★ There was also complete equipment for the company, including horseshoes, armor and salt.

The disaster which followed was of epic proportions. For tortuous months the expedition struggled over frozen mountain passes and through steaming jungles, fighting Indians and losing Indians, until it faced starvation at the headwaters of the Amazon. A contingent of fifty-seven Spaniards and two Indian slaves under the command of Captain Francisco de Orellano was sent out in a hastily constructed brigantine to search for food. They were ordered to return in twelve days, but after finding no food they continued, fighting, foraging (losing thirteen of their number), until they reached the Atlantic Ocean, thus accomplishing the first historic descent of the Amazon. (The river, then called the Marañon, is said to be named for a band of women warriors encountered on this journey.) Orellano, with forty-three soldiers and two Negro slaves, finally reached the pearling island of Cubagua, off the coast of Venezuela, on September 11, 1542, after one hundred and fifty-nine days afloat.

Gonzalo himself, with his eighty remaining Spaniards, finally forced his way out of the jungle and reached Quito in June, 1542, where he denounced Orellano as a traitor. For the final word I quote the eminent Chilean historian, José Toribio Medina: "Pizarro's expedition was a disaster of such magnitude that none like it in America can be recalled."†

Another interesting tale of Quito tells how the beautiful Cantuña Chapel got its name. According to this tale Francisco Cantuña, an Indian, owed his life to a Spanish soldier who rescued him when his straw house was set afire and he was too sick to move. Cantuña became the servant of the Spaniard, and out of gratitude presented him with gold from a secret horde with which to pay his debts and live in luxury, bequeathing him more when he died. When the Spaniard himself was about to die, he realized how much he owed to his servant, Cantuña, and so left his fortune for the erection of a magnificent chapel to be designed and decorated by the finest artists of the day, on the condition that it would be named for the Indian. All that remains to testify to the truth of this story is a slab in the chapel which bears the simple inscription: "This is the sepulchre of Francisco Cantuña and his heirs—year of 1669."§

★Horses, which had to be brought from Spain or Cuba or Tampico, at that time cost between five hundred and one thousand pesos, and a peso was worth from ten to fifteen dollars.

†This absorbing tale is vividly recounted in *A Crossbowman's Story*, a historical novel by George Millar. The excerpts from the fifty source books in his bibliography provide satisfying evidence of its authenticity.

§One authority, B. Gento Sanz, thinks the story grew out of the inscription.

The preceding tale may have some basis in fact, but the legend which follows is clearly Quitonian fiction.

The Indian, Francisco Cantuña, impelled by either the thirst for gold or the desire for fame, rashly made a solemn promise to construct a grand *atrio* (atrium) for the Chapel of Cantuña adjacent to San Francisco. The date set for completing the structure drew near and the work was only half done. It was humanly impossible to finish it within the time allotted. Finally there remained but eighteen hours in which his promise could be fulfilled. The dreams of fame and fortune which had animated the poor Indian were dashed by the terrible reality. He would end in a prison cell, taunted and abused by everyone. His pride had caused his downfall.

The afternoon died in a fiery twilight. The church bells issued their call to prayer, and the streets were deserted except for the few people who turned to answer the call. At that instant Cantuña saw in the distance some strange and diabolical figures. Weary and distressed, this miserable one ran with swift steps to his house believing that neither prayer nor supplications could avail him. He then thought he heard a mysterious voice exhorting him to appeal to Heaven, and he obeyed. As the prayer came to his lips a balm of ineffable peace seemed to descend upon him and he returned to the chapel beside the Church of San Francisco. A secret hope led him to believe that the Heavenly Father had heard his prayer and that the work would be finished on time.

At the corner of the plaza, out of a heap of stones a mysterious personage in a red coat appeared. His countenance was dark; an enigmatic smile played upon his enormous mouth. He wore boots with turned-up toes, also red. The phantasm approached the stupefied Indian. "Cantuña," he said, "I know your trouble. This very morning you will be disgraced. But I am able to help you in your affliction. Before dawn the atrio will be finished. You, in turn, will sign this contract. I am Lucifer and I desire your soul. Do you accept? Speak!"

The Indian, without hesitation, accepted the offer. "But," he said, "if at the break of dawn, before the sound of the last stroke of the Ave Maria, the atrio is not finished, if there lacks one stone to be placed, only one, hear well, my contract with you is void."

"Done. Sign the contract," answered Lucifer.

A little later, exhausted and jeered at, Cantuña returned sadly to his home. Copious tears fell on his breast. Fervently he implored Heaven to pardon his sin and provide a remedy for his soul.

The Forteleza from El Panecillo

When dawn began to break the following day, Cantuña went at high speed to the Chapel. Work was just being completed by millions of red devils who passed like tongues of fire through the atrio, which now rose majestically. But the soul of the poor Indian was lost. His lips uttered a prayer, filled with faith and penitence. The Devil smiled. Day was dawning. A pale violet light began to fill the firmament, causing the cocks to crow. The sun appeared behind Ichimbia. Cantuña contemplated the scene. The atrio appeared to be finished. Slowly, solemnly, the four bells of the Ave Maria sounded, the heralds of the dawn.

"Victory," boomed Lucifer.

"Victory for *me*!" exclaimed the Indian. "One stone is lacking!"

In truth, one stone *was* lacking and the soul of Cantuña was saved. Lucifer, muttering, fled back to the infernal regions with his helpers. The promise of the Indian

Palacio del Gobierno (governor), Arch of Carondolet on the left

was fulfilled and, like a marvelous answer to prayer, the majestic structure stood in all its glory before the people of Quito. In the years following, countless children have sought the location of the missing stone.

Devised centuries ago by Quiteños to explain how the atrio was built, this interesting variant of the old Faustian theme has been retold through the years.

Don Ricardo Palma, that wonderful raconteur and author of *Peruvian Traditions*, in 1856 went ashore from a naval vessel in Paita, Peru, and was introduced to Manuela Saenz, the one-time mistress of Simon Bolívar. At the time, Palma was twenty-three years old and she was in her sixties—corpulent, poor, arthritic, living in retirement.

But Ricardo Palma found her gracious and easy in conversation; even in poverty she clearly showed that she had once belonged to aristocratic society. He sketched the facts of her life briefly.

Doña Manuela Saenz was born, out of wedlock, of distinguished Quitonian parents. After being educated in a convent in Panama she was married in 1817 to Dr. Don Jaime Thorne, an Englishman. After a few years they moved to Lima, but in about 1822 Doña Manuela returned to Quito and was one of one hundred and twenty Caballeresas del Orden del Sol, an exclusive order.

After the victory of Pichincha, won by Sucre on May 22, Bolívar came to Quito; there Manuela met the Liberator, who became enamored of her. When he went to Lima she stayed in Quito, where, at the head of a squadron of cavalry, she overcame a mutiny in the streets. All of the generals of the Patriot army treated her as though she were Bolívar's wife.

After the battle of Ayacucho, Manuela joined Bolívar in Huaura, but when he went back to Colombia she stayed in Lima, always guarding his dispatches and letters. Finally, the Governor of Lima asked her to leave when sentiment went against Bolívar, and she then joined the Liberator in Bogotá. Providence made her the savior of Bolívar when conspirators under Santander sought to murder him. After the death of Bolívar in 1830 (he was then in exile in Soledad, Colombia), the Congress of Peru and one of the three governors of Colombia assigned a pension to "La Liberadora." But this evidently lapsed and, as her family prevented her from acquiring her patrimony, she was forced to live in poverty. Don Jaime Thorne had died at the hands of three assassins in 1840. Why Manuela retired to one of the dreariest places in Peru is a matter for conjecture. *

*Her story is the subject of *The Four Seasons*, a historical novel by Victor von Hagen.

Entrance to the beautiful Torre Tagle Palace, Lima

Chapter Six

LIMA, PERU
The City of the Kings

Lima, the chief city and capital of the Republic of Peru, is a handsome progressive metropolis with over a million inhabitants, situated on a coastal plain only seven miles from the seaport of Callao. Its avenues and plazas are lined with trees and statues, embellished with fountains and tropical flowers. A broad avenue follows the course of the twelve-foot adobe wall erected in the seventeenth century as a protection against pirate raids. The old Lima—a city of straight and narrow streets—lies within the new. Its heart is the Plaza de Armas, an historic Colonial square which contains a bronze Baroque fountain dated 1650; the massive stone or concrete buildings of Spanish descent, however, are chiefly reconstructions on the original sites. Nowhere in South America, in spite of a superabundance of leveling earthquakes and revolutions, is the power and splendor of the Spanish Colonial period more apparent than in Lima, the seat of the first and most important viceroyalty. The city is still the aristocrat of the continent.

Vivid witnesses to Colonial life exist in unexpected places. There is, for instance, on Giron Ancash the Trece Monedas, a restaurant which preserves its Spanish heritage for the delight of the contemporary tourist. You will find it behind a rococo door on a side street near the Plaza Inquisición—a unique one-story house which has been restored for its present purpose but retains many of its original features. A stone horse block stands in the small courtyard behind this door and over the entrance is

The Cathedral Basilica on the Plaza de Armas, Lima

an unidentified coat of arms displaying thirteen coins. The carved wooden chairs and tables are at least seventeenth century, as are the paintings in their mirror-encrusted frames and the sculptures. There is even an eighteen-inch carved tabernacle. And the nude over the bar does not seem out of place, although it is actually a polychrome saint from an early church.

Façade of Church of San Francisco

Sacristy of San Francisco Church

Trece Monedas has dark-beamed ceilings and a beautiful example of a *teatina*, a dormer-like window for admitting light and air. In the brick-floored kitchen the original wood-burning stoves glow under the bright copper pans, providing ideal grills for the superb food. You will find this charming restoration of a Colonial home an excellent starting point for an expedition into old Lima.

But don't wait too long to gaze upon the remnants of Lima's past: the ancient *quincha* walls built to undulate with earthquakes show here and there their reeds and mud, but they are surrounded by modern buildings, except in part of the Rimac area. There is no doubt that the days of *quincha* construction are numbered. Now that the cloisters of San Agustín are being converted into shops and the original buildings of San Marcos University are being abandoned for modern structures, one sees the handwriting on the wall for Colonial landmarks.

Yet today, even among the new buildings, and sometimes in the midst of squalor,

188

View of the ceiling and high altar of San Francisco from the choir loft

Entrance to the Convent of Saint Augustine

ancient structures may still be found that retain the carved wooden balconies and lovely grilled windows, the signature of the Moorish influence on Colonial Spain. There are still many *quintas*, or enclosed places, which once were farms outside the city; hacienda houses are still in evidence, as are parts of beautiful old churches and convents that attest to the past. History, moreover, remains visible in Lima not in buildings alone, but in names that evoke people and events of an earlier time—names of streets and plazas, of commemorative parks, statues, and fountains.

You do not need to be a professional antiquarian to enjoy the heritage of the centuries in Lima, but to appreciate these memorials fully you will want to know something of Lima's history. ★

Lima was founded January 18, 1535, on the site of an Indian settlement in the

★For a detailed and authoritative account see the four volumes of *Lima, Fourth Centennial of 1935* or the 1,117 invaluable pages of *Peruvian Traditions* of Ricardo Palma.

189

Courtyard entrance to the restaurant, Trece Monedas, formerly a palace built for the aristocratic Perez y Rodolfo family. Note the thirteen coins (trece monedas) on the coat of arms above the door.

Interior view of the teatina (dormer window) of Trece Monedas

valley of the River Rimac (Lima is a corruption of Rimac) by that doughty old conqueror and gold digger, Francisco Pizarro. Since he had selected the site on January 6, the Feast of the Epiphany, he named it Ciudad de los Reyes, the City of the Kings, in honor of the three kings who followed the Star to Bethlehem. After six years of turbulent, yet constructive rule, Pizarro himself was brutally assassinated by followers of his rival, Almagro. His life was a fitting prelude to his death; but he lifted the curtain of the fabulous viceregal period which extended from his day to the proclaiming of the Republic of Peru by General San Martín on July 23, 1821, or, more exactly, to the final victory of the Patriot forces under General Sucre at the Battle of Ayacucho, December 9, 1824. But throughout the city the names most often encountered are those of Simon Bolívar, hailed as the Liberator of Peru, and of José San Martín the Protector; that of the Conqueror was noticeably absent until quite recent times. Even Pizarro's body, hastily and secretly buried, was not properly placed in the cathedral he had founded until the 1890's, and not until 1935, on the occasion of the city's fourth centennial, was an equestrian statue, the gift of the wife of an American sculptor, erected on the plaza he had laid out.

Lima: The City of the Kings

In 1537, two years after its founding, Charles V of Spain bestowed upon the city a coat of arms composed of three crowns and a star, the symbol of the Magi, or Three Kings. At the same time he bestowed upon Pizarro a coat of arms and the title of Marqués of Atavillos; he had already made him governor and virtually viceroy. Little exists now of Pizarro's city. The governor's palace is on the site of the home he built for himself; in one of its four patios is the fig tree he planted, near which he died. Other mementos of the sixteenth century include: the olive trees of the Hacienda of San Isidro, planted in 1560; La Casa de Pilatos (House of Pilate) on Calle Zavala, which is pure sixteenth-century Spanish; parts of the old churches and convents; and two paintings in San Pedro by Bernardo Bitti—"La Candelaria" and "Coronation of the Virgin." Since the sixteenth century the destruction wrought by man and nature has taken a heavy toll.

A prison cell and a beautifully carved mahogany ceiling alone attest to the activities of the Inquisition, established in Peru under the Dominicans, with headquarters on the plaza named for it. Its work was carried on more vigorously in Lima than in any other city in South America (Ricardo Palma records that one poor foreigner was burned for being a Lutheran).* But it was finally abolished, unlamented, in 1820. Today the Museum of Bolívar and San Martín, known also as the Colonial Museum, is the principal building on the Plaza Inquisición.

The colored tiles of Santo Domingo Church are dated 1606 and the old stone bridge built by Viceroy Marqués de Monteclaros in 1610 is still standing. But chiefly what we have left to study of Colonial Lima belongs to the period after 1746. In that year the most devastating of earthquakes practically demolished the city (it is recorded that it killed 40,000 people and in nearby Callao all but 200 of its 4,500 inhabitants: an almost incredible statistic).

The twelve-foot city wall, built in 1669 to protect the city from pirate invasions, was used in time mostly for promenades, and after much earthquake damage was torn down by Henry Meiggs, called the "Yanqui Pizarro," in 1867. The present highway between Lima and Callao was built under the thirty-sixth viceroy, Ambrosio O'Higgins, at the beginning of the nineteenth century.

The varying styles of church architecture in Peru continue to fascinate the intelligent traveler as well as the architectural historian. A number of styles are represented, but chiefly the Baroque in its different phases which appeared first in Cuzco about 1650 and developed alternately in that Inca city and in Lima during the seven-

*Op. cit.

The High Altar of the Cathedral. The choir stalls are spoiled by being moved from the transcoro.

Altar in the choir of San Pedro Church

teenth century. This was its great period, though it extended into the eighteenth. It is in the grand manner, intense, exuberant, even theatrical, yet possessed of a dignity that is achieved in part through its use of color and diffused light and in part through an inner spiritual vitality. It was followed and overlapped by the Rococo, a style which emphasized lavish and sensuous decoration to fantastic or bizarre extremes (the church of El Corazón de Jesús in Lima is an example).

The Churrigueresque (a late Baroque style named for a Spanish architect) can be studied in the famous façades of La Merced and San Agustín, which have been plastered over and recarved but are still beautiful.

Of the oldest convent in the city, that of Santo Domingo, it has been said that it "conserved a little of the sixteenth century, enough of the seventeenth, and a great deal of the eighteenth." The notable features of the church are its roof, one of the few works of brick which survived the 1746 earthquake, the assembly hall, the carved ceiling of the library, the sacristy, the cloister arches, and the early seventeenth-century tiles.

192

Frescoed ceiling in the Jesuit Chapel of San Marcos University

Sta. Brigida, Religiosa, on frescoed ceiling of Jesuit Chapel of San Marcos University

The Cathedral of Lima is the most recent successor of the little church of adobe and thatch whose cornestone was laid by Pizarro in 1535. Restorations have followed the recurring earthquakes, but the floor plan of Francisco Becerra, the distinguished Spanish architect of the late sixteenth century, who also designed the cathedral and La Compañía of Cuzco, has never been materially modified. After 1746 a Jesuit from Prague, Juan de Rher, was put in charge of the extensive restoration; hence the structure today belongs almost entirely to the latter part of the eighteenth century. The façade, however, is in the early Baroque style of the Spanish sculptor Pedro de Noguera's original design of 1687.

The interior of the cathedral lacks the magnificent furnishings of an earlier period, but it boasts a glorious Immaculate Conception by Diego Aguirre, leading sculptor of Peru in the late seventeenth century, and a series of early Baroque choir stalls, designed by Pedro de Noguera in 1623, which were transferred from the nave to the sanctuary in 1895. These stalls are important not only for their excellent craftsmanship but also for their influence on later work; the stalls of San Francisco Church at

Tapadas (concealed ones) of Lima

Jewelled painting of Saint Rose of Lima (Santa Rosa)—1746— in a silver frame with the inscription "made in thanksgiving by the Conde de Superunda, Viceroy of Peru, for being saved in an earthquake." Collection of Pedro de Osma

Cuzco are virtually copies. In design, workmanship and decoration they bear comparison with almost any in Europe, and are undoubtedly the finest in Peru. Among the figures carved in relief is a lovely "Santa Rosa de Lima."

The chapel in the cathedral most visited by tourists is the one in which the shrunken remains of the once mighty conquistador, Francisco Pizarro, lie in a glass casket for all to gaze upon. The mosaic decoration on the walls depicts his coat of arms and the dramatic episode on the island of Gallo in which he offered his fifty-odd disheartened followers the choice of staying with him or of returning to the rescue ship which had been dispatched for them. The thirteen who chose to stay are ranked with him as the founders of the Viceroyalty of Peru.

194

Although the first Franciscans arrived with the founders in 1535, their earliest church was not erected until 1546, and since that year has been rebuilt many times. However, the designs for the "new" church, completed in 1674, have not been entirely superseded; the ground floor and vaults have outridden a number of earthquakes, making San Francisco the oldest church in Lima, and the only one which retains a cane and plaster roof. Its Baroque retable façade is particularly fine but somewhat dwarfed by the heavy dimensions of the towers. The Renaissance interior, through misguided nineteenth-century restoration and upheavals of nature, has been stripped of its wonderful Baroque retables and silver altars, but is still impressive. Further damage was done by the earthquake of 1940.

The main cloister of the Monastery of San Francisco, begun in the sixteenth century, is probably the oldest in the city and also the most beautiful. The monastery itself is a treasure house of the past and, in fact, maintains the Museum of Religious and Colonial Art. Among its most unusual features are the staircase leading to the upper cloister, the restored Mudéjar cupola★ over the grand stairway leading to the choir, the choir stalls and the retable behind them. Of exceptional interest are the chapter house, which contains a series of paintings of Franciscan saints and martyrs in gilded frames and, in the cloisters, the marvelous collection of Sevillian tiles dated 1620, also a legacy from the Moors in Spain.

The story of these tiles and of the beginning of tile-making in Lima has often been told. One version claims that the celebrated Doña Catalina Huanca, descendant of the Indian *cacique*, Apu Alaya, wishing to bestow some of her great wealth upon the new cloister, brought or had imported from Seville a large collection of colored tiles. Unfortunately, no one could be found to lay them properly, and they might have remained boxed indefinitely had not the prior, listening to the last confession of one Alonzo Godinez, learned that the condemned man was an architect and also skilled in ceramics. At once the prior hastened to the palace, where he persuaded the viceroy to commute the death sentence to life imprisonment in the monastery. Hence it was that the prisoner Godinez spent the rest of his life creating a "porcelain garden" that has been called the most beautiful in the world. When it was completed he turned to the making of new tiles for the further embellishment of the Monastery of San Francisco.

Another favorite story concerns the church bells of Lima. It seems that a number of them had names, such as "La Purisima" of the cathedral, and "La Abuelita" of the

★This collapsed in 1940.

Doorway of the Casa de Pilatos (House of Pilate). This is the oldest mansion in Lima.

tower of San Pedro, and they were rung to announce baptisms, weddings, funerals, as well as fiestas, victories, proclamations, and salutes to viceroys. On one occasion the bell ringer of San Agustín, Jorge Escoriquez, failed to ring a bell for Don Luis, Duke of Alba de Liste. The offended viceroy complained to the prior who summoned the bell ringer and gave him a word lashing. One night not long afterward, when the city was still, Escoriquez caught sight of the viceroy slipping through the street in disguise and called attention to him by ringing all the bells in the tower. Thereupon the viceroy called the bell ringer to the palace and they drew up a "non-aggression pact."

Two places in particular evoke the flavor of old Lima, though it is one of past glory: La Alameda de los Descalzos and Quinta Heeren. Across the Rimac River from the Plaza de Armas is a formal park which in Colonial times was romantic and fashionable but is now shabby and dilapidated—La Alameda de los Descalzos (Park of the Barefoot Ones), named after the adjacent Franciscan convent. The broad central avenue is still there with the old trees and the classical statues on their pedestals; but the fountain has ceased playing, the marble benches are disintegrating, the iron fence is rusting, and in the park where fashionable ladies, in carriages with gold-edged leather fittings and accompanied by well-appointed horsemen, once took part in a colorful promenade, I found only poor students and beggars. It has been called a "skeleton of the past impregnated with sadness, a cemetery of memories." In the neighboring patios of the convent the padres still feed the pigeons and dispense rations to the poor.

Quinta Heeren, a smaller park with statues off the Street Carmen Alto, still exists —but one wonders for how long. While I was there in 1958, an ancient fig tree toppled from its roots and fell over the quincha wall of a run-down apartment house. Across the way was a paddock with riding horses and, nearby, the ruins of a once fine hacienda. Behind an interesting old gate I saw a few large restored houses defying the prevailing decay, but, in general, the future of the once charming park seemed in doubt—toppling, one might say.

Among the important landmarks of Lima is one which represents its present and future as well as its historic past. San Marcos University, the oldest in the New World, antedating Harvard by almost a century, was inaugurated on May 12, 1551, by the royal decree of Charles V of Spain. It started to function the following year under Fray Tomás de San Martín, first Provincial of the Order of Santo Domingo, and became for Peru what Oxford was for England, Padua for Italy and Heidelberg for Germany. The Indian languages, such as Quechua, were taught at San Marcos, as well as the conventional subjects: theology, philosophy, grammar and, later, medicine and music.

The oldest and most beautiful feature of the university, the chapel, was built by the Jesuits and named for them; at present it is the Salon of Arts of the Faculty of Letters. It is famous for its frescoed ceiling, which depicts a group of seventeenth-century theologians. On my visit to this historic chapel I was accompanied by the cultural attaché of the American Embassy, Dr. Albert Giesecke. He had ridden in a car just behind that of Richard Nixon when the vice-president was greeted with insults and rocks in 1958 by the communistically-inclined students of San Marcos, a reception that was very much decried by the solid citizens of Peru. I looked around expecting a bearded one to cry "Yankee, go home," but received no attention whatsoever.

THE MANSIONS OF LIMA

From the few remaining examples of luxurious Colonial mansions I could see that not all the wealth of the viceregal period—the gold wrested from the conquered Incas, the silver dug from the mines of Potosí—was poured into the building and adorning of the churches and convents of Lima. A large amount of it was used for the erection of public buildings and monuments, and still more for the sumptuous homes of the nobility. These homes, or mansions, which were described by José Santos Chocano as "part oratory and part harem,"* are an integral part of the luxury and elegance of the period. The influence of the cloisters can be seen in the elaborate series of capitals and arches of the more pretentious mansions, but the interior arrangement, at least at first, followed a basic pattern. The ground floor was designed for the servants' quarters and the transaction of business; the second floor was for the family and was usually entered by an outside stairway in the patio. In general, the construction was adapted to the material at hand, and, since this did not include stone or hard woods, the first floor was likely to be of adobe ornamented with wooden beams, and the second of quincha. A coat of clay covered the flat roof.

More impressive features were introduced in the eighteenth century: the formal salon, decorated with the Rococo medallions and wreaths of Louis XIV and Louis XV, and the private chapel or oratory. Styles varied with the centuries. The *rejas*, or grill work, over the windows were of turned wood from Central America up to 1650; after that they were of wrought iron. Balconies, like suspended cages, stood

*Hector Velarde, *Arquitectura Peruana*, p. 106.

198

Casa de los Marqueses de Oquendo y Osambela where General San Martín lodged after he proclaimed the Independence of Peru, July 28, 1821. Restored in 1962. It will be the seat of the government tourist agency.

Stairway leading from entrance patio of the Torre Tagle Palace

on either side of the doorways and were hardly ever of the same size. In the seventeenth century these were composed of four parts: the lower part or body, often decorated with Mudéjar designs, the frieze, the lattice, and the balusters.

There is an explanation for the presence in Lima of closed Oriental balconies. Beatriz, the Moorish slave of García de Salcedo, conquistador and one of the founders of Lima, later became his legitimate wife. It was she who, with other Moorish women, brought an exotic flavor to the scene of Lima and influenced its architecture, which according to Buschiazzo "was above all Oriental and somewhat feminine."*

The complement of the latticed balconies, with their atmosphere of Moslem se-

*Mario J. Buschiazzo, *Estudios de Arquitectura Colonial*, p. 120.

200

Patio of the Torre Tagle Palace

clusion, was found in the renowned *saya* and *manto* of the ladies of the upper class. The *saya* was a full skirt; the *manto* was a kind of shawl or mantilla which was brought over the head and across the face, hiding all but the eyes. Dressed in this fashion the ladies of Lima were known as *Tapadas*, or concealed ones, and could go about practically incognito. The practice could and did lead to amorous adventures which, in turn, had to be revealed in the confessional. Indeed, so startling were the disclosures that the Church finally prohibited the wearing of these garments, although not until the middle of the nineteenth century was the prohibition effective. Thus ended a custom that for three hundred years prevented men of Lima from seeing, in public, more of a lady than an elegantly turned foot and a pair of sparkling eyes.

Inner court of the Casa del Conde de Fuente González

As mentioned before, a very interesting feature of Lima houses were the *teatinas*, or windows raised above the roof. They were like ventilators turned to the south to catch the breeze, but were decorative architectural items besides. I was much intrigued by these and was surprised to find that friends in Lima had never noticed them. The lookout tower, or *mirador*, much like a captain's tower in New England, was of Moslem origin. A balcony was also called a mirador. The teatinas and miradors are rapidly disappearing from the scene as the old buildings are being torn down.

My first discovery of an old mansion was La Casa de Pilatos, or House of Pilate, so called, according to an account which I read, because it resembled a house of the same name in Córdoba, Spain. It is one of the few examples of classic Spanish archi-

Salon of Casa del Conde de Fuente González, 1824. Furniture was Isabelino II (XIXth century)

tecture in Peru and was the pride of the old viceroyalty. Built in 1590, it is the oldest mansion in Lima. The leftover materials of the Church of San Francisco, opposite, supplied the materials for its solid construction; the same architect was employed for both buildings. The house was connected by a subterranean gallery with the Convent of San Pedro where the Jesuits lived, and this gave rise to many stories. The stone façade is beautifully composed with rusticated columns, a balcony over the doorway, two coats of arms and a very fine cornice. One distinguishing feature is the stairway opposite the entrance; another is the typically Spanish patio, which is exceptionally large and has arches above Doric columns (these are characteristic of only the most distinguished homes).

Coronation of the Virgin at Church of San Pedro, by Diego Quispe Ttito, one of the few paintings of the sixteenth century in Lima

Façade of Church of La Merced, Union Street

The House of Pilate was built by a rich merchant named Diego de Esquivel who had been a companion of Pizarro. Until 1635 the house was rented and served as an inn for Portuguese miners and merchants. There was even a time when fruit merchants occupied the patio. Doña María de Esquivel y Jarava, daughter of a Spanish general, inherited the house, and when she died the Inquisition held it for a credit of 800 pesos. Her nephew, Don Diego de Esquivel y Jarava, a native of Cuzco who, in 1687, obtained the title of Marqués de San Lorenzo de Valle Umbroso, did not wish the house to go out of the family and paid up all of the creditors' 28,000 pesos. After the Independence, primogeniture ceased and the house passed out of the family to other proprietors. The story of how this house obtained its name is told by Ricardo Palma. *

*Op. cit., p. 361.

In August, 1635, in the middle of the night a servant named Truhan, an habitual drunkard, was passing by this house and discovered the door unbolted and ajar. He heard sounds within and out of curiosity ascended the stairs to find out what was going on. In a room above he saw a beautiful life-size crucifix. Nearby, under a canopy sat a rich Portuguese Jew named Don Manuel Bautista Peréz; about one hundred compatriots on benches listened to him in reverent silence. The drunkard testified that when Peréz stopped talking the listeners arose and advanced toward the image and each one gave it a strong blow. Peréz, like Pilate, authorized with his impassive presence this mocking chastisement. The spy, not wishing to see any more blasphemy, escaped and went with his tale-bearing to the Inquisition, which a few hours later incarcerated the group of Portuguese Jews. After that the Limeñans gave Peréz the nickname Pilate and the house remained under the name La Casa de Pilatos.

Historic documents in the Library of Lima tell of the trial of the Jews which lasted three years, and give their crime as profanation of images. Peréz and ten of his co-religionists were burned in an auto-da-fé in 1639 and fifty more, all of them wealthy, were put in prison. La Casa de Pilatos now houses a school.

In contrast, the Torre Tagle Palace is the epitome of viceregal elegance. Although it was built early in the eighteenth century, it held to the style of the seventeenth and was pure Limeñan, influenced by the Andalusian, Moresque, Creole, and even Asiatic, but with none of the Churrigueresque or Rococo of its own period. This architectural gem in palaces was built by the Marqués José de Tagle y Drache, whose family occupied it until it was taken over by the Foreign Office of Peru. It was the home of General Torre Tagle, Patriot President of the Republic of Peru in 1823, who went over to the side of the Spaniards and died in the Fortress of Callao before its surrender in 1826 to Republican forces.

The carved balconies of this palace are typical Mudéjar, with elaborately turned balusters and lattices, but with Asiatic influences revealed in the magnificent brackets which support them. The beautiful doorway is an enchanting combination of Baroque and other styles incorporated into a harmonious whole. The palace is noted also for its stairway leading directly up from the entrance, its rich decoration throughout, its patios, and finally its mirador, with Moorish cupola—Lima's *sine qua non* of the period. The name of the architect is not known. Luckily, the 1746 earthquake did little damage to the palace, although extensive restoration was deemed necessary in 1957–58; this was carried out under the direction of the distinguished Spanish architect, Don Andrés Boyer Ruiz, who had just finished working on the

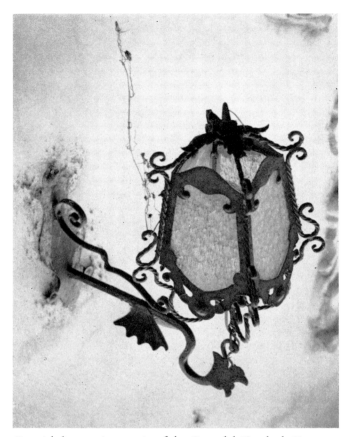

Moorish patio of the Casa del Conde de Fuente González, last governor of viceroyal Peru; now a private residence

Spanish lantern in a patio of the Casa del Conde de Fuente González

restoration of the Cuzco Cathedral after their earthquake of 1951. Unfortunately, I was not able to see the final restoration.

Less restored and more imbued with the spirit of its past owner, Conde del Villar de Fuente is the historic home at Jirón Callao 380, now the property of Señor Manuel Fernando Barbieri, who holds himself responsible for its conservation. Conde del Villar de Fuente was the last governor and captain general of the Viceroyalty of Peru. He died a prisoner in the Fortress of Callao on the eve of Independence, 1825, and was thus a companion, perforce, of Torre Tagle. The two men must have sighed for the beautiful homes they had left behind. This magnificent home has eighty-six rooms, fifty-six upstairs and thirty downstairs. Señor Barbieri rents out some of the upper rooms to various organizations, but the main floor with its original furnishings is carefully preserved. The elaborate suite of furniture in the main salon had been ordered for Queen Isabella the Second of Spain. This salon adjoins the chapel which was used for family services and for special occasions. In the patios the original

Original chair and jar (tinaja) of the Casa del Conde de Fuente González

Grilled window of inner court of the Casa del Conde de Fuente González

lanterns, the *maceta* jars in wrought-iron stands, the Spanish tiles, and the iron gratings over the windows create an antique atmosphere as one patio leads into another and another. Tropical plants and flowers enhance the picture. The entrance to this home does not give much notice of the interest within.

A historic property, known formerly as the House of Paz Soldan, is now occupied by a women's club dedicated to cultural improvement and called "Entre Nous." First called "Biblioteca Entre Nous," the organization promoted many good causes and occupied several *ventanas de rejas*, grilled windows—a quaint expression designating temporary quarters. Then, under the leadership of Señorita Belén de Osma and with the assistance of the distinguished architect, Don Rafael Marquina Bueno, the club acquired this beautiful old home and restored it in 1952. It is on Riva Street and was in the same block with the residences of many illustrious families in the mid-seventeenth century.

The excellent restoration accomplished by Entre Nous has preserved many of

Entrance to the Hacienda of San Isidro with its two cannons. It is now occupied by the Moyrera family.

Interior of the private chapel of the Hacienda of San Isidro

the features of Colonial mansions. The imposing entrance has a carved religious inscription—"Praised be the Sainted Sacrament of the Altar"—and two upright bronze cannons to bid welcome. The entrance patio has elaborate window gratings and hanging lanterns, tile dadoes and a stairway leading up to the second floor. The *mampara,* or screened door, at the entrance to the Salon Dorado is exquisitely designed, and beyond it one sees the handsome chandeliers with their blue glass and crystal prisms. In an alcove off the salon is a beautiful altar and retable. A well-proportioned auditorium has been provided, and a well-equipped library with Colonial bookcases and beamed ceiling. A connecting patio, typical of Lima, has cloister-like arches, tiled walls, grilled windows, and flower beds and a tiled fountain in the center. The building is an exhibit in itself, besides being a *casa de cultura.* José Galvez, in his *Calles de Lima,* gives an account of the many families, titled and otherwise, which have occupied this lovely old residence.

In October, 1959, at the time of the Festival of El Señor de los Milagros, Entre Nous held an important exposition of the Art of Viceregal Peru which displayed inlaid furniture, paintings of the Cuzco School, two hundred forty-eight water colors

Governor's Palace built by Pizarro in 1538*

of Pancho Fierro, silver, and popular folk art, including *urnas*, *santos*, and *huamanga* stone carving. The exhibits came largely from private collections. Of particular interest was a set of porcelain used by Simon Bolívar at a banquet to celebrate the Proclamation of Independence. A "figure of welcome" was a *tapada* wearing a Spanish mantilla which characteristically left only the eyes showing. One of the most distinguished pieces shown was a *maqueta* (lacquered chest) loaned by the Church of San Francisco, Lima, but owned by the Dibos Dammert family. Materials used in it were mother-of-pearl, tortoise shell, agate, gold, silver, and ivory with inserts of paintings. The Latin inscription on a silver plate is, in translation: "Made

*From 1535–1538, Pizarro with his wife Doña Inés Yupanqui, descendant of Huayna Ccapac, and their daughter Doña Francesca lived in "the Casa de Cadena (chain)." They lived in his new palace (shown here) until 1541 when Pizarro was assassinated. Then the wife and daughter returned to Casa de Cadena and remained there until 1550. This palace was torn down by Governor Augusto B. Leguía.

Cabinet of Prayer (Amrario—Oratorio). Note Saint Rose of Lima in glass on right. Hacienda of San Isidro

Glass cabinet of Jacaranda wood—Portuguese style. Hacienda of San Isidro

by Giovanni de Espinoza, Painting by Bartolomeo Murillo, 1657, Seville." I had left a year before the exhibition at Entre Nous!

Through the kindness of an American friend residing in Lima, I had the pleasure of visiting the Hacienda de San Isidro. Built in the seventeenth century in the center of a large encomienda, it is all that remains of a once vast property. At one time the whole district of San Isidro belonged to the hacienda, but all of it has been sold during the last twenty-five years except the main building with the gardens in front and back. Its modern swimming pool is an anachronism.

The Count of San Isidro died without issue, and his home was acquired by members of the distantly related Moreyra family who still occupy it. In June of 1958 Señorita Luisa Moreyra★ was my gracious hostess and guide. I was delighted to tour this wonderful old walled country mansion which stands but a short distance from the Park of the Olive Trees. The house was built on a mound, the kind used by the Indians for their shrines, and on either side of the entrance gate cannon are embedded —as they are in front of the Torre Tagle Palace and Entre Nous—symbols of refuge and welcome within. From the front piazza there is a fine view of the tower of the neighboring church of Santa María Magdalena.

★"Paco" Moreyra, Luisa's brother, would be eligible for the title "Conde de San Isidro" if he were to present his documents of proof to the Spanish government.

210

Library of the Hacienda of San Isidro. On the left is a portrait of an official of the Inquisition.

Silver mirror from Cajamarca. Rococo with Indian touches. Alzamora Collection

The tower of the adjoining family chapel was destroyed in 1746 but was rebuilt within the year. In this chapel hangs a document attesting that, in 1775, Pope Clement XIV granted the family the privilege of holding private Mass. The main floor of this historic chapel is composed of ancient tiles, and along the two sides are benches for the peons. In the balcony facing the fine altar and retable are carved *prie-dieus* for the family. Large framed religious pictures hang on the right wall. As of old, a wedding was about to take place when I was there in 1958.

The patio contains benches made of tile and immense oil jars, which, from time to time, have been dug up on the grounds and are now used for flower pots. Inside the house are heavy Spanish doors, some of them original, others replacements for those eaten by termites. The beamed ceilings have been replaced during the last three years for the same reason. Family portraits hang all about the place, each with the coat of arms in the upper left-hand corner; one subject in a long black coat was an official of the Inquisition. In one room a choice hand-illuminated book tells the story of the different escudos, each depicted on parchment. The present Señor, Don Francisco Moreyra y Riglos, has kept the entire collection of family papers intact for his nephew and heir. The furniture, rugs, and objects of art are all very choice. There are sixteenth-century Aubusson rugs; a French chest of the time of Henry the Second; an Italian ebony and mother-of-pearl cabinet of the seventeenth century;

Framed portraits of conquistadors on huamanga stone from Ayacucho. Pizarro is in the center with Spanish coat of arms above him. Alzamora Collection

Statue of Our Lady, La Purisima—1666—is from Granada. The silver brazier was a present from the Conde de Lemos to his wife Anna de Borja. The chairs are vice regal. From the collection of Pedro de Osma

Flemish, English Sheraton, and Spanish pieces. Meissen figurines are in abundance.

All things considered, I have seen no more fascinating Spanish Colonial home than the Hacienda of San Isidro, surrounded as it is by modern dwellings but with the sixteenth-century olive trees for company.

The next opportunity was that of visiting the home of Don Pedro de Osma. One of the finest collections of Spanish Colonial art in South America belongs to Don Pedro and is housed in his block-long palace on Pedro de Osma Avenue in Barranco, one of the suburbs of Lima. The house is enclosed by a wall and is built around a palm-lined inner court, in the corner of which are the owner's sumptuous living quarters. The tour he conducts of the priceless collection for selected guests invariably winds up in his own quarters, in a room whose panels were taken from a cloister.

Most museums in South America, at least those in Bogotá, Quito and Cuzco, are housed in what were originally private homes, complete with galleries and patios. The Pedro de Osma collection of rare paintings (largely of the Cuzco School), exquisitely carved images and other art objects is not, at present, on view for the public. But Don Pedro intends to leave his home—its fifteen rooms filled with priceless

212

objects—to his country. He keeps four craftsmen constantly restoring the gilded, glass-incrusted frames and silver entablements. On July 23, 1960, the Provincial Council of Lima honored Don Pedro de Osma with a parchment declaring him an "Ambassador of National Art." When the first Museum of Art was opened on August 1, 1961, he gave forty pieces to the city. This museum was organized by Dr. Carlos Neuhaus Ugarteche, president of the Lima Art Foundation, and exhibits six thousand pieces covering twenty-five hundred years of culture. It is located on Grau Plaza at Pasal Colón in a building which had been restored for a French exhibit several years before. The second floor, devoted to Colonial art, contains thirteen areas displaying, besides the whole collection of the Prado family, those of Don Pedro de Osma, the family of Don José Antonio de Lavalle, the Pancho Fierro collection of the Municipality of Lima and donations from many other individuals.

A house worthy of preserving is La Casa de Nicolás de Rivera el Viejo, a precious example of the seventeenth century whose stone porch is typical Limeñan and whose long balconies are among the most beautiful in the city. No law in Lima assures the protection of historic houses as yet; thus the preservation of such mansions as La Casa Rada, Mansion de Oquendo,★ and the Instituto Riva Obuero depends upon their enlightened owners.

The description of a Latin American city is not complete without mention of the religious processions which for four hundred years have held an important place in the lives of the people. Of all the processions in Lima the most impressive is that of El Señor de los Milagros (Lord of Miracles) in October. Inaugurated soon after the terrible disaster of 1746, it has continued to express the ever-present dread of earthquakes and grief for the destruction they cause. It represents also the response of the Church to this fear and sorrow, and the many miracles acclaimed since.

The procession always follows the same route: starting on October 18 from the Church Las Nazarenas, proceeding to Santa Domingo, then to the cathedral, and on to La Concepción. At night it is in Los Descalzos de San José and by noon the next day it reaches Santa Catalina. The people say that El Señor sleeps in Los Descalzos, lunches the first day in La Concepción and the second in Santa Catalina. The entrance into a church is always a solemn moment. All the bells ring, and in the choir the monks or nuns intone psalms. The silver incense pots, some decorated with a pea-hen, the emblem of El Señor, fill the air with a spicy sweetness.

The cortege accompanying the Lord of Miracles is composed of all classes—rich

★In 1962 this was restored under the direction of architect Hector Vilarde. It will be used as the seat of the Corporación de Turismo.

Room of the Pedro de Osma residence whose decorations were taken from a 17th-century cloister. The old portraits are of archbishops of Lima.

and poor, masters and servants, penitents and beggars. The *zambos* (natives of mixed Negro and Indian blood) wear their characteristic lavender garb; the penitents are in coarse clothing and march barefoot reciting the rosary. Held aloft in the procession are the ponderous antique *andas* (platforms or litters), richly decorated and covered with flowers and ex-votos, which bear the sacred images. The *anda* carrying El Señor has a silver arch which swings above the image like a gleaming halo. (The effigy is modeled upon an eighteenth-century painting in Las Nazarenas.) There is a tradition that each year one of the bearers collapses and dies under his heavy burden, but there are alway sturdy *zambos*, Indians, and mestizos who welcome this way of increasing their chances of getting to heaven. During the frequent rest stops the people on the streets dance and sing and patronize the food vendors.

Private altar with Virgin of the Immaculate Conception. Bought in Lima from an old Cuzco family. Alzamora Collection

Don Pedro de Osma (portrait taken in his residence in Lima in 1948)

A different festival, similar to a Mardi Gras, is held on the last days before Lent. The streets are richly adorned for the occasion; tapestries and woven stuffs hang from the balconies; flags and banners are everywhere. Now is the time for general merry-making, for masquerades and practical jokes; grotesque figures dart in and out of the crowds; bowls of water are emptied from the balconies on the passers-by and eggs are tossed by men riding by on horseback.

The Good Friday procession, which also dates back to the Colonial Period, originated in Surco, a settlement of the nearby suburb of Barranco. Its solemnity was never marred by merriment. The central figure is that of the crucified Christ, which was carried first on a scaffold-like ladder and then borne in a recumbent position, the head crowned with flowers, the body bleeding from its wounds. After this second image is carried into the church the faithful pay homage to it, approaching with lighted candles and offerings of coins and praying far into the night. An effigy of the Virgin Mary in her role as Mater Dolorosa also presides over this procession. She holds a silver cross over her heart which is pierced by seven swords, symbols of the seven deadly sins.

The artist who most graphically portrayed these processions was a Creole,

Elaborate altar in the residence of Pedro de Osma, Archbishop of Lima. Salon de Goyerreche

Pancho Fierro, 1817–79. He has been called the Peruvian Goya, but in his accurate, though often sardonic and ruthless depiction of the life of his time he seems to me rather a Peruvian Cruikshank or Hogarth. His paintings provide a memorable record of the death agonies of the viceroyalty and the birth struggles of the Independence. He was so close an observer of the varied types of people about him that he captured their inner spirit—the grace and verve of the splendid ladies of the court, the bravado of the ragged street vendors. Through his work we know in detail the dress of the period: the *saya* and *manto* of the society matron, the robes and hoods of the different monastic orders, the colorful variegated costumes of the dancers. His medium was crayon or water color, never oil.

Examples of Fierro's work formerly owned by the father of Angela Palma, who had them from his father, are now in the museum Pinacoteca Municipal in Barranca, Lima. I saw my first Fierro original in the Lavalle collection in Lima in 1958. ★

For collectors in Lima there are pre-Inca pottery and weaving; pottery bulls of Pucará (miniature replicas of the great bulls which the natives dress with flowers for the fiestas); paintings of the Cuzco School; and—for the sheer fun of it—aquarelles of Pancho Fierro. A real find would be a book illustrated by Fierro.

No Colonial Theatre remains except that of Perricholi, which is described later. However, the seventeenth century was a brilliant period for the Limeñan theatre, and both plays and actors held a secure place in popular affection. In the early years of the century, plays of Calderón and Lope de Vega were presented in open yards, such as the yard of the Convent of Santa Domingo and of the Hospital of San Andrés. The street on which the Monastery of San Agustín stood was formerly called the Street of the False Door or the Street of Old Comedies, because of the fact that comedies were frequently presented in the corral of the monastery. In 1662 an elliptical-shaped building, long after referred to as Maison Blanco, was built in front of the false door. It stood there for some time, but by 1738 it had disappeared and the Street of the False Door of San Agustín became Plazuela del Siete de Septiembre (Seventh of September) in commemoration of the first armed action of the populace against the Spanish General Canterac, who advanced toward Lima during the 6, 7, and 8 of September, 1821. It was the first expression of the people's desire for liberty. The day also commemorated San Martín's disembarcation at Paracas in the same month of the preceding year.

★There are about 240 pages on the Creole master in the two-part volume, *Lima— Tipos y Costumbros por Pancho Fierro*, by José Antonia de Lavalle; this is the best source for the study of Spanish Colonial costume that can be found.

El Teatro Principo, the principal theatre of this period, was built in 1662, destroyed in 1746, and then rebuilt. In 1852 it was expropriated by Governor Echenique; it burned down in 1883. In its day it was noted for its opulent silver boxes and lavishly decorated rococo ceiling. Its magnificent silver chandelier was the focus of sharp criticism, partly because of the drippings from the many wax candles but chiefly because at whatever level it was hung it obstructed the vision of some part of the audience. Yet gas was never permitted in this theatre.

Due to the insistent demand for comedies the companies were obliged to present three new ones each month, in addition to one each Sunday and one for each festival. During the Octavo of Corpus Christi in June, 1617, two companies played two performances a day, one in the palace for the viceroy and the other in the atrium, or porch, of the cathedral.

The traditional theatre of Lima had sustained a severe blow on October 8, 1621 when a dispatch from Spain announced the death of Philip III. The Royal Audiencia and the viceroy at once arranged for the display of rich tributes and other manifestations of public grief, and banned all dramatic productions until after Lent, 1622. This decree worked hardship for both playwrights and actors.

Bull fighting was one of the last popular diversions introduced by the conquistadors. Every memorable event in Lima was celebrated in this way, at first on Sundays but later, at the instance of the Church, on Mondays. (Today they are on Sundays again.) They were often gorgeous spectacles, particularly in the early days when a series of fights was held in honor of the canonization of Santa Rosa de Lima and again in 1790 in honor of the coronation of Charles IV. The first bull fights were staged in the main plaza of the city and in the plazuelas of the convents. La Plaza de Acho, built in 1768, is the oldest bull ring in America, and still functions across the old bridge on the Rimac side of the city.

The procedure of the bull fight followed a formal pattern. It opened with a military pageant and reached a high point when a trumpet announced that the first bull was entering the ring. The custom of having the actual fight preceded by display drills in which smartly uniformed soldiers marched in circles, squares, and other geometric forms lasted a long time. According to an anecdote related by Ricardo Palma in his *Tradiciónes*, this custom was challenged on the occasion of a bull fight given in honor of Bolívar, who was about to depart from Peru. After Bolívar was seated in the official box beside General La Mar the proceedings began as usual; the national anthem was played, the cornet sounded, and a platoon of soldiers entered, stood at arms, and saluted their captain. Then, in protest against the parade, the

Retablo—a Tableau of the Bible with miniature wood carvings*

cornet sounded taps and the soldiers at once dispersed and sought seats among the spectators. There was a general uproar from the people who felt cheated of their traditional spectacle, but Bolívar proclaimed that the captain was right and General

*In the foreground, left to right, are the Annunciation, the Garden of Eden, the Baptism of Christ in the Jordan. Second level depicts, left to right, the Three Kings, the Nativity, Presentation of Christ Jesus in the Temple. Top background shows the Trinity in Paradise and beneath an orchestra of angels. Made in Ayacucho, the whole retablo can be folded up into the form of a chest. 17th century. Pedro de Osma Collection.

Juanita Breña with bull in Acho

The vendors of fish

The strolling place of the mayors

The breadmaker

La Mar agreed with him. The name of the officer in charge on this occasion was Felipe Santiago Salaverry, a noted patriot in the Independence movement.

THREE LEYENDAS (OR STORIES) OF LIMA
La Perricholi and Viceroy Amat

The favorite secular legend of Lima concerns the love of the Viceroy Manuel de Amat y Junient for the actress La Perricholi. She was born Micaela Villegas of humble parentage, but her beauty, her wit, and her talent made her the toast of Lima and gave her the protection of its most exalted personage. She was the foremost actress in all Spanish America. It all happened some two hundred years ago, but is kept alive by existing mementos—the theatre in which she acted exclusively for the viceroy and his friends, and the Paseo de Aguas, a park inspired by Versailles, which her aging lover created for her delight (and perhaps also to compensate her for the slights she had received from Limeñan society in the once fashionable Alameda de los Descalzos). Through the graceful arches of her park one can still see the balcony from which her bright eyes looked out on the garden.

Across the Rimac River, near Cinco Esquinas in Old Lima, stands a charming eighteenth-century chateau called Quinta Presa, built on the property of Count Fernando Carrillo y Abornoz in 1776–77, which may have been designed by the viceroy himself and in which he entertained the actress. The rococo structure is now a museum, and in one of its elegantly furnished rooms one can gaze upon the bed of La Perricholi.

The estate of Quinta Presa covers an area of some 15,000 square meters, partly occupied by barracks; behind the well-designed residence, with its fine double stairway, is a garden containing a variety of fruit trees and other plants. There is a special fountain providing water for the main pool and comfortable seats around another fountain at the lower end of the garden. The viceroy built a bathing pool for La Perricholi and above it a high rustic pavilion from which, according to one story, he removed a few boards in order to secretly observe her bathing below. The pavilion is still there; at the time I saw it, it was slightly marred by soldiers' laundry airing on the stairs. A marble bust, presumed to be of her, was dug up behind Quinta Presa and was placed at the edge of a pool surrounded by flowers in the garden. (Only one small portrait of La Perricholi is known to exist in Quinta Presa.)

When the viceroy brought Micaela Villegas for brief visits, fancy dress balls were staged in the second-floor salon, which at the time had mirrors on the inner door of the salon. It was here, according to the story, that Micaela, while dancing with the

Small painting of La Perricholi in the ballroom of Quinta Presa

Don Manuel Amat y Junient painted by Cristóbal Aquilar in 1771

Bust of La Perricholi in the garden of Quinta Presa

viceroy, made gestures and faces behind his back much to the amusement of those present. The viceroy, catching her in this act, raised a scene at which he is supposed to have called her by a name which the Lima public translated into "Perricholi." The real statement seems to have been made of two words: *perra* (bitch) and *chola* (lower-class Indian).

Wealth came easily to La Perricholi and she distributed it with open hands. One story tells of her impulsively selling a gilded coach, a gift of the viceroy and a rarity in Lima, in order to bestow the proceeds upon a group of beggars who had aroused her sympathy. In another version she presents the coach to the cathedral (after first riding in it to the indignation of the titled aristocrats who considered a coach their sole privilege), so that priests could carry the Blessed Sacrament to the dying more speedily. Her compassion for the poor and scornful ridicule of the rich have been celebrated in verse and prose in Offenbach's opera, *La Périchole*, Prosper Merimée's

223

Rear view of Quinta Presa, a country house frequented by Viceroy Amat y Junient and La Perricholi

play, *Le Carrosse du Saint-Sacrement*, and Thornton Wilder's well-known novel, *The Bridge of San Luis Rey*.

From 1773 to 1775, Viceroy Amat and La Perricholi were separated because of a scandal; during that time she was forbidden to perform in public. When Don Manuel de Guiror became viceroy in 1776, Manuel de Amat retired to Spain. La Perricholi then resumed acting and had for a companion a Spaniard named Fermín Vicente de Echarri, whom she married privately a year after Amat died. She was then forty-seven years old and her son by Amat was twenty-six. After eleven years of married life, Fermín Vicente de Echarri died, and until her death on May 17, 1819, La Perricholi led a Christian life, devoting herself to charitable works.

Of the mansions which the viceroy gave her, only the last, Palacio de Retiro, remains. It is back of the Prado Cloister in Barrio Altos and is owned by the fathers of the Convent of Santo Domingo. Dr. Cesar has headed a movement to restore the

Paseo de Aguas (Fountain Promenade). Built by Viceroy Amat for La Perricholi

ancient ruined palace which was once the most elegant one in Lima. It is principally of the rococo style which was much used by Viceroy Amat.

The theatre La Perricholi made famous is now an unprepossessing structure at 225 Huamiles Street which houses a Catholic school, a carpenter's shop, and a bakery. Near the bakery, which was formerly a chapel, is a room which in the viceroy's time was richly furnished and frescoed in blue. The border of female busts for which it was noted has been painted over, uncovered, and finally obliterated. As I stood one Sunday in a gentle rain, unusual for Lima, photographing this building, a religious procession with an image and a bass drum moved down the street, and the bystanders looked amazed at my interest in this nondescript old building.

In San Isidro, Amat Avenue runs romantically into Perricholi Street.

Santa Rosa de Lima

The city of Lima has its own saint, the first in the New World, and one of the few of Spanish American origin, Santa Rosa. A favorite subject of artists and sculptors,

Trysting place of Viceroy Amat and La Perricholi at Quinta Presa. Her bathing pool was below.

La Perricholi's bed preserved at Quinta Presa

she is renowned for her austere life and virtuous deeds. Isabel Flores de Oliva was born April 30, 1586, of a Puerto Rican father and a Peruvian mother. Her father had his quarters on the grounds of a small hospital built for sailors, and here Isabel loved to work in the garden where flowers grew profusely—with the exception of roses, which had not yet been imported from Spain. One day, to her delighted surprise, she miraculously found a rose bush in her garden and cultivated it with loving care. This incident accounts for her name and for the fact that she is always represented wearing a crown of roses.★

Another story concerns the turning point in her life. One day she went to the Church of Santo Domingo to ask the priest to give her a palm which had been blessed, but he refused. Sorrowfully she knelt before the Madonna in the garden and said, "God does not wish me to receive a palm from mortal hands. You shall give me one that will never fade and make me happy forever." Then the Child in the arms of Mary said, "Rose of my heart, you shall be my bride," to which she replied "I shall be your slave. Me, a poor sinner, to be the bride of Christ, the Redeemer!"

★Other Saints of the New World are: San Pedro Claver of Cartagena and the mulatto, San Martín de Porras, who was born near Lima in December 1579. The latter was the son of Don Juan de Porras, Caballero de Alcántara, Governor of Panama, and Ana de Escarcena, a freed slave. He was made a friar at the age of twenty-four. Notice of his beatification arrived in Lima in 1835.

226

As a result of that mystical passage in the year 1606 Isabel became a nun of the Third Order of Dominicans, taking the name of Rosa. The rest of her short life was spent in prayer and penance (she practised the most severe austerities), in nursing the sick and tending her garden. It was the life of a religious mystic in love with God. She died in 1617 when she was thirty-one, crying, "I go to Thee, O Lord, to the eternal nuptial." Dressed in a white habit and black veil and holding a rosary, the body was placed in an open hall for everyone to see. Rich and poor alike mourned, "A saint has died," and prostrated themselves before her bier. The archbishop himself claimed the honor of taking charge of the remains.

When the funeral cortege moved to Santo Domingo the throngs were so dense that the viceroy had to call in halberdiers and archers to keep order. Mourners of all ranks crowded to touch the corpse with rosaries and other pious objects. The habit of the dead nun was snipped by frenzied women, who concealed scissors beneath their mantos, and had to be changed six times on the route. Streets and houses were decorated as for a festival or solemn procession; the balconies were hung with sumptuous tapestries and from them came showers of roses. At the door of the church the archbishop, his cross held high, received the body, but so great was the tumult the service had to be postponed until the following day. Then, at a Solemn Requiem Mass, attended by the highest dignitaries and members of the Royal Audiencia and the Holy Office of the Inquisition, the body of the future saint was taken to the Sala Capitular and there interred.

Today the Church of Santa Rosa de Lima, built on the site of her birthplace, is one of the most venerated of all South American sanctuaries. Visitors to it are shown the well into which she threw the key that fastened her disciplinary belt of barbed wire, the infirmary where she cared for the sick, and the nearby garden of Santo Domingo where she believed herself betrothed to the Christ Child.

The Pizarro Monument

The first and, I believe, the only monument to Francisco Pizarro in all Peru was erected in 1935 when the mayor of Lima included it in the elaborate preparations for the four-hundredth anniversary of the founding of the city. The monument, an equestrian statue, was obtained through the generosity of the widow of Charles Cary Rumsey, a North American sculptor, who had previously donated the original to Pizarro's native city of Trujillo in Spain.

With the arrival of the statue, the mayor's problems had begun. At first the president of the Republic barred it from the center of the Plaza de Armas on the grounds that it could provide shelter for a small group attempting to storm the palace. His

B. ROSA DE Sᵗᵃ MARIA

St. Rose of Lima in Dominican habit and crowned by roses, with the Christ Child in one arm and model of City of Callao in the other. From the Hacienda Mondragón near Potosí, Bolivia

Saint Rose of Lima with silver decoration. Collection of Dr. Lizardo Alzamora

Hermitage made by Saint Rose of Lima and her brother in the garden of her Sanctuario

objection to having it set up in the patio of the palace itself was even stronger. The archbishop didn't at all approve of having it on the steps of the cathedral, but finally gave provisional consent. Once it was there, the critics took over. There were those who thought it did not harmonize with either the palace or the cathedral; moreover —and this was more serious—it was irreverent for Pizarro and his steed to turn their backs on the chief ecclesiastical structure in the country. There were those who were convinced that the statue was not authentic—the horse resembled one of Dürer's, the helmet was Teutonic, and so on. At any rate, others declared, on this four-hundredth anniversary of his arrival Pizarro should be represented as founder, not as conqueror.

It required years for the Church to have the monument removed, but one day in 1952 it crossed the ancient plaza and was anchored in a plazuela between the government palace and the post office. The amazing part is that there is any statue of Pizarro at all in Lima—there is none of Cortés in Mexico—for the Spanish conquerors are not held in loving regard by the countries they once conquered.

View of the Plaza de Armas (main square), Cuzco, with the Cathedral flanked by Churches Jesús María and El Triunfo. La Compañía church is at right.

Chapter Seven

CUZCO, PERU
The City of the Clouds

THE ancient city of Cuzco, once the seat of the extraordinary empire of the Incas, lies in a fertile Peruvian valley, 11,300 feet above sea level, surrounded by the towering Andes. As we flew along the snowcapped mountains in 1957, breathing oxygen through tubes, we marveled that our pilot could find the place. Guided by the Inca fortress of Sacsahuaman he *did* find it, and like a condor our plane dipped down to a landing.

Several other places of interest besides Cuzco lie in this valley on the Urubamba River, known to the Incas as the Sacred Valley. Here are Pisac, the site of a famous ruin and also of a colorful Sunday market; the massive fortress of Ollantaytambo; Urubamba with its imposing church and *posada*, or government inn; and, above all, the matchless deserted city of the Incas—Machu Picchu—discovered and named by the North American explorer, Hiram Bingham, in 1911. Unknown to the Spaniards of the Conquest, this Inca city is now connected with Cuzco by an auto-carril which travels seventy miles in three hours to the base of the cliffs upon which it is built. From the government hostelry, reached by bus, there is an unsurpassed view of the celebrated ruins and of the Andes.

En route to Machu Picchu we saw Indians in tall white hats and red ponchos, herds of llamas, reed-constructed suspension bridges of Inca origin, threshing operations employing oxen, mules, and horses, and a gorge as deep as the Grand Canyon.

231

We also gazed upon solid white granite cliffs covered with air plants or Spanish moss; stone Indian huts with smoke curling through the thatched roofs; and gorgeous flowers—orchids, lilacs, begonias, and, in the valley, yellow Scottish broom. There are Inca terraces cut in the hillsides, bits of the Inca road, fields of wheat, corn and even tea. The whole valley is a region of breath-taking beauty.

Although the same claim is made for Quito, it is possible that to Cuzco belongs the distinction of being the oldest continuously inhabited city in the Americas. In comparing other ancient cities Lord Bryce makes the following comment: ★

> Cuzco belongs to that category of historic cities which have once been capitals of kingdoms and retain traces of their ancient glory, a class which includes Moscow and Krakau, Throndhjem and Upsala, Dublin, Bagdad, Toledo and Granada. Cuzco was the capital of an empire vaster than was ruled from any of these seats of power.

Doctor Arnold Toynbee states that there have been twenty-six fundamental cultures in the world's history, and the twenty-sixth he calls the Andean-Peruvian civilization with its center at Cuzco, under the Inca regime.

The Colonial city rose on the foundations of the Inca and exists at present chiefly in religious structures (Cuzco has more than its complement of churches) and in narrow stone streets designed rather for llamas than for wheels. The population of the city at the time of the Conquest was reported to be 200,000, a figure that is undoubtedly exaggerated but suggests a large and thriving metropolis. Decline set in under the oppressive rule of Spain, and the city did not regain its importance until recent times. By 1934, through forced work and disease, the population had been reduced to 30,000. By 1955 it was back to 80,000.† The terrible earthquakes of 1650 and 1950 caused widespread destruction and loss of life, but the significance of Cuzco to historians and archeologists—as well as to tourists—is now recognized, and its existing monuments and treasures are being carefully restored and preserved.

Anyone interested in examining the remains of once powerful civilizations will delight in Cuzco. The Spanish conquerors looted and destroyed as thoroughly as they could, erecting their own brick buildings on top of Inca walls and foundation stones. But although they superimposed the Spanish way of life and the Catholic religion upon the Indians, evidences remain of the older culture. So deeply was it imbedded that in spite of the instruction in religion and the training in arts and crafts

★James Bryce, *South America*, p. 95.

†In 1912 students of the University of Cuzco, under the rector, Dr. Albert Giesecke, took the census of the Province of Cuzco. The census showed a population of 28,000.

View of a stair-like street in Cuzco

Famous Cuesta de la Armagura (Painful Laborious Ascent) was important in the military history of the Incas.

given by dedicated friars, native traditions and customs, and even dress, persist after three hundred years.

The oldest and best-known written source for the history of the Incas is the celebrated *Royal Commentaries*, written by "Inca" Garcilaso de la Vega, the son of a Spanish aristocrat, Captain García Lasso de la Vega, Governor of Cuzco from 1553 to 1556, and an Inca princess, Isabel Chimbbu Ocllo, niece of Emperor Huayna Capac. Mixed marriages were inevitable in the early years of the Conquest when Spanish women had not yet come to the New World, and Garcilaso was an illustrious representative of the new mestizo race then emerging. He studied the classics at a school established for the sons of the conquistadors, but tales of the glorious past of the Incas related to him by his Inca uncle made a lasting impression. When he was

233

twenty he was sent to Spain to continue his education, and there distinguished him-self as an officer in the army of Philip II, as a writer, and later as a cleric in Córdoba. At the age of seventy, when he had been away from his native Peru for fifty years, he wrote his *Royal Commentaries*. The book was published in Lisbon in 1601 and brought out again in Madrid in 1723.

Part I of this book deals with the marvelous achievements of the Incas before the Conquest, Part II with the daring exploits of the Spaniards, particularly of individual leaders. Later historians have accused Garcilaso of an over-exuberant imagination, but his work is basic for an understanding of Peruvian history and makes absorbing reading today. The pro-Inca sentiment evoked by Part I was so strong that when a revolt against Spanish tyranny erupted in Peru in the latter part of the eighteenth century, the book had to be suppressed by royal decree.

Of all the Inca legends that Garcilaso heard from his uncle and treasured through the years, the one concerning the founding of Cuzco has the most appeal for me.

Our Father, the Sun, seeing the human race in such a primitive state, sent down from heaven a son and a daughter to instruct them in the knowledge of our Father, the Sun, that they might adore him and adopt him as their god; also to give them precepts and laws by which to live in houses and towns, to cultivate maize and other crops, to breed flocks and to use the fruits of the earth like rational beings instead of living like wild beasts. With these commands and inten-tions our Father, the Sun, placed his two children at Lake Titicaca, which is eighty leagues from here; and he said to them that they might go where they pleased but that at every place where they stopped to eat or sleep, they were to thrust a sceptre of gold into the ground, which was half a yard long and two fingers in thickness. He gave them this staff as a sign and token that in the place where, by one blow on the earth, it should sink down and disappear, there it was the desire of our Father, the Sun, that they should remain and establish their court. And uncle went on to say what the Father declared: "I take care to go around the earth each day, that I may see the necessities that exist in the world, and supply them as the sustainer and benefactor of the heathens." Having declared his will to his children our Father, the Sun, dismissed them. These children set out from Titicaca and at last came to a small resting place which is called Paccau-Tampu. From this place he and his wife and sister, our queen, advanced to the valley of Cuzco, which was then covered with forests. On the hill called Huanacouti the sceptre of gold buried itself in the ground with great ease and was never more seen.

Those first rulers set out in different directions to call people together and the first place they pressed their feet, the temple was built in memory of the Sun's act of benevolence per-formed for the world. The prince went northward and the princess went southward to tell the peoples the Sun had sent them to be rulers of the land, to bring them together into villages and to eat the food of men. The people, seeing them with their ears bored and wearing different dress, thought that they were the children of the Sun and obeyed them as kings.

234

Andean Choza (house) near Pisac, displaying signs for chica, whiskey and bread

Arch of Santa Clara, Cuzco (showing two Condors). The two churches in the background are Sta. Catalina and San Pedro.

So the people began to settle this imperial city and divided it into two parts: Hanan Cuzco above, settled by followers of the King, Manco Capac and Hurin Cuzco below settled by those gathered together by the Queen, Ccoya, Mama Occllo Huaco.

At the same time the city was being peopled, our Inca taught the Indians those occupations which appertain to a man, such as breaking up and cultivating the ground, sowing corn and seeds, which he pointed out as fit for food and useful. He also taught them to make ploughs and other necessary instruments, he showed them the way to make channels from brooks which flow through the valley of Cuzco, and even instructed them how to make the sandals which we now wear. On the other hand, the Queen employed the Indian women in such work as is suitable to them, such as to sew and weave cotton and wool, to make clothes for themselves, their husbands and children and to perform other household duties. In fine, our princes taught their first vassals of everything needful in life, and Inca making himself King and master of men, and the Ccoya being Queen and mistress of the women.

Other passages in the book explain some of the Inca customs. In one we learn that the Inca bestowed upon his noble followers the privilege of wearing fringed

235

Early Cuzco painting of a Corpus Christi procession before an imaginary cathedral, showing Spaniards and Incas. Alzamora Collection

Marriage of Inca princesses to nephews of St. Ignatius Loyola and of St. Francisco Borgia. The Incas have Spanish faces. By an unknown Cuzco artist

headdresses, of shaving their heads (with a stone knife) except for a finger-sized tuft on the crown, and of boring their ears for the insertion of large wisps of straw or wood to permit the wearing of heavy gold discs. This last practice results in the extension of the lobes and accounts for the name "Big Ears" given them by the Spaniards. Seventeenth-century paintings of a Corpus Christi procession still preserved in the Indian church of Santa Ana reveal these characteristic features.

The Inca ceremonial costume seen in the paintings has changed remarkably little. Women still wear the *pullo*, a shawl in which they carry all their burdens, including the babies; the *montera*, a wide-brimmed hat very much like the one worn by the men; and, for adornment, *tupas*, pins of copper in alloy with silver or gold. Their *uncuna*, or bag, is a woven article used to hold small objects of value and the coca leaves they love to chew. The men's bag is called a *chuspa*. Spanish modifications appear in the woven skirts and in the blouses trimmed with imported ribbons. Men wear trousers but still make use of the *lliclla*, the elegantly woven poncho of Inca origin, for carrying bundles and as an overcoat. In the Andean highlands, trousers with odd openings and pockets in the rear, and long socks, sometimes three pairs at a time, afford protection against the cold. *Llanques*, shoes made from fox skins, are also still worn. One can understand how Indians, dressed in this homespun fashion, their only weapons spears and slingshots made of llama or alpaca wool, could be easily overcome by a small force of mounted Spaniards in armor shooting guns that spat fire.

Before the Conquest thousands of Indians were required to serve the temples and many of them resided on the grounds. The high priests were drawn from the Inca nobility, as were the priestesses, or Virgins of the Sun, who tended the sacred fire and took vows of chastity. Prescott does not use the term Chosen Women, but it was from this larger group, who were also of high birth, that the Lord Inca selected his secondary wives and concubines and bestowed others upon his nobles and favorite captains. Both groups of women were trained from childhood to serve the Incas—to weave robes and hangings of the finest vicuña wool for the temples and palaces and to prepare *chicha*, the popular drink. They have been compared with vestal virgins and with nuns, but in most ways the comparison does not seem an apt one.

The most revered spot in the Inca empire, Coricancha, the fabled Temple of the Sun, was the richest edifice to be despoiled by the conquerors. Its marvelous stone walls proved so difficult to raze that they became the foundation for one of the first Christian churches, Santo Domingo. Coricancha—in Quechuan language the

"Garden of Gold"—is glowingly described by Prescott with details gleaned from Garcilaso and other early chroniclers. In his account the main temple had a number of smaller "chapels" adjoining it which were dedicated to the Moon, the Sister-Wife of the Sun; the Host of Stars; the Avenging Spirits of Thunder and Lightning; and the Rainbow. All were fashioned of the finest masonry and lavishly adorned with gold and silver. The interior was literally a "gold mine." The east wall was covered by the image of the Sun god, a human countenance from which emanated rays of light, all engraved on a massive gold plate thickly studded with emeralds and other precious stones. Everything possible was made of gold—the immense vases, censers, ewers, and agricultural implements, even the pipes that carried the water to the gold fountains in the gardens.

The gardens themselves were filled with gold and silver votive offerings to the Sun: exquisitely fashioned replicas of animals, plants, and vegetables, in particular the Indian corn, or maize; a dazzling variety of flowers and birds and creeping things; and a great deal more. Prescott himself wonders if the chroniclers might not have exaggerated and later historians have been frankly skeptical, but the archeologists have unearthed a surprising amount of evidence.

The goal of the conquerors was to find gold, and in Cuzco they found it beyond their wildest imaginings. They stripped whole sheets of the precious metal from the walls of the temples. But whenever possible, the natives hid their treasure from the enemy. The fabulous gold chain made for Inca Huayna Capac, father of Atahualpa, which was reputed to be long enough to stretch around the great square of Cuzco, was thrown into Lake Urcos and never recovered. ★

The Spanish conquerors, who had endured and barely survived incredible hardships before reaching Cuzco, were now richly rewarded. In the division of spoils, which included sections of the city with portions of its treasures, the major share went naturally to the leaders, beginning with the Pizarro brothers. Other conquistadors received what was considered their just allotment, and the remainder was divided among the troops. Except for a few objects of unusual interest, all the gold and silver was melted down and recast in bars to permit equal distribution. One fifth, called the "royal share," was reserved for the Crown.

★Huayna Capac had the great chain made for the festivities when his son, Huascar, should have his lock cut, be weaned and given a name. The chain, described by Garcilaso's uncle, was of gold dancers linked together by the ears and was estimated to be 700 feet long—the length and breadth of the market place. It took two years to make, and the links were of the breadth of a wrist.

Silver altar of the Cathedral   *Christ of the Earthquakes*

Not all who shared in the booty enjoyed it for long. Pedro del Barco, one of the first to enter the Imperial City, was given half of the House of Chosen Women, but the man to whom he sold it discovered under the pavement a cache of gold valued at 72,000 ducats. Another leader, Antonio Altamirano, was allotted part of the palace of Inca Huayna Capac and found in the patio a large golden jar for brewing chicha, as well as other treasures valued at 80,000 ducats. However, both del Barco and Altamirano met their deaths because they chose the wrong factions in the Spanish civil wars over the control of Cuzco.

To Mansio Serra de Leguisamo fell the golden disc of the sun wrested from Coricancha. Mansio, a notorious gambler, lost the precious emblem in one night of play, from which stroke of misfortune came the saying, "He played away the sun before dawn." He was more fortunate in his subsequent career, for he was elected

239

Façade of La Compañía

Retable of Our Lady of the Consolation, 1760–1780, La Compañía

alcalde of the city, an office he held for a number of years. He married an Inca princess, Doña Beatriz Nusta, and their son was a schoolmate of Garcilaso, the historian. His importance in history rests chiefly upon his deathbed confession, dated 1589 and addressed to Philip II, which concluded with these words: "I pray to God that He will pardon me, for I am the last to die of all the conquerors and discoverers; it is well known that there are none surviving except I alone, and now what can I do to relieve my conscience?" He then testified to the excellence of the Inca government and to the good disposition of the Incas themselves and confessed to all the cruelty and oppression in which he had participated.

Inca uprisings against oppression were as inevitable as they were futile. The most serious and protracted revolt broke out in 1536 when Manco II, acknowledged by Pizarro as the rightful Inca but divested of all power, attempted to recapture his capital city of Cuzco. Although his troops numbered close to 200,000 and those of the Spaniards were under 200, the latter were far better trained and equipped and were led by the redoubtable brothers, Hernando, Juan, and Gonzalo Pizarro. (Fran-

Temple of La Merced of typical Mestizo Cuzco style *Beautiful cloister of the Convent of La Merced*

cisco was then in Lima, his new capital.) During a three-month siege the city was burned more than once, and deeds of daring and valor were performed by both sides. The Spaniards were saved, according to legend, by the apparition of a beautiful Madonna which threw the Indians into disorder and caused them to withdraw to an almost inaccessible mountain stronghold called Vilcabamba.★ There, with his three sons, nobles, priests, and Chosen Women, and with selected troops nearby, Manco II established a Neo-Inca state which was to endure almost forty years.

From this stronghold and from Vitcos, a military outpost, Manco and, later, his sons were able to harass the Spaniards by continuous raids. While under the rule of Túpac Amaru, the last of the royal Incas, Vilcabamba was at last penetrated by a Spanish army dispatched by Viceroy Francisco de Toledo (1569–81); the Inca was brought to Cuzco in chains with his principal wives and chiefs and there convicted of treason. His execution was considered noteworthy even in those days of refined

★This miracle is the subject of a famous picture to be seen in El Triunfo Church built on the spot where the conquistadors were besieged. The picture shows them being saved by the apparition of Our Lady.

241

cruelty. It also had its moments of high drama, for just before the end an Augustinian bishop and five friars fell on their knees before the viceroy pleading for mercy and asserting that since Túpac Amaru was a king in his own right he could only be tried by his peer, the King of Spain. Toledo, however, was adamant and the blow fell. At midnight of that day the square was still filled with kneeling Indians.

Almost two hundred years later the name Túpac Amaru II was assumed by José Gabriel Condorcanqui, the last man to claim Inca blood. In 1781 he led the Indians in a very bloody revolt which was finally suppressed two years later. In the same plaza he was torn to pieces by four horses. That was the last uprising, "the most important movement for emancipation by the Indians—and Túpac Amaru II is the greatest figure in Indian-American history." ★

Bitter quarrels among the conquerors themselves and particularly between Francisco Pizarro and Diego de Almagro, two of the three original partners, erupted during the period of conquest. Jealousy over rank and division of spoils, especially the possession of Cuzco, resulted in the execution of Almagro in 1538 by the order of Hernando Pizarro. Almagro's son, known as "the Lad," avenged his father's death by conspiring in the assassination of Francisco Pizarro, now marquis and governor, in his palace in Lima in 1541.

Gonzalo, when the youngest and last of the Pizarro brothers in Peru, Juan Pizarro, was killed at the siege of Cuzco and his brother Hernando was taken to Spain as a prisoner, returned from his desperate but fruitless quest for Inca treasure (recounted in the Quito chapter) to find he must fight for his rights. He did so by heading the faction which defied the "New Laws," conniving in the death of the viceroy who had attempted to enforce them, and making himself master of Peru. His forces were decisively defeated in a major battle on the plains near Cuzco in 1547, and he was beheaded in the Plaza Mayor, together with his crafty, cruel lieutenant, Francisco Carvajal. With his death the civil wars in Peru came to an end.

What were the visible results of these events of Cuzco's early history? All that remains is the old plaza, no longer surrounded by a gold chain but by arcaded buildings and by four fine churches—the cathedral, with El Triunfo and Jesús y María on either side, and La Compañía at an angle. In the center of the plaza is now a peaceful nineteenth-century fountain surmounted by the figure of an American Indian which was supposed to have been sent to Mexico but instead reached Cuzco. When we had arrived in the city which the explorer Hiram Bingham called "one of the most interesting places in the world," an automobile took us over cobbled streets to our

★Dr. Luis Valcarcel.

242

Cloister wall and ceiling of La Merced. Painted allegory by Basilio Pacheco

hotel; there, from a large window at the end of a corridor, we looked out over this historic plaza which had been the scene of so many religious processions, fiestas and beheadings. This had been the center of a great rectangle, of which Miriam Kropp writes as follows:

Only members of the royal families and those connected with the religious cult of the Inca lived in the ceremonial district, about a mile long and a quarter of a mile wide. Within this district were the palaces of the Incas, schools for the youths of the royal blood, splendid plazas and religious edifices. Today's Plaza de Armas is but a part of the great rectangle, Haucaypata, which was the center of this district. With each reign, the aspect of the capitol was altered, as it was the custom for each successive Inca to choose a new site for his imperial palace. Central Cuzco was entirely redrawn and rebuilt by the ninth emperor, Pachacuti, in the fifteenth century.

That Cuzco now is a principal center of Hispanic architecture in Latin America is due chiefly to Don Manuel de Mollinedo, the son of a noble and wealthy family in

243

Calle San Agustín, with remains of an Inca palace
LEFT: *Renowned Monstrance of La Merced, with over a thousand pearls, diamonds and other jewels*

244

Madrid, who became Bishop of Cuzco in 1673. *During his episcopate of twenty-six years, and under his influence, the city was largely restored and rebuilt after the disastrous earthquake of 1650. He himself endowed more than fifty new churches in the diocese and was the donor of numerous retables and paintings which represent the great period of the Cuzco school of art. The portrait of this Lorenzo de Medici of Peru appears in the painting, "Madonna of Almudena," which is near his tomb in the cathedral, and in a number of other churches.

It is not possible in this chapter to give more than a few of the outstanding features of the principal old churches of Cuzco.† First there is the cathedral, which such a recognized authority on architecture as Dr. Harold E. Wethey considers the finest church in the Western Hemisphere.§ Others may disagree, holding that La Compañía has more style and certainly finer towers (those of the cathedral are widely separated as a protection against earthquakes), but for "magnificent proportions, austere simplicity, and majesty" Dr. Wethey considers the cathedral unsurpassed. "The whole mass of the church," he continues, "is rectangular and powerful, and the virile ruggedness of the brown Andean stone, called andesite, adds in no small measure to the solemnity and grandeur of the exterior." This stone, characteristic of Cuzco churches, came from the Inca fortress of Sacsahuaman.

It has been established that the first church in which the first bishop of Cuzco said Mass was a chapel built on a site now occupied by the small church of El Triunfo next to the cathedral. The chapel continued to function as a cathedral until March 11, 1560, when the first stone of the cathedral was laid on the new site—the ruins of the palace of Viracocha Inca, which had originally been allotted to one of the conquerors, but sold by him to the Church. Later, in 1723, on the right side of the big new cathedral a chapel called El Jesús y María, or Chapel of the Holy Family was built. Plans for the building were drawn up and altered by a number of architects over a long period, but the ones finally adopted are believed to be those of Becerra.

Francisco Becerra, the greatest architect Spain sent to her colonies, was born about the middle of the sixteenth century near Trujillo, Spain. His father was an architect there, and his grandfather, Hernán Gonzáles, was the famous chief architect of Toledo

---

*Information about the bishop was obtained from the testament of his nephew recently discovered by Dr. José García of Cuzco.

†Our knowledge of the builders comes mainly from J. M. Covarrubias Pozo, Padre Vargas Ugarte and José García in Cuzco, and from Emilio Harth-Terre of Lima.

§See Bibliography.

Cathedral. In the New World, Becerra worked in Mexico, Quito, and Lima and, in 1582, was sent by the viceroy to take charge of the plans at Cuzco. Almost one hundred years after the laying of the cornerstone, the structure was finally completed under Bishop Ocon. It typifies the last phase of the Spanish Renaissance and reveals the sober influence of Juan de Herrera, distinguished architect of El Escorial outside Madrid.

That the cathedral has been almost alone among Cuzco churches in sustaining earthquake shocks with relatively minor damage must be due to the rugged quality of both exterior and interior noted by Dr. Wethey. The magnificent façade is Baroque; the portal is said to have set the standard for the entire school of Cuzco during the second half of the seventeenth century. Cuzco's cathedral, like Lima's, which it closely resembles, has a vaulted Gothic ceiling of brick. Its choir, in the center of the church, contains a beautifully carved bishop's throne and an almost complete set of choir stalls, the work of Diego Arías de la Cerda. These stalls Dr. Martín Soria, also an authority in the field, calls "Baroque carving at its best."

The city is famous for its bells and bell towers. The north tower of the cathedral contains its most celebrated bell, María Angola, named for the noble lady who tossed twenty-five pounds of gold into a crucible at the Monastery of San Francisco, where the bell was being cast for the second time. Other devout women followed her example, and the combined gold, silver, and bronze produces a resonant tone which can be heard for miles. "It seems on ringing," writes the historian Buschiazzo, "to take up the very voice of Cuzco surging up from the immeasurable past." * The clock in the north tower is reached by a stairway hewn in part from a monolith once used as a throne by the Incas. On the crown of the tower are balls and pyramids, survivals of the late Renaissance, an ornamentation similar to that on fortified castles of the same period in southern France.

Among the priceless treasures of the cathedral are a monstrance incrusted with jewels, the silver frontal of the high altar, and the famous statue of Christ of the Earthquakes. This statue, medieval in spirit, has been used in religious processions since 1650. In addition to the previously mentioned "Madonna of Almudena," painted by the Indian Basilio de San Cruz, there is a remarkable series of the twelve months, painted by Diego Ttito Quispe, a major artist of the Cuzco school.

The next finest church in Cuzco is La Compañía, now on the Plaza Mayor west of the cathedral. The Jesuits' first church, which was erected over the ruins of

*Mario J. Buschiazzo, *Estudios de Arquitectura Colonial*, Editorial Kraft LTDA, Buenos Aires, 1944.

Tower of Santo Domingo Church

Renaissance apse built over Inca stone work on site of the Temple of the Sun (Cori–Cancha)

Inti Raymi celebration given annually on June 24th at the Fortress of Sacsahuaman

Amarucancha, the palace of Inca Huayna Capac originally assigned to Hernando Pizarro, was destroyed in the 1650 earthquake. Two years later, rebuilding on the new site advanced so ambitiously that the canons of the cathedral, fearing that the Jesuit church would surpass their own in both size and beauty, instituted suit against the Order. The Jesuits, however, by working rapidly and reducing the size of their structure by one aisle and one nave, succeeded in finishing the church before the courts could hand down a decision.

What La Compañía lost in size by this curtailed construction it gained in the height of its towers and in the magnificence of its façade. The façade is in high Baroque retable style in three tiers with arches and decorated columns. On either side of the main portal are carved stone crosses. The same andesite was used as for the cathedral. The towers with their elliptical openings and unusual dome, the first of its kind, give added distinction to the exterior. Its cloister, with the Tuscan Doric columns, reminiscent of La Merced at Quito, now houses part of the University of Cuzco. The interior of the church is equally majestic. The elaborate and refulgent Baroque carving of the high altar is the finest in Cuzco, if not in all Colonial Peru, an area which included Ecuador, Bolivia, and Chile, in addition to the whole of present-day Peru. This altar, as well as the all-gilt pulpit, has been attributed to the leading sculptor-architect of the second half of the seventeenth century, Diego Martínez de Oviedo. The statues of Saint Jerome and Saint Francis, which decorate the Altar of the Immaculate Conception, mark a high point in Colonial sculpture. In the sacristy of the church is a set of four pictures illustrating the life of Mary Magdalene, believed to be by Basilio de San Cruz.

On opposite sides of the entrance to La Compañía are two large paintings which have great documentary value, since they exhibit both Spanish and Inca fashions. On the right side is depicted the wedding of Don Martín de Loyola, nephew of the founder of the Jesuit order, and Doña Beatriz Nusta, princess of Peru, and daughter of Inca Sayri Tupa. The daughter of this marriage, Doña Lorenza Nusta de Loyola, went to Spain and married Don Juan Loyola de Borja, thus linking the two Spanish houses with the Inca emperors. With considerable artistic license this second wedding, including in the background the Incas Sayri Tupa and Tupu Amaru, is shown on the left of the picture. Across the entrance a similar painting depicts the weddings of two other Spanish grandees with Inca princesses, the later descendants of whom are the Dukes of Granada and the Counts Xavier.

La Merced in the Plaza de Cusipata was begun in 1536 on the basis of donations from Francisco Pizarro, Diego Almagro, Inca Cayo Tupa, and many others. It is noted for having the finest tower in the city, the loveliest cloister, and an invaluable monstrance. This latter epitomizes the wealth which poured into the city from the surrounding mines—mercury from Huancayo, silver from Potosí, gold from Cerro de Pasco. Created in 1720 by Juan Olmos, assisted by an Indian, it weighs twenty pounds and contains 1318 diamonds, 615 pearls, emeralds, and rubies. A single Baroque pearl forms the body of a mermaid, a fascinating feature.

The cloister of La Merced, completed in 1670, may well be the finest in Latin America. Its open proportions and the golden color of its stone led Dr. George Kubler to call it "the happiest enclosure of the city." The carving on the Plateresque two-story columns is in the best mestizo style. Although similar carving can be seen on the tower and on the retables in both La Merced and La Compañía, it originated and flourished in the churches of Arequipa, Pomata, and Juli, where the Indians were under less restraint and could follow their own ideas in applying the animals and flowers of the countryside. The art collection contains notable paintings by Chacón and a "Holy Family" by Rubens.

The church and monastery of Santo Domingo were begun in 1534 under the same Fray Vicente de Valverde who became the first bishop of Cuzco. The church was built over the Temple of the Sun, the monastery over the walls of the smaller temples of the Moon and Stars. Originally allotted to Juan Pizarro, this hallowed site was presented by him to the Dominicans. The most notable part of the church's Baroque exterior is the massive curving wall of Incaic construction which now supports the apse behind the high altar, but which once marked the location of the throne of the Sun. *

Munificent donations in the form of money, land, art objects, and jewels poured into Santo Domingo, as into other churches, from the time of its establishment to the close of the seventeenth century. It is interesting to learn the names of the earliest benefactors and their gifts as set down in the original records. One donor was Doña Anselma Huaco-Ocllo, widow and niece of Tupan Inca Yapanqui, who, in 1579, gave in perpetuity all of the lands, houses, and woods of seven localities to the church; another was that well-known Maecenas of Peru, Bishop Mollinedo, who gave Santo Domingo eight hundred pesos for the crown of the Virgin del Rosario y el Niño and the wood for the retable of the high altar.

The church and monastery of San Francisco also date back to the first year of the occupation of Cuzco; they were begun at that time by Padre Pedro Portuguez and other Franciscans who had accompanied the conquistadors. On the present site (Plaza de San Francisco) the first church, completed in 1574, was of stone with three naves and a brick roof. Of this building only the principal cloister remains. Although severely damaged in the 1950 earthquake, it has been restored along the lines and in the spirit of the original and is probably the oldest structure surviving in Cuzco— one of the few remaining examples of sixteenth-century architecture in all Peru. The style is Plateresque, simple but very fine, with traces of Moorish influence. The beautiful choir stalls carved by Padre Luis Montes can be reached only through the principal cloister and so are concealed from female eyes.

Destructive as have been the earthquakes, the church suffered even greater loss

---

*The destruction caused by earthquakes has had one redeeming feature: the disclosure of further sections of pre-Columbian stonework. So extensive was the damage to the church in 1950 that adequate reconstruction will require many years and considerable money.

Coro de San Francisco

about 1900 when its friars sold all their priceless Colonial altars, retables, paintings and marquetry furniture in order to raise money to redecorate in the prevailing, showy Italian Gothic style. They were caught up, according to Dr. Wethey, in "a wave of Neoclassic modernization," which affected nearly all the churches in the area, with the deplorable result that almost nothing is left of sixteenth-century work and very little of seventeenth.

San Francisco contains the earliest dated pulpit in Peru, perhaps in Latin America. Made by Padre Gómez in 1678, it is unique in its use of inlay with carey wood, ebony, and ivory. There are also beautiful pulpits in the cathedral and in La Compañía —the period in Cuzco has been called "the golden age of pulpits"—but the most celebrated is in San Blas, a rather primitive adobe church in northeast Cuzco. Its pulpit, carved by an unknown artist between 1680 and 1695, marks the climax of the exuberant Cuzco style, and is widely considered one of the finest works of art produced in Latin America. In the words of Dr. Wethey: "The pulpit of San Blas deserves its wide renown . . . as a major manifestation of the high Baroque at its

Beautiful entrance of the House of the Four Busts, showing Inca wall. Above the coat of arms, a Moorish arch has been superimposed.

Famous pulpit of San Blas Church

fantastic best." Cossia del Pomar calls it a "Bacchanalian tempest of form." Here is Dr. Soria's description:

> The saints in their niches are flanked by small twisted columns supporting hemispherical domes of concentric skirt-like circles, topped by spiral scrolls. The wall niche, flanked by fern-like arabesque flaps, leads to a tremendous conical canopy of many skirts and above it statues of saints and angels in two rows and finally a dominating image of St. Paul. The impression is of teeming, crawling life and dynamic change of form.

On the picturesque Plaza de Nazarenas is the House of the Serpents. It is now the convent of the Nazarenas, but it was started in 1598 with eighty students as a school for the children of Inca nobles. For two and a half centuries it existed as a general seminary until Bolívar ordered it removed from clerical jurisdiction and transferred to its present site, the cloister of La Compañía, where it is now part of Cuzco University. Next to the convent, Bishop Mollinedo started to build the Chapel of San Antonio Abad (Saint Anthony the Abbot). It was finished in 1699 and carries the shields of Spain and of Bishop Mollinedo over the doorway.

The simple little plebeian church of Santa Ana was founded in 1560 as a parish church for the Indians and was located at the foot of the hill of Piccho. In front was a narrow entrance street through which the Spaniards entered and took possession of the city. In the middle of the little plaza stands a wooden cross on which were carved the names of the conquistadors. Santa Ana contains Cuzco's most precious pictures, those of the Corpus Christi processions.

Cuzco has three principal convents: Santa Clara, under the Franciscan Order; Santa Catalina, under the Dominican; and Santa Teresa of the Order of the Carmelites. The oldest is Santa Clara, founded in 1549, mainly for the care of mestizo orphans and descendants of the Incas. The buildings on its present site, the Alameda de Santa Clara, were completed by 1622. Since Santa Clara, like the cathedral, withstood the shock of the 1950 earthquake, its church is the oldest in the city and an important example of Colonial architecture. Its attractive features include a dignified freestanding tower, probably of the late seventeenth century, four lovely cloisters, and a striking Plateresque portal fitted into an Inca stone wall. In the interior one's eyes are dazzled by light reflected from hundreds of small mirrors adorning the five modern retables built over original altars. The nearby arch of Santa Clara, bearing two condors aloft, commemorates the Confederation of Bolivia, 1836–38.

Santa Catalina was founded in 1600 through the generous bequest of one Doña Isabel de Padilla. The first structure, raised over the foundations of the House of Chosen Women, was destroyed in 1650, and the present one was built soon afterward with the help of Bishop Mollinedo. The church has two splendid retables, both of rich Churrigueresque style, which were restored in 1922 under the direction of Cossio de Pomar. Its fine choir, like that of Santa Clara, is unfortunately screened from view, but it possesses gilded Moorish balconies from which Creole ladies used to hear Mass, and a series of early paintings of the life of its patron saint. The convent of Santa Teresa, which was not established until 1673, is noted for its Spanish wall tiles, a series of paintings of the life of Teresa of Ávila, who reformed the Order, and a sacristy ceiling which rivals any in Cuzco.

Each year in Cuzco there are three outstanding events: the two great religious processions of Christ of the Earthquakes and of Corpus Christi, and the celebrated Indian pageant known as Inti Raymi, or the Harnessing of the Sun.

253

18th-century Cuzco painting entitled "Christ on the Way to Calvary." Prado Museum, Lima

Meeting of the Conquistadors with King Atahualpa at Cajamarca. It shows the Archangel at left and Santiago at right and Bishop Valverde with the Cross. Collection of Alayzo Paz Soldan

First in order comes the procession of Christ of the Earthquakes, which takes place the Monday before Easter; that is, on the first day of Holy Week. The powerful figure of the crucified Christ, which is deeply venerated by the Indians, is the central figure in the procession. It was presented to the city by Charles V and has been regarded with increased fear and fervor ever since the 1650 earthquake. About two o'clock in the afternoon it is placed on its silver *anda* before the cathedral and there blessed before being borne in solemn procession on a route covering ten blocks, with scheduled stops at churches and convents. On its return at dusk the cathedral is dark, the doors closed, and the plaza crowded with kneeling figures murmuring prayers. As the clock strikes seven the doors are opened, lights are turned on, and the Image is carried to its place within. Not until the doors are again closed and the lights extinguished does the crowd disperse, happy in the belief that since the statue had

254

returned safely there would be no earthquakes during the coming year. It is an ancient custom, faithfully observed. Only the illumination belongs to our day.

The festival of Corpus Christi, first observed in Flanders in the twelfth century, was instituted in Cuzco by the viceroy, Francisco de Toledo, some four hundred years later. Since the first Thursday after Trinity Sunday, the date of the Corpus Christi procession, is close to June 24, the established date for the Indian festival of Inti Raymi, the viceroy attempted to harmonize the two, thus bringing the Indians closer to the practice of Christianity. Each festival, Christian and pagan, holds first place in the hearts of believers.

For the Corpus Christi procession the statue of La Linda, the beautiful patron saint of the cathedral, is carried out on her silver litter, wearing a jeweled crown and accompanied by the silver tabernacle from the altar. Other statues from the neighboring churches join her during "visiting week," the time of Corpus Christi: Santiago (Saint James) from his church in north Cuzco; El Belén (Our Lady of Bethlehem) from the southwest, sparkling with the gems bestowed upon her as the favorite patroness of the city; San Sebastian from his church in the east; La Candelaria, Virgen Purificada from San Pedro; Santa Barbara from Poroy in the west; San Cristóbal (Saint Christopher) and San Blas (Saint Blaise) from the churches named for them and San Antonio from his seminary. Our Lady of Bethlehem stays nine days at the Convent of Santa Clara for a novena before joining the others. Saint Jerome makes his first stop at El Belén, and when he arrives his handsome scarlet robes are protected by a linen duster. Each year when he reaches the plaza of San Sebastian there is a struggle for precedence between the two saints, Jerome and Sebastian. After the procession the statues of the principal saints are placed between the piers of the cathedral. In 1957 we saw these principal figures so placed with the *andas* nearby, and it was a beautiful sight.

The date of Corpus Christi depends upon that of Easter, but the Indian festival of Inti Raymi, held since the time of the Incas at the ruined but still formidable fortress of Sacsahuaman, always falls on the twenty-fourth of June. (This date corresponds with December 24, the winter solstice in northern latitudes, where primitive people also feared that the sun was leaving them forever and must be brought back by prayer and sacrifice.) The event starts early in the day in Cuzco. At seven o'clock the conch blowers in gay native dress march through the streets, summoning all to the festival. A nine-thirty Mass is celebrated in the cathedral, followed by a sermon by the archbishop, who thus bestows the blessing of the Church upon the occasion. Later, in front of the atrium, he reviews the folk dancers as they file past him in colorful native costumes. Particularly picturesque is a group which circles with tall, brightly tipped poles. At half-past one, performers and spectators, as many as 50,000 people, converge upon the esplanade of the Inca fortress to watch the dancers, known as folklore groups, go through the age-old rhythmic patterns of their race. Traditional music is furnished by *pututeros* (conch blowers), flutists, drummers, and other players, these days broadcast through loud speakers.

At a fixed moment, down the path on the opposite rock-strewn hill, through the throng of awed spectators, long lines of Indians come in brilliant Inca attire to play their part in the pageant of the Harnessing of the Sun. This is the main theme, the focal point of the festival: *Inti*, the Sun, has gone too far north and must be brought back, "harnessed," by the Inca. As part of the ceremony a fine herd of llamas is driven across the level field, one of which is selected and decorated for the ritual sacrifice. In the days of the Incas the llama was slain, its entrails ceremoniously removed, and its blood drunk from golden bowls. Today most of the rites are simulated, and chicha, the native drink, is substituted for blood. The drama of appeasement is brought to a close when the Indian impersonating the emperor addresses the Sun in sonorous Quechuan, imploring him to return and bring food, children, and prosperity to the land.

From our seats in a grandstand, erected over ancient monoliths, we looked across the immense mountain-ringed parade ground to the place where richly garbed "Inca nobles" were grouped around a sacred platform on which, in ceremonial robes, stood the "Lord Inca" himself. We were told—and found it easy to believe—that in this majestic setting we were gazing upon the finest folk festival in South America. Both participants and spectators were drawn to it from towns and villages miles away—even from countries overseas. In the days before the Conquest, the Inti Raymi festivals were held simultaneously in different parts of the Empire, the one at the capital city of Cuzco being the most important. In every Temple of the Sun, thanks were offered for the preceding harvest, and an augury, divined from the blood and entrails of the slain llama, was prepared by the priests for the year to come. If the omens were favorable, as they invariably were, the feasting and dancing might continue for days.

We returned to the city by way of Giesecke Road, so named because an American, Dr. Albert A. Giesecke, was responsible for its construction during his terms of office as Mayor of Cuzco.

The next points of interest on a visitor's agenda are the various houses which

Virgen de Belén (Bethlehem)—prize example of the Cuzco School of Painting in the Viceregal Museum

Our Lady of Victory of Málaga, 16th-century Cuzco School

have historic or architectural significance. The colonial houses of Cuzco are built almost entirely upon Inca foundations with Inca cut stones, the native masonry being utilized in places up to a height of seven or more feet. Above that point the material is adobe or mortared brick, and the architecture is Spanish of the sixteenth to eighteenth centuries. In the older parts of the city the typical street is a narrow passageway between Inca stone walls, punctuated by doorways and barred windows, sometimes by latticed balconies beneath heavy overhanging tile roofs. Within the houses there are arcaded courtyards and stately salons, but seen from the street the characteristic feature is the ornamented doorway, usually displaying an armorial shield on its lintel.

Those interested in tracing old Cuzco will find the houses noted here well worth a visit, if only for a few features.

257

Casa del Almirante is widely considered the finest colonial mansion in Cuzco. Its name, House of the Admiral, stems from a seventeenth-century admiral of the Spanish nobility; but the house was rebuilt after 1650 by the Count of Laguna, whose arms are over the door. The doorway itself, framed in ornamental rosettes and intricately carved, is as handsome as any in the city and may antedate the great earthquake. The style is Plateresque, as it was transferred to the Indies, and recalls other sixteenth-century examples. Leading from the regal arched patio are salons with fine Mudéjar ceilings. A graceful stairway rises to the second floor. The damage this edifice suffered in 1950 has been repaired, and it is now used for classrooms by the University of Cuzco.

Casa de los Marqueses de Buenavista has been rebuilt and restored as the archepiscopal palace. The platform, or enormous terrace, on which it rests was occupied in the fifteenth century by the palace of Inca Roca, and the Inca masonry which is now visible on three sides is most impressive—indeed, second only to Sacsahuaman, according to George Kubler, who directed the reconstruction after the 1950 disaster. Embedded in this wall is the celebrated twelve-angled stone, long regarded as a marvel of joinery. The most striking feature of the house, though, is a corner window with a balcony and heavy overhanging eaves.

Casa de Siete Culebras was originally bestowed upon Mansio Serra de Leguisamo, the conquistador who gambled away the golden disc of the Sun, but is now the convent and chapel of the Nazarenas. The building, a happy blend of Inca and Spanish construction, has an imposing trapezoidal doorway, over which is an armorial shield supported by two sirens. The seven serpents which gave their name to both house and street are carved on the side wall. On the other side of the narrow street is the chapel of San Antonio Abad.

Casa de los Quatro Bustos derives its name from the busts of four unidentified men in sixteenth-century dress which adorn the lintel of its handsome doorway. The rosettes in the pilasters of the door are of the same period and design as those on the House of the Admiral. The carving reveals Indian influence in the treatment of flowers and masks and merits close inspection. Over the lintel are the quartered arms of several noble families, including the Bazán. Of special interest is the patio with its double arches on the upper story. Since 1922 the house has served travelers as an inn.

The reputed birthplace of Garcilaso de la Vega, the Peruvian chronicler, is of interest for its association rather than for intrinsic merit. Records indicate that the elder Garcilaso owned a house on this site, and a plaque bears the legend: "Inca

258

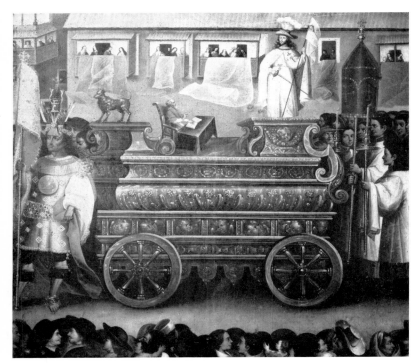

Processional Figure of Santiago, one of a famous series of paintings in the Church of Santa Ana. At left is the Inca Sairi Ttupacc.

Our Lady The Queen of Angels. Late 16th century

Cuzco School of Painting depicting earthquake from the Church of El Triunfo

Virgen de la Natividad by Juan Tomás, Cuzco, 1680, in Almudena Church

The Virgin of the Distaff. 16th-century Cuzco School

Garcilaso de la Vega. Born here 1539. Died in Córdoba 1616." A simple doorway studded with heavy iron nails has two armorial shields on the lintel. The whole building was badly shaken in 1950 and has not been restored. To visit it you must receive permission of Señor Lambarry, who has a shop next door.

Still other homes will reward the visitor in search of Colonial Cuzco. Casa de los Pumas is a three-story house, unusual in Cuzco, with Inca masonry visible on the second floor. It is best known for its six pumas, a sacred symbol of the Incas, carved on either side of the doorway.

Casa Valleumbroso has the arms of its original owner, Rodríguez de Esquivel, Marquis of Valleumbroso, graven in stone over the Renaissance portal. Colonial balconies with characteristic overhanging eaves adorn the two-story façade.

Casa Concha, built for a historic family, has Cuzco's loveliest balcony, a seventeenth-century doorway, and a courtyard with arcades on three sides. Unfortunately, it is now an office and warehouse.

Don Joaquín Tadeo Zarate, Secretary of the Bishop of Heras. Collection of Dr. Albert Giesecke, Lima, Peru

Casa Jara, once the residence of the Marqueses de Jara y Palma, has a rare wooden balcony with carved spindles that are undoubtedly native work, and a lovely stairway rising from the double-arch patio to the second floor. It is one of the best preserved of these homes and is now accessible as an inn.

Casa de San Borja displays the arms of Francisco Borja, who belonged to the family of the Jesuit saint of that name. The house was built as a school for the sons of Inca nobles. Bolívar "slept here."

The importance of the Cuzco school of art, like that of the Quito school, which it closely resembled, was recognized throughout the New World. It has been estimated that during the Colonial period more than 200,000 works from this school enriched not only the churches, museums, and private collections of the city but were exported, chiefly through Lima, to all the Spanish possessions and to Europe. Under the influence of the Catholic Church, Cuzco became an even greater ecclesiastical workshop than Quito and was "the main center," according to Soria, "of pictorial production in South America." Here, too, the painters and sculptors were practically all mestizos and Indians—the architects alone were Spaniards—trained by the missionary friars who had accompanied or closely followed the conquistadors. The Church, which looked upon religious art as an effective tool for converting and retaining the soul of the Indian, continued to prescribe both the choice of subject matter and the interpretation of dogma, and it is in this context that the work should be judged. Pál Kelemen extracts the essence of Colonial art in two sentences:

> The art of Colonial Latin America is characterized by the sincerity and power which marked the early Christian spirit; expressed in the current idiom—the flamboyant Baroque—it achieved a unique flavor. . . . The art was a social expression of the time, missionary, anecdotal, catechistic, picturesque and ingenuous.

During the greater part of this period Cuzqueño productions were largely imitative. It was not until the late seventeenth or early eighteenth century that the Indian began to draw freely upon his own heritage. European prints, engravings, or inexpensive reproductions provided the models. Since the Indies were a melting pot of many races and cultures, these were not even predominantly Spanish but chiefly Flemish and Italian, with a smattering of French and German. The development of a distinctly native style was gradual. In the sixteenth century, Soria points out, works of art were addressed to and commissioned by connoisseurs, churchmen and laymen; by the seventeenth century they appealed to the people as a whole. It is his belief that Cuzco attained the highest mestizo culture of all the Spanish colonies.

View of the main salon of Casa Orihuela, showing arms collection and picture of St. Christopher

Two of a series of four paintings depicting the life of Christ

Fine example of Cuzco craftsmanship: a carved cabinet. Orihuela collection

Cuzco chest with an example of Señor Orihuela's collection of Keroes or Chicha Cups

The Cuzco school of art, using a style of mannerism, decorative and flat, began soon after the Conquest and lasted almost three hundred years, during which paintings were produced mostly by anonymous artists. Its peculiar characteristics were the introduction of native flora, flat colors, and gold trimming, but with realistic detail which rendered the processional paintings of great ethno-historical value. However, even when Cuzco painters copied a European picture, they added so much of their own feeling that the results showed originality and freshness. Delightful are their archangels—dressed as soldiers of the time of Charles II with swords or guns and great wings added.

Perhaps "mannerism" should be defined, or at least an attempt made in that direction. In mannerism a way of painting is adopted from another painter or school so that the general approach is repeated and stylized, and through that becomes more decorative. In the Cuzco school of painting, angels in clouds and cherubim hanging from draperies became very realistic, but the conception was actually surrealist (expressing the subconscious mind). The fantasy world of the native painter became more and more evident. Mannerist grotesques, first introduced in Italy, according to Soria, "present what never was, never will be or can be, impossible, and surrealist inventions stemming from the world of dreams. The New World offered to all, Europeans, Creoles, Negroes, mestizos and Indians, an outlet for suppressed desires and creative invention."★ The Cuzco school is like a biological mutation, a spon-

★*Art and Architecture*, p. 182.

264

taneous departure from the main stem which develops its own characteristics, retaining attributes of the parent plant, which in this case was the European influence blended with that of the Indian.

A really magnificent primitive Cuzceño painting comes from the collection of Dr. Lizardo Alzamora of Lima. It portrays a Corpus Christi procession in the Plaza Mayor in front of the Cuzco Cathedral. In the middle distance are five images on their silver floats: San Cristóbal, San Sebastian, La Virgen de la Concepción, the Madonna and Child, and, to the far right, Santiago on horseback with sword aloft. The Virgins are both crowned and sumptuously garbed in period costumes, as are the Incas, who wear the golden breastplates of the Sun. At the right in front of La Compañía, which the artist has taken the liberty of moving into his composition, is a group of Spanish prelates and lay notables. At the back of the picture the uncovered balconies are crowded with spectators and hung with fluttering draperies. The enormous amount of detail and the pervading air of festivity make this painting, if not a masterpiece, certainly amazingly interesting.

Few of the humble, religiously inspired native artists signed their names, and of those who did, little is known. Only their work remains to testify to their piety and zeal. Their best and most characteristic work belongs to the eighteenth century, when they were less concerned with bodily form and facial expression than with embellishment. Gold leaf sprinkled lavishly on fabrics, then tooled in intricate rococo patterns, became a distinguishing mark of the school; the process was called estofado. ★ Garments themselves became so important that actual textiles were sometimes woven into the composition, and actual jewels were hung from the Virgin's ears and inserted in her crown.

The "Madonna of the Little Candle" by Carlo Crivelli of the fifteenth-century Venetian school, now in the Brera Gallery in Milan, shows the gold tooling, garlands of fruit, vase of flowers and architectural background which characterize the more stylized work of the Cuzco school. (Its style is purer and more serene, however.) Art historians have traced this emphasis on decoration to the influence of sixteenth-century Byzantine icons, popular at the time, and to that of Chinese lacquer and Indo-Chinese batiks, in which richness of color and variety of design were of primary importance.

The creative imagination of the Colonial artist might be held down by restrictions of subject and the tenets of the Church, but it often escaped in a variety of in-

★This has been described in the chapter on Quito.

genuous ways. Lack of professional training, including ignorance of anatomy and perspective, led to conceptions that are as charming as they are absurd. One example is a Cuzco primitive painting in the Prado Museum in Lima of "Christ on the Way to Calvary." Here Christ is shown above a half moon lighted by eight candles. Arranged on a stairway are four delightful but unorthodox archangels gorgeously attired in ballet skirts, plumed hats and sweeping wings, and the kind of full billowing sleeves that I have seen worn by steel band players in the Caribbean. The lower corners of the picture are filled with vases of flowers tied with bows, and in the bottom center is a highly stylized Madonna and Child. The technique is superb, but imagination has run riot.

Perhaps the finest example of the Cuzco school and the highest form of folk art is the "Virgen de Belén" (now in the Viceregal Museum). She is rigid with gold leaf, scarcely human, but magnificent. Displayed almost anywhere she would be a decoration and an inspiration.

When the Cuzco painters tried to be original they often became naïve. "The Childbirth of the Virgin" in the Chapel of Huaran (Province of Calca) depicts the Blessed Virgin lying in a richly adorned bed, Saint Joseph in attendance, while a midwife gives the Holy Infant his first bath in a rough trough. Virgin and Child are almost always over-dressed in the later paintings, even to the point of wearing large Spanish hats as they do in the "Madonna as a Pilgrim" in the Viceregal Museum. Both decorative and fanciful is the "Virgin of Coherces" in the Casa de Dromeda in Potosí—a crowned Madonna on an *anda*, set in a Flemish landscape incongruously peopled with Spanish Colonials. Also richly robed and fanciful is the "Virgin of Copacabana" in Bolivia, which was painted in 1694, but, interestingly, shows the altar as it was in 1634. Even more imaginative, though in the European tradition, is a charming "Holy Family" in the José Orihuela collection, in which four baby angels are seated on a log while a fifth sits cross-legged in a tree strumming a guitar (this last touch is Indian).

Some of the best work of the Cuzco school was in portraiture. The artists, influenced by Flemish and Venetian models, produced some memorable characterizations of the descendants of the conquistadors and other notables. An excellent example of such a character study is in the collection of Dr. Albert Giesecke, cultural attaché in the American Embassy at Lima. The title of the portrait is not the least impressive thing about it: "Don Joaquín Tadeo Zarate, natural de la ciudad de La Paz, Caballero de la Flor de Lis de Francia y de la Orden de Isabel la Catolica, Secretario del Obispo de Heras." In Dr. Alzamora's collection there is a painting of an

Archbishop's palace on right, Calle Hatun Rumiyoc　　*Casa de Almirante (Admiral)*

historical portrait gallery, of which there are variants. Largely imaginative, and captivating, it presents an unbroken line of Incas ending with Atahualpa, and of Spanish monarchs beginning with Charles V.

Throughout this period the Cuzco school continued to be affected by European art and artists and to follow a similar tradition, one distinct from the primitive or popular style. Prominent among the foreign artists was Bernardo Bitti, a Jesuit lay brother who came to Lima in 1575 after his studies in Rome, and whose influence on Peruvian art extended into the eighteenth century. He was considered one of the major artists in South America; according to Soria his "linear purity and idealization of features seem a last reflection of Raphael."★

Probably best known of the native painters in the sixteenth century is the Indian,

★From *La Pintura del Siglo XVI en Sud America*, Buenos Aires, 1956.

267

Panorama of Machu Picchu

Diego Quispe Ttito (1548–1610), himself the pupil of the most professional painter South America ever produced, Melchior Pérez de Holquín of Bolivia. What the cathedral still possesses of Quispe's remarkable series illustrating the Parables of Christ and dedicated to the twelve months and four seasons, dated 1601, as well as a signed painting, are believed by Martín Soria to have been influenced by the engravings of Bosch and Jeronimo van Aiken. Quispe's "Holy Family" Soria traces to an engraving by Ralph Sadlier after a painting, "The Vision of the Cross," by Martín de Vos.

A few other names should be mentioned. One is that of Juan Espinoza de los Monteros, who, with his son, produced a series on the life of Santa Catalina for the

Indian woman with primitive spindle

Sunday Market at Pisac, 9 a.m.–2 p.m.

convent dedicated to her and, in 1655, a genealogical tree of Franciscan saints for the cloister of that Order. In the Monastery of San Francisco also are various examples of the work of the Spanish friar, Juan Basalio de Santa Cruz, who immigrated to Cuzco before 1684 and whose pupil, Inca Juan Zapata, imitated his style.

The sculptors of the Quito school were not as widely known or as influential as the Quito masters, but their productions showed virility and less of the sentimental sweetness found in the other school. Here, as elsewhere in the New World, the chief outlet for their work was in the great churches, particularly in the retable, a monumental arch structure which framed the altar and became the focus of decoration during the Colonial Era. It was a structure that called for the skills of architect,

269

Llamas who have brought their 100 pounds of grain to Cuzco (after unloading)

Doorway of a street in Pisac showing Andean hat styles, one of an Indian covered with flowers. Cholo hat in doorway

painter, and sculptor, although two or three of these skills could be combined in one man. The sculptor was needed to fill the numerous shelves, brackets, and niches of varied dimensions with statues, the painter to clothe or adorn them. The favorite subjects were again, of course, all religious—Christ, the Virgin, saints and martyrs —in particular, patron saints; angels, including the chief archangels Michael, Gabriel, Raphael, Uriel. In addition, there were the purely decorative motifs, among them columns and bosses, garlands of fruit and flowers, symbolical birds and beasts, caryatids, cherubs, and a profusion of *putti* (angel heads).

On the whole, the sculptor was more creative in his expression than the painter, although he too used models, such as the woodcuts by Albrecht Dürer, or the Flemish engravings from Martín de Vos to Rubens. The Baroque spirit permeated all art, but, while in Europe the Baroque in art is flamboyant and emotional, in the colonies it was less so, tempered by native influences of placidity and suffering. In the sixteenth century emotions were restrained; faces express affection and grief, never joy or sensuality. Later, many figures were carved in dramatic attitudes and could be painfully realistic: the Virgin and the Magdalene weep real tears; the wounds of Christ drip real blood; the three nails which pierce His hands and feet are of iron. It has been suggested that the Indian sculptor identified his own sufferings with those of the crucified Saviour, and so found an outlet for his emotions.

270

The Cuzco sculptors carved choir stalls and pulpits of exceptional beauty. The double-tier stalls of the cathedral, La Merced, and especially San Francisco have been mentioned with the names of their makers, as well as the marvelous pulpit of San Blas. The most celebrated single piece of sculpture in the city is "Nuestra Señora de Almudena" (1686), in the chapel of that name. It was created by Juan Tuyru Tupa, an Indian of noble lineage, who was both sculptor and architect. (In 1701 he was appointed chief architect of Cuzco, a signal honor for one of his race.)

During the early years of Peruvian independence, religious art fell into such disfavor that paintings and sculpture were disposed of in wholesale lots; it has been estimated that as many as 10,000 objects of art left the city during the nineteenth and early twentieth centuries. Happily, large numbers remain to be enjoyed and studied in the churches and the Viceregal Museum, where they are now zealously cherished. Many of the finest examples are in private collections in Cuzco as well as in all parts of South America and countries overseas.

The United States is fortunate in having a few collections of Spanish American art, mainly of the Cuzco school, such as the Morley collection in Santa Fe and the Gerhardt Bading collection in the Milwaukee Museum. But the most important one belongs to María Engracia Freyer of Denver, the widow of Captain Frank Freyer, who headed the American Naval Mission to Peru in 1920 and later became chief of staff of the Peruvian navy. In recognition of the services rendered the country by both Captain and Mrs. Freyer, the Peruvian government permitted them to assemble a noteworthy collection of Cuzqueño art—probably the last collection of any importance to be allowed to leave Peru. It was first exhibited in the United States in 1924.

Among the twenty-five or so paintings of the Cuzco school in the Freyer gallery in Denver, Colorado, are two sixteenth-century works of special distinction. The first, "Mary with a Distaff," a charming mestizo composition, shows the child Mary seated on a chair holding a distaff or spindle. On her head is an Inca headband and over her shoulders an Inca shawl. Both shawl and lace-edged dress have characteristic estofado decoration, and the picture is bordered with a garland of flowers. The other painting, "Our Lady of Victory," is a copy of a celebrated statue which was presented to the cathedral in Málaga by Ferdinand and Isabella. It is noted for its rich estofado, and is an example of the use of the liquid gold which the Indians called Oro de Concha after the shells in which it was kept. Its use is a lost art, but it is believed that gold mixed with quicksilver was brushed over sizing made by a ruby-toned substance (similar to the pigeon-blood glaze the Chinese applied to porcelain).

A sixteenth-century bed in Mrs. Freyer's gallery is covered with this same liquid gold; it is of true viceregal elegance.

Of the private Peruvian collections none, with the exception of Pedro de Osma's, is finer than that of Don José Orihuela, present head of one of the oldest families in Cuzco. The first member of the family to come to Peru was José Aviles de Orihuela, *hijodalgo*, an imperial courtier, who in 1534 was entrusted with letters to Diego Almagro from Emperor Charles V. The collection is fittingly housed in a new building at the ancestral hacienda, Huayucari (Quechuan for "hanged man"), which is set high on an Inca terrace between Pisac and Urubamba, about fifty miles north of Cuzco. From the terrace it commands a superb view of the Andes.

The art objects were assembled by Don José's grandfather and father and augmented by his own purchases during the last forty years. One of the prized items is a portrait of Ponce de León, dated 1695, which Don José inherited from his great-great grandmother, herself a descendant of the famed explorer who lent money to Pizarro and Almagro for their first expeditions to Peru. There are not only valuable paintings in this collection, but also rare examples of Peruvian furnishings: *arcons* (chests), a gold-leaf bed made for the family in or before 1630, religious images, weapons, mirrors, specimens of polychromed or gilded doors and picture frames. A number of the gilded frames are decorated with small sections of mirror; the process was a specialty of the Cuzco school.

Outstanding among the paintings is a series based on four episodes in the life of Christ: "The Annunciation," "The Birth," "In the Cradle," "In the Garden." The name of the painter is not known, but his sources have been identified by Soria, who traces the first composition to an anonymous Flemish engraving, the second to a Cornelius Cort engraving copied from a 1567 painting by Taddeo Zuccaro, the third and fourth to engravings by Hieronymus Wierex. The pictures are all in heavily carved and gilded frames, their Salomonic columns (an architectural feature) lavishly adorned with flowers. Other important paintings include three of the Virgen de Belén, patron saint of Cuzco; a sixteenth-century Madonna, Byzantine in style and the oldest in the collection; a Cuzco primitive showing an Indian's idea of the cathedral before it was built; a San Cristóbal carrying the Christ child and staff, half European, half Cuzqueño in style.

Especially interesting also is Don José's collection of *keroes*, wooden libation vases, with and without handles, made during Inca and Colonial times. These vases are curiously carved, many in the shape of human or animal heads, and may have been used by the Incas in their sacrificial rites. In the Spanish Era decorations were

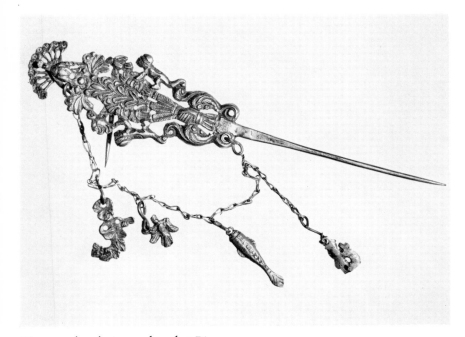

Tupu or shawl pin purchased at Pisac

Montera (hat) and chuspa (bag) purchased at Pisac

added that were previously unknown to the natives: horses, mules, firearms, and figures recognizable as Spaniards or Negroes. These *keroes*, illustrating both the Inca and post-Inca periods, were exhibited in 1923 at the Institute of Peruvian Art in Lima.

Of the 2,500 acres which comprise the Orihuela estate, 250 are irrigated on Inca terraces in the Inca manner. We were driven over this section in an International truck from Chicago, and Señor Orihuela pointed out his fine white corn which was drying on the ground preparatory to being shipped for popcorn to San Francisco, California. The Indians tipped their hats in feudal fashion as we went by, and Don José spoke to them in Quechuan. They were sorting corn barefoot, but I noted that their sandals piled by the side of the road were made from discarded automobile tires (called "yanquis").

Back at the hacienda, my companion and I spent the afternoon photographing all we could of the magnificent art collection. We dined with our host at the banquet table in the main salon, surrounded by ancestral treasures. A last look at the terrace-draped Andes, an inadequate but sincere "gracias" to Don José for his hospitality, and we left Huayucari, aware that we had been accorded a great privilege.

Sunday morning is the time to drive out to the Pisac fair, for then one can see the mayors of the neighboring villages carrying their staffs of office at the head of the procession which issues from the church after high Mass. In this colorful parade the

273

Retable purchased in Cuzco: reputed to be 200 years old. The primitive pictures on the doors resemble some of Picasso's. *

El Torito de Pucará †

Madonna is borne on her anda and lusty music is provided by the conch blowers. The fair itself is held among the great trees bordering the main plaza, with an array of merchandise presided over by Indians in local garb and attended by llamas, donkeys, and chickens. Here one can find folk art, some of which still displays designs used in Colonial times, and can buy the hats of the region—the velvet *monteras* of the Indians, the white felt hats of the *cholos*, showing Spanish influence, the intricately knitted wool caps with ear flaps for the high Andes—as well as woven *ponchos*, *pullos* and *chuspas*. A specialty of the fair is a rug made of pieces of llama or alpaca skin decorated with a design of shepherds and shepherdesses in variegated colors. On

*A painting with similar figures was recently found in an Andean village and called a "sensational discovery." It was reported in the newspaper *Caretas* printed in Lima, April 19, 1960.

†The festival of marking the herd was held in Pucará near Puno in the olden days. The most beautiful young bull was chosen to be marked and decorated. First his feet were tied together and cuts made on his back in the outlines of saddle and harness. Into these cuts were placed ashes, colors and even gold powder. The back of the ribs were whitewashed and half moons were cut in the eyelids. The ear was cut and blood gathered to be mixed with wine to be drunk. Cuts were also made above the lips and on the fat of the neck, making flaps. These cuts were then all treated, and when the bleeding ceased the bull was decorated with garlands of flowers and fruit. Chili pepper was put under the tail, and it was then that he broke his bonds and bounded around the field as fires of coca leaves at one end gave out clouds of incense to create feelings of happiness and to extinguish sorrow. Later came the music, dancing and feasting.

When the grazing fields dried up and the water sources disappeared, the herds diminished so that the people had to move and were impoverished even to the point of selling their sons. The Pucará pottery bulls have been made ever since in memory of the festivals at Pucará; the replicas are characterized by a handle, a hole in which to pour chicha or water for flowers, the saddle and harness markings, the whitewash and the flaps down the fat necks.

274

one side of the fair is the grocery department, displaying neat piles of beans and peppers, and hidden coca leaves whose sale is forbidden. Two jarring notes were struck at the time of my last visit, though I may have been the only one disturbed. A truck with a loudspeaker gave a Punch and Judy show followed by a raucous commercial for Coca Cola; an automobile drove up and distributed political pamphlets.

One can rent a horse and ride up to the historic Inca fortress, but the altitude of Pisac is high, more than 13,000 feet, and I passed up the opportunity to go higher. Instead, we had a little more time in the village. A number of the houses we passed bore signs corresponding to the ice and bread cards once used at home. The Indian signs are more picturesque: a waving plume of grass for *aguardiente* (whiskey), a tan bunch of straw with a dash of red for *chicha* (beer), and a graceful green wreath or a basket for *pan* (bread). Ice is not among the obtainable commodities.

Since the Independence closed the Colonial Era, after three centuries of Spanish domination, we shall close this chapter with the words of Simon Bolívar, the Liberator, uttered soon after his triumphal entrance into Cuzco on December 9, 1824. On that day, while the bells of twenty churches pealed their welcome, Bolívar rode under decorated arches, over rich carpets, past balconies hung with mantles, down a route lined with people showering him with flowers. His handsome steed, its saddle gleaming with gold and brilliants, was a gift from his admirers. From the hand of the wife of the governor, he received the gold crown which Cuzco offered to him, the Liberator. ★ At the cathedral, where the bishop awaited him, a Te Deum was sung in his honor. He then received the blessing of the Church and was presented with a jeweled belt and a gold cross studded with precious stones.

On the next day, in the Palacio de Almirante, Bolívar voiced his impression of the ancient city of Cuzco.†

Yesterday I reached the classical country of the Sun, of the Incas, of fable and of history. Here the true sun is gold; the Incas are the viceroys or prefects; the fable is the history of Garcilaso; the history is the account by Las Casas of the destruction of the Indians . . . Manco Capac, the Adam of the Incas, left his Titicaca paradise and founded an authentic realm, without a mixture of sacred or profane fable . . . God made him man; he made his kingdom, and history has told the truth; because the stone monuments, the long straight roads, the primitive customs and the genuine tradition make us witnesses of a creation about which we had no idea, no model, no copy. Peru is unique in the history of mankind.

★The Cuzco crown was later taken to La Paz and given to Sucre, victorious general of the Battle of Ayacucho, but Sucre claimed that the last battle was the work of General Córdoba and placed the crown on Córdoba's head. Córdoba gave it to his native city, but on his death it passed to the Museum of Bogotá.

†From an article by Dr. Jorge Cornejo Bouronclo in *La Crónica*, Lima, July 28, 1953 (p. 11).

PHOTOGRAPHIC CREDITS

GERHARDT BAKKER: 273, 274 *left.*

MARTIN CHAMBI: 230, 240 *left*, 241 *right*, 251.

CRESCENCIO CARRILLO Y ANCONA LIBRARY, MÉRIDA: 47, 64.

DEPARTMENTO DE BELLAS ARTES OF THE UNIVERSITY OF PUERTO RICO: 29, 31 *left.*

ENGRACIA FREYER DOUGHERTY: 260 *right.*

JON ENGLE: 75, 77, 78, 81, 85 *top*, 85 *left*, 89, 93, 94, 97 *left*, 98, 103, 104, 140, 143, 144, 148, 149, 151 *right*, 152, 155, 156, 158, 161, 162, 163, 165, 169 *right*, 170, 173, 175 *right*, 176, 178, 181, 187, 188, 189, 192 *left*, 193, 194 *right*, 196, 199, 201, 202, 203, 206, 207, 211 *right*, 212, 214, 215, 216, 219, 223 *right*, 224, 225, 226 *right*, 229, 233 *left*, 235 *left*, 236 *top*, 239 *right*, 240 *right*, 241 *left*, 243, 244, 247 *left*, 252 *left*, 254 *right*, 260 *left*, 261, 263, 264, 269, 270, 274 *right.*

JOHN C. FREYER: 257 *right*, 259 *top right*

ALEXANDRE GEORGES: 27 *left.*

DR. ALBERT GIESECKE: 190, 208, 209, 210, 211 *left.*

A. GUILLEN: 267 *right.*

FREDERICK L. HAMILTON: XII

INSTITUTO DE CULTURA PUERTORRIQUEÑA: 31 *right*, 32 *right*, 34 *right.*

INTERNATIONAL BUSINESS MACHINE CORPORATION: 169 *left.*

LIBRARY OF CONGRESS: 4.

LISA LITTLE, THE MUSEUM OF PRIMITIVE ARTS: 42, 49, 58.

PUERTO RICO NEWS SERVICE: 2, 7 *left*, 10, 14, 26 *right*, 35 *left.*

M. GONZALEZ SALEZ: 200.

SAMUEL A. SANTIAGO: 10 *bottom*, 16, 19, 20, 22, 24, 25, 26 *left*, 28 *right*, 32 *left*, 33

A. SCHMIDT, THE MILWAUKEE PUBLIC MUSEUM: 166.

DR. MARTIN SORIA: 151 *left*, 192 *right*, 204 *left*, 223 *left*, 228, 236 *bottom*, 254 *left*, 257 *left*, 259 *top left.*

HAROLD WETHEY: 259 *bottom.*

BERTHA KITCHELL WHYTE: 7 *right*, 27 *right*, 34 *left*, 35 *right*, 36, 38, 41, 44, 50, 53, 55, 56, 61, 62, 65, 67, 68, 70, 72, 85 *right*, 86, 90, 97 *right*, 100, 106, 108, 111, 112, 115, 117, 119, 120, 123, 124, 127, 128, 129, 131, 132, 134, 136, 137, 138, 147, 186, 204 *right*, 226 *left*, 248.

BODO WUTH: 163 *right*, 175 *left*, 182.

BIBLIOGRAPHY

GENERAL

ANGULO, DIEGO. *Planos de monumentos arquitectonicos de America y Filipinos.* (Sixteenth century.) Sevilla. 1933 and 1939.

BAUDIN, LOUIS. *A Socialist Empire: The Incas of Peru.* Princeton, N.J. D. Van Nostrand Co., Inc., 1961.

BEVAN, BERNARD. *History of Spanish Architecture.* N.Y. Scribners. 1939.

BOSSOM, ALFRED C. *Architectural Pilgrimage in Old Mexico.* N.Y. Scribners. 1924.

BOTTOMLEY, WILLIAM L. *Spanish Details.* N.Y. Wm. Helburn, Inc. 1924.

BRIGGS, MARTIN SHAW. *Baroque Architecture.* N.Y. McBride Nast Co. 1914.

BUSCHIAZZO, MARIO J. *Estudios de arquitectura colonial.* Buenos Aires. Hispano Americana Editorial Guillermo Kraft Ltda. 1944.

CROW, JOHN A. *Epic of America.* N.Y. Doubleday. 1946.

DORTA, MARCO. *Fuentes para la historia de arte Hispano America.* Vol. X. Instituto "Diego Velásquez" Sección de Sevilla. 1951.

HERRING, HUBERT. *History of Latin America.* N.Y. Alfred Knopf.

KELEMEN, PÁL. *Baroque and Rococo in Latin America.* N.Y. MacMillan Co. 1951.

KUBLER, GEORGE, and SORIA, MARTIN. *Art and Architecture in Spain and Portugal and their American Dominions, 1500–1800.* Penguin Books. 1959.

MADARIAGA, SALVADOR DE. *The Rise of the Spanish American Empire.* N.Y. MacMillan Co. 1949.

———. *Bolívar.* N.Y. Pellegrini and Cudahy. 1952.

SANFORD, TRENT E. *Story of Architecture in Mexico.* N.Y. Norton.

TAULLARD, A. *El mueble colonial sudamericano.* Buenos Aires. Ediciones Peuser.

WETHEY, HAROLD. *Colonial Architecture and Sculpture in Peru.* Harvard University Press. 1949.

WORCESTER, DONALD, and SCHAFFER, WENDELL G. *Growth and Culture of Latin America.* Oxford University Press. 1956.

OLD SAN JUAN

BUSCHIAZZO, MARIO. *Historicos monumentos de Antiguo San Juan.*

CALVAN, MANUEL DE JESÚS. *The Cross and the Sword.* (Fiction.) Translated by Robert Graves. Bloomington, Indiana. Indiana University Press. 1954.

DOOLEY, ELIZA B. K. *Old San Juan.* San Juan, P.R. Pan American Book Co. 1955.

KEITH, NATHANIAL, and FEISS, CARL. *A Report on the Renewal Possibilities of the Historic Triangle of the City of San Juan.* For the Municipal Housing Authority of the Capital of Puerto Rico. May, 1955.

MADARIAGA, SALVADOR DE. *The Rise of the Spanish American Empire.* N.Y. MacMillan Co. 1949.

MERCADO, OSIRIS DELGADO. *Sinopsis historica de las artes plasticas en Puerto Rico.* San Juan. Instituto de Cultura Puertorriqueña. 1957.

MORISON, SAMUEL ELIOT. *Christopher Columbus, Mariner*. Boston. Little Brown and Co. 1955.

PALM, ERWIN WALTER. *Los monumentos arquitectónicos de la española*. Vols. I and II. Ciudad Trujillo. University of Santo Domingo. 1955.

PHILLIPPO, JAMES M. *Jamaica: Its Past and Present State*. London. John Snow. 1843.

SLUSSER, MARY. "Tropical Christmas," *Americas* (Pan American Union, Washington D.C.), Vol. 5, No. 12 (December, 1953).

STEWARD, JULIAN H. (ed.) *People of Puerto Rico*. University of Illinois Press. 1956.

MÉRIDA

BOLANOS, LUIS VEGA. *Catalogo de construcciones religiosas del Estado de Yucatán*. Talleres Graficos de la Nación Mexico. 1929–1939.

BROOKS, VAN WYCK. *Fenollosa and his Circle*. N.Y. E. P. Dutton and Co. 1962. (Contains a biography of John L. Stephens.)

CERAM, C. W. *Gods, Graves and Scholars*. N.Y. Alfred Knopf. 1956.

CHAMBERLAIN, ROBERT S. *The Conquest and Colonization of Yucatán, 1517–1550*. Washington D.C. Publication 582 of the Carnegie Institute. 1948.

COGOLLUDO, FR. DIEGO LOPEZ. *Historia de Yucatán*. 1656. (A third edition, dated 1867, is in the Crescencio Carrillo y Ancona Library, Yucatán.)

EMMERICH, ANDRÉ. "Savages Never Carved these Stones," *American Heritage*, February, 1959.

FUENTE VEGA, A. *Plano guia de Mérida*. 1956.

HIJUELOS, FAUSTO A. *Mérida*. Mexico City. Ediciónes Centro Yucateco. 1946.

LANDA, FR. DIEGO DE. *Relación de las cosas de Yucatán*. Mexico City. Editorial Porrua, S. A. Eighth edition. 1959. (Written in 1566.)

MORLEY, SYLVANUS GRISWOLD. *The Ancient Maya*. Palo Alto. Stanford University Press. 1956.

REDFIELD, ROBERT. *The Folk Culture of Yucatán*. University of Chicago Press. 1941.

SOLIS, LIC. MOLINA. *Historia de Yucatán durante la dominación española*. Mérida. Juan Francisco. 1913.

STEPHENS, JOHN L. *Incidents of Travel in Yucatán*. London. 1843.

THOMPSON, J. E. S. *The Rise and Fall of the Maya Civilization*. University of Oklahoma Press. 1954.

CARTAGENA

ARRAZOLA, ROBERTO. *Historia de Cartagena*. Cartagena. 1933.

BOSSA HERAZO, DONALDO. *Quia artistica de Cartagena de Indias*. 1955.

DORTA, ENRIQUE MARCO. *Cartagena de Indias*. Sevilla. 1951.

GRAHAM, CUNNINGHAM. *Cartagena*. 1926.

JIMÉNEZ MOLINARES, GABRIEL. *Los martires de Cartagena de 1816*. I & II. 1950.

MARTINEZ FARDO, EUSTORGIO. *Cuentos y Leyendas*. Cartagena. Editorial Mundo Nuevo. 1948.

Smith, Robert. *Latin American Republics.*

QUITO

Hagen, Victor Wolfgang Von. *South America Called Them.* N.Y. Duell, Sloan and Pearce. Boston. Little Brown and Co. 1955.
———. *The Four Seasons of Manuela.* London. J. M. Dent and Sons, Ltd. 1952.
Kelemen, Pál. *Baroque and Rococo in Latin America.* N.Y. MacMillan Co. 1950.
La Orden Miracle, Ernesto de. *Elogio de Quito.* Madrid. Cuadernos de Arte. 1950.
Llerena, José Alfredo. *Quito colonial y tesoros "artisticos."*
Millar, George. *A Crossbowman's Story.* (Fiction.) N.Y. Alfred Knopf. 1955.
Moscoso, Cardenas Alfonso. "Between Earth and Sky," *Americas* (Pan American Union, Washington D.C.), Vol. 10, No. 5 (May, 1958).
Ulloa, Anthony, and Juan y Santacilla, George. *Seven Years in Peru.* Boston. Albert J. Wright, printer. 1878.
Vargas, Fr. José María, O. P. *Arte religioso ecuatoriano.* Quito. Ediciónes Casa de la Cultura Ecuatoriana. 1956.
———. *María en el arte ecuatoriano.* Quito. Impr. Romero. 1954.

TUNJA

Buschiazzo, Mario J. *Estudios de arquitectura colonial, hispano americana.* Buenos Aires. Guillermo Kraft, Ltda. 1944.
Correa, Ramón C. *Quia historica (Para el turismo en Boyacá).* 1953.
Rojas, Ulises. *Escudos de armas e inscripciones antiguas de la Ciudad de Tunja.* 1939.
———. *Campana libertadora de 1819: Batallas de Pantano de Vargas y Puente de Boyaca.* Departmental Tunja. 1951.
Rubio y Manuel Briceno, Ozias S. *Tunja.* 1909.
Soria, Martín L. *La pintura del siglo XVI en Sud America.* Buenos Aires. 1956.
Vincente, Restrepo. *Los Chibchas.*

CUZCO

Bingham, Hiram. *Lost City of the Incas.* N.Y. Duell, Sloan and Pearce. 1948.
Bryce, James. *South America.* N.Y. MacMillan Co. 1912.
Camacho, Fabio. *Cuzco.* Empresa Publicitario, Expresión Peru.
Cossio de Pomar, Felipe. *Arte de Peru colonial.* Buenos Aires. Fondo de Cultura Economica. 1958.
———. *Pintura colonial (Escuela cuzqueña).* Cuzco, Peru. 1928.
Covarrubias Pozo, Jesús M. *Cuzco colonial y su arte.* Universidad del Cuzco. 1958.

GARCÍA and GIESECKE. *Artistic Guide to Cuzco*. Lima. 1925.

HARTH-TÉRRÉ, EMILIO. *Las tres fundaciónes de la Catedral del Cuzco*. Buenos Aires. 1949.

KROPP, MIRIAM. *Cuzco: Window on Peru*. N.Y. Thomas Y. Crowell and Company. (Studio Publications.) 1956.

KUBLER, GEORGE. *Cuzco (A Report)*. Tours, France. Unesco. 1951.

LA RIVA, AQÜERO JOSÉ DE. *La historia en el Peru*. Cuzco.

LA VEGA, INCA GARCILASO DE. *Royal Commentaries of the Incas*. Translated by Clements R. Markham. London. The Hakluyt Society. 1869. (The original, *Los comentarios reales de los Incas*, was dedicated to the Duchess of Braganza of Portugal in 1609.)

PARDO, LUIS A. *Historia y arqueología del Cuzco I y II*. Cuzco. 1957.

PRESCOTT, WILLIAM H. *Conquest of Peru*.

ROZAS, L. EDGAR ALBERTO. *Cuzco*. 1955. Second edition in English, 1960.

SITWELL, SACHEVERELL. *Golden Wall and Mirador*. London. Weidenfeld and Nicolson. 1960.

VALCARCEL, DR. LUIS. *The Incas and Pedro de Ciego León*.

WETHEY, HAROLD E. *Colonial Architecture and Sculpture in Peru*. Cambridge, Mass. Harvard University Press. 1949.

LIMA

COBO, BERNABE. *Historia de la fundación de Lima*. (The author was a padre in San Francisco convent from 1629 to 1639.)

CIEZA DE LEÓN, PEDRO DE, *Cronica del Perú*, Vol. XXVI, Madrid. 1833.

"EL PERU EN FOTOS," *El Comercio-Lima*, Friday, April 10, 1959.

Festival de Lima. Edición Antologia. Concejo Provincial de Lima. 1959. (Ten small volumes.)

GALVEZ, JOSÉ. *Calles de Lima*. Lima. Presented by International Petroleum Co. Ltd. 1943.

HARTHE-TÉRRÉ, EMILIO. *Artifices en el Virreinato del Peru*. Lima. 1945.

———. "Nota para una historia del balcon en Lima," *Revista del Archivo Nacional del Peru*, Eretrego II, Tomo XXIII, Lima, 1959.

JIJÓN Y CAAMAÑO, JACINTO, *La Religion del imperio de los Incas*.

LIMA. *Precolumbia y Virreinal*. Artes Graficas Lima. 1938.

MARIATEQUI, JULIO CESAR, and LA FUENTE CHAVEZ, GERMAN DE. *Lima en el centenario de su fundación*. Lima. Editorial Minerva. 1935.

MEANS, PHILIP AINSWORTH, *Fall of the Inca Empire and Spanish Rule in Peru*. 1530–1780. N.Y. 1932.

MONTESINOS, FERNANDO, *Memorias del Perú*, 1652. Translated by P. A. Means, Hakluyt Society Publications, Series II, No. 48.

PALMA, RICARDO. *Tradiciónes peruanas*. Madrid. Aguilar. 1957.

QUESADA, AURELIO MIRO. *Artes y oficios del Peru*. Lima.

"Remozamiento y Jerarquia Nacional de 'Entre Nous'," Turismo año, XVII, No. 164 (May–July), 1952.

Sanz, Benjamin Gento. *San Francisco de Lima*. Lima. Imprenta Lorres Aquirre, S. A. 1945.

Valcárcel, Daniel. "La creación de San Marcos," *Fanal año*, Vol. VI, No. 26, 1952.

Valcárcel, Luis E. *Historia de Cultura antigua del Perú*. Lima. 1943–49.

Velarde, Hector. *Arquitectura peruana*. Mexico City. Fondo de Cultura Economica. 1946.

———. "La restauración del Palacio de Torre-Tagle," *Fanal año*, Vol. XIV, No. 54, 1958.

Wethey, Harold E. *Colonial Architecture and Sculpture in Peru*. Cambridge, Mass. Harvard University Press. 1949.

INDEX

Italicized titles indicate names of works of art. Italicized numbers indicate illustrations.